THE NOTORIOUS ELIZABETH TUTTLE

NORTH AMERICAN RELIGIONS

Series Editors: Tracy Fessenden (Religious Studies, Arizona State University),
Laura Levitt (Religious Studies, Temple University), and
David Harrington watt (History, Temple University)

In recent years a cadre of industrious, imaginative, and theoretically sophisticated scholars of religion have focused their attention on North America. As a result the field is far more subtle, expansive, and interdisciplinary than it was just two decades ago. The North American Religions series builds on this transformative momentum. Books in the series move among the discourses of ethnography, cultural analysis, and historical study to shed new light on a wide range of religious experiences, practices, and institutions. They explore topics such as lived religion, popular religious movements, religion and social power, religion and cultural reproduction, and the relationship between secular and religious institutions and practices. The series focuses primarily, but not exclusively, on religion in the United States in the twentieth and twenty-first centuries.

BOOKS IN THE SERIES:

*The Notorious Elizabeth Tuttle: Marriage, Murder, and
Madness in the Family of Jonathan Edwards*
Ava Chamberlain

The Notorious Elizabeth Tuttle

Marriage, Murder, and Madness in the Family of Jonathan Edwards

AVA CHAMBERLAIN

NEW YORK UNIVERSITY PRESS

New York and London

NEW YORK UNIVERSITY PRESS
New York and London
www.nyupress.org

References to Internet Websites (URLs) were accurate at the time of writing.
Neither the author nor New York University Press is responsible for URLs
that may have expired or changed since the manuscript was prepared.

Chamberlain, Ava.
The notorious Elizabeth Tuttle : marriage, murder, and madness in the family of Jonathan
Edwards / Ava Chamberlain.
p. cm. — (North American religions)
Includes bibliographical references and index.
ISBN 978-0-8147-2372-2 (cl : alk. paper)
ISBN 978-0-8147-2373-9 (ebook)
ISBN 978-0-8147-2374-6 (ebook)
1. Edwards, Jonathan, 1703-1758—Family. 2. Tuttle, Elizabeth, b. 1645—Marriage.
3. Edwards, Richard, 1647-1718—Marriage. 4. Tuttle family. 5. Edwards family. 6.
Families—Mental health. 7. Divorce—Connecticut—History—17th century. 8. Murder—
Connecticut—History—17th century. 9. Connecticut—Biography. I. Title.
BX7260.E3C48 2012
285.8092—dc23
[B]
2012010671

New York University Press books are printed on acid-free paper, and their binding materials
are chosen for strength and durability. We strive to use environmentally responsible
suppliers and materials to the greatest extent possible in publishing our books.

Manufactured in the United States of America
10 9 8 7 6 5 4 3 2 1

To my mother, Evelyn L. Chamberlain,
my siblings, Tommy, George, and Emily Chamberlain,
and the memory of my father, Hiram S. Chamberlain III

CONTENTS

ACKNOWLEDGMENTS

This project was conceived during an NEH Summer Seminar on "Early American Microhistories" that was held at the University of Connecticut in 2005, when Richard D. Brown, the seminar's director, remarked, "Two murders in one family! There *must* be a story here." Without his encouragement, and the introduction to the literature and methodology of microhistory this seminar provided, this story would have never been told. Participants in the *William and Mary Quarterly*-Early Modern Studies Institute Workshop on "Writing Early American History," convened at the Huntington Library by Fred Anderson and Andrew Clayton in the spring of 2008, provided important additional direction. One comment made during this workshop, that I must make the reader "care about this woman," led me to reconceptualize the story's organization entirely.

The bulk of the research for this book was conducted at the Connecticut State Library in Hartford. Summer after summer I arrived at the library and in a frenzy of activity collected the sources I needed for another year's work. The expertise and patient assistance of the staff of CSL's History and Genealogy Unit made these research trips both enjoyable and productive. I especially wish to thank Mark H. Jones, the State Archivist, and Carol Ganz, Bonnie Linck, Jeannie Sherman, and Mel Smith, the reference staff, for all their help over the years. I am also grateful to the staff of Wright State University's Paul Lawrence Dunbar Library, particularly Diana Kaylor and Piper Martin, for their many forms of assistance. In addition, the staffs of the American Philosophical Society, the British Library, the Connecticut Historical Society, the Franklin Trask Library at Andover–Newton Theological School, the Massachusetts Archives, the Massachusetts Historical Society, the National

Archives of the United Kingdom, the Northamptonshire Record Office, the Plimouth Plantation, the Sterling Memorial Library at Yale University, the Whitney Library of the New Haven Museum, and the Dayton, Ohio, East Stake Family History Center provided research assistance. A visiting fellowship at the Beinecke Rare Book and Manuscript Library permitted me to conduct extended research in its Jonathan Edwards Collection.

In more ways that I can name, I am deeply indebted to Kenneth P. Minkema, Harry S. Stout, and the entire staff of the Jonathan Edwards Center at Yale University. During my time as a research editor at the Center, transcribing manuscripts for *The Works of Jonathan Edwards*, I acquired both the technical skills and the historical knowledge that ultimately made this book possible. Over the years Ken has generously provided both moral support and ready assistance with all manner of research questions. Having read and commented on the entire manuscript, he has made many insightful suggestions for improving its argument.

Wright State University facilitated the research and writing of this book in several areas. David L. Barr, the chair of the Departments of Religion, Philosophy, and Classics, and Charles S. Taylor, the dean of the College of Liberal Arts, both worked diligently to ensure that I have had the resources necessary to pursue this project. A professional development leave as I was beginning the research and a nonteaching quarter as I was completing the manuscript gave me time to focus more on the small mysteries of the past than the large challenges of the present. The university has also provided ongoing financial assistance for this project in the form of travel and professional development grants. In economically challenging times, such generous institutional support is especially welcome.

I am blessed to be surrounded by supportive colleagues and friends who have been ever-ready to turn a critical eye to portions of the manuscript, to discuss methodological problems, and to provide less tangible, but even more important, forms of assistance. I have known Laura Levitt, Tracy Fessenden, and David Watt, the editors of the North American Religions series at NYU Press in which this volume appears, since 1996, when we participated together in the Young Scholars in American Religion Program sponsored by the Center for Religion and American Culture at Indiana University–Purdue University, Indianapolis. This book is in important ways the fruit of the ongoing scholarly nurture that all my colleagues in this program have provided over the years. Ellen Fleischmann has closely read and commented on every chapter, patiently discussing with me over innumerable lunches and teas issues as small as the choice of a single word or as large as the value of studying ordinary women's lives. Amanda Porterfield, who has been a generous supporter of my academic work, read and thoughtfully commented on the entire text, as did an anonymous reader for NYU Press. Jennifer Hammer and Despina Papazoglou Gimbel, the editors at NYU Press responsible for this book's production, helped transform my often-undisciplined prose into clear text. Many other scholarly friends reviewed portions of the text, including Joseph Conforti, Carol Herringer, Noeleen MacIlvenna, Marjorie McLellan, Valerie Stoker, Rachel Wheeler, and Mary White. Cornelia Dayton graciously invited me to be a guest in her home during several research forays to Connecticut. Cheri Adams, the Director of Astronomy at the Boonshoft Museum of Natural History in Dayton, Ohio, re-created the colonial Connecticut night sky for me in the museum's planetarium. Patrick Craig, Kyle Farley, Bill Keegan, Cheryl Meyer, and John van Epps also provided various forms of research assistance. Finally, I wish to thank Ed Fitzgerald for his support throughout this project, for discussing with me the many legal issues that complicate this story, and for helping me see just how much, and how little, has changed in American jurisprudence over 400 years.

NOTE ON SOURCES

Quotations from manuscript sources have retained the erratic spellings and capitalizations found in the originals. The many abbreviations and contractions common in seventeenth-century writings have, however, been silently expanded, and modern usage has been followed for the letters *u, v, w, j,* and *i.* Some punctuation has been added to quotations of unpublished materials to increase clarity, and excessive italicization has been silently removed in quotations from early modern publications. Dates also have been altered to conform to the Gregorian calendar, which begins the year on 1 January, instead of the Julian calendar—still in use by English colonists in the seventeenth century—which began the year on 25 March.

INTRODUCTION

> History is crucially distinguished from fiction by curiosity about
> what actually happened in the past. Beyond the self—outside the
> realm of the imagination—lies a landscape cluttered with the detri-
> tus of past living, a mélange of clues and codes informative of a
> moment as real as this present one. When curiosity is stirred about
> an aspect of this past, a relationship with an object has begun.[1]

Who was Elizabeth Tuttle? The most common answer to this question cites a
genealogical relationship: Elizabeth Tuttle was the paternal grandmother of
Jonathan Edwards. Colonial America's greatest theologian was born in 1703,
the only son of Elizabeth's second child. He began his career as the pastor
of the Congregational church in Northampton, Massachusetts, and, through
his powerful preaching and popular revival writings, he became a leader of
the international evangelical movement that transformed Protestant Chris-
tianity in the eighteenth century. After a theological dispute forced him to
leave Northampton, he took a post at the Indian mission in Stockbridge,
Massachusetts, where he wrote lengthy treatises defending such traditional
Calvinist doctrines as original sin and divine sovereignty. In the nineteenth
century, his disciples founded on these doctrinal writings a new theological
movement, and as evangelicalism swept the country, his importance grew. In
the mid–twentieth century, he emerged as the central figure in the modern
academic study of colonial American intellectual history. Constructed as a
misunderstood genius whose writings were "so much ahead of his time that
our own can hardly be said to have caught up with him," Edwards has generated an outpouring of scholarship that eclipses in size and scope the work
on any other figure in American religious history.[2] Social historians have
reduced this outsized image to a more manageable scale, but the Edwards
myth endures, appropriated most recently by theologians building an intellectual foundation for the modern evangelical tradition.[3]

Elizabeth Tuttle plays but a small role in this idealized construction of Jonathan Edwards. His is a large—and very male—story of powerful intellects
and clashing theological ideas. The women who inhabit its periphery, like

Elizabeth Tuttle, have not received sustained attention, for their inarticulate, thinly documented lives appear insignificant to the intellectual historians and theologians who regularly write about Edwards. This project came into focus only when I shifted my gaze from the central story to its margins. From this perspective, my attention was quickly drawn to the figure of Elizabeth Tuttle. Modern biographers of Edwards have routinely depicted his paternal grandmother as a rebellious woman who by her mad threats and promiscuous behavior drove her long-suffering husband to petition for a divorce. Ola Elizabeth Winslow's Pulitzer Prize–winning study, which appeared in 1940, established this crazy-grandmother story as a standard feature of the Edwards myth. Subsequent biographers from Perry Miller to George Marsden have invariably followed Winslow's lead, portraying her as the antithesis of the puritan goodwife.[4] This misbehaving woman added a pinch of spice, a whiff of scandal, to Edwards's pious moralism, but she also seemed a bit too convenient, a straw man dressed in cap and petticoats. Her gendered identity aroused my curiosity and led me again to ask, Just who was Elizabeth Tuttle?

The historical answer to this question consists of a series of dates: Elizabeth Tuttle was an ordinary puritan woman who was born in the New Haven colony in 1645. In 1667 she married a cooper named Richard Edwards and moved to Hartford, where her new husband lived. Less than seven months after the marriage she gave birth to an early baby, the first in the expected succession of children. In 1691, she separated from her family when the Connecticut General Court granted her husband's petition for a divorce. After this date she disappears; no record even notes the date of her death.

These dates reveal very little about the person whose life they represent. Laurel Thatcher Ulrich, who has contributed more than any other colonial American historian to the study of ordinary lives, recognizes this inadequacy. In her book *A Midwife's Tale*, a diary provides access to the "real story" of Martha Ballard's life. "[H]er biography would be little more than a succession of dates," Ulrich admits, without this meticulous first-person source.[5] It rescues this ordinary woman from the obscurity of numberless persons of the past whose lives have made only scant marks on the historical record. With Elizabeth Tuttle I am not so fortunate. No diary remains to trace the tedium of her daily life; no cache of letters provides a glimpse of the interiority of her existence. She left behind no first-person writings at all, not even a signature on a document. Shall we conclude from this absence that her life is irrecoverable, and move on? If not, how shall we fill this void?

Because Elizabeth Tuttle's story cannot be told directly, we must adopt an indirect approach. This method begins with the recognition that ordinary people in colonial America occupied clearly defined locations within the web of relationships that constituted the family. These relationships, although unequal, were reciprocal. They "tied men and women together in a complex series of mutual dependencies."[6] As interdependent pairs, husbands and wives, parents and children had relational identities, determined primarily by the duties and obligations that adhered to the role each performed in the family. This book takes as its object of study, therefore, Elizabeth Tuttle not as an isolated individual but as a member of a family. Beginning her life as a child in her parents' household, she became at marriage a member of the Edwards family, a new identity reinforced by her change in physical location. As Richard Edwards's wife, she became the female head of her own family defined by new reciprocal relationships. When he divorced her, she lost that role and was left without a visible place in any family, neither Tuttle nor Edwards. Because these interrelated and shifting family structures formed the framework within which she lived her life, reconstituting them can tell us something about who Elizabeth Tuttle was.

Sources documenting the Tuttle and Edwards families in their first and second generations are plentiful. Although Elizabeth made only meager tracks, many of the men and women to whom she was joined by ties of blood and marriage left behind more robust records of their colonial lives. From these materials a picture can be formed of the family she grew up in and the family she married into. These were migrant families, bringing with them to the New World identities already formed in the old, identities that shaped in many ways who they became after settlement. A reconstruction of this transatlantic identity must, therefore, begin with the complex of religious and economic motives that led these families to risk migration. Although the Tuttles, like most colonists, left no record of their decision-making process, the factors that pushed the Edwardses out of England are well documented in a rare collection of letters. For both families, however, sufficient information can be recovered to obtain a clear sense of their social locations in England, and of how successfully they embodied the puritan family ideal after settlement in the colonies.

The normative family in puritan New England has been described in a rich literature. Classic studies, such as Edmund S. Morgan's *The Puritan Family* and John P. Demos's *A Little Commonwealth*, have produced valuable portraits of the religious and cultural expectations defining the different roles each member of the family occupied.[7] Such abstract descriptions of the ideal type form useful standards of judgment, but they provide little information about how particular men and women actually behaved. To explore this disorderly reality I have adopted a method fruitfully employed by social historians studying the dynamic of town life in early New England. Like town studies, this book takes the extant colonial records as its textual foundation, but it reduces the scale of observation from the families that inhabited a particular town to two intertwined families. Colonial court records contain a plethora of information about the many members of Elizabeth Tuttle's interconnected kin network. Civil court records, which preserve such routine activities as probating an estate or suing out a debt action, identify times when her relations were flourishing or struggling in their worldly affairs. Criminal court records are an even richer source because of the unusual number of transgressions—ranging from small sex crimes to spectacular murders—that occurred in her extended family. These sources tell us more about how she and her relations misbehaved than how they lived their daily lives. Such exceptional moments reveal, however, a fragile and tragic dimension of Elizabeth Tuttle's experience that tells us much about who she was.

Central to this identity was gender. As a socially constructed category, gender is not defined in isolation but is performed in relationships. Focusing on Elizabeth Tuttle as a woman embedded in a web of personal relationships accents the gendered dimension of her experience. More specifically, it uncovers repeated examples of gendered conflict and violence in her extended family. Each of the pivotal moments in these men's and women's lives was gendered. The migrations of both families to the American colonies were driven at least in part by the difficulty of achieving the patriarchal ideal of manhood in seventeenth-century England. Once settled in Connecticut, the heads of both families struggled with differing degrees of success and failure to model this ideal. The crimes that shattered the Tuttle family in its second generation likewise can be understood only by reconstructing the gender expectations that constrained their perpetrators. And Elizabeth Tuttle's marriage broke down because of the gendered failures of each of the parties. When her increasing incapacity as a goodwife impeded her husband's patriarchal ambitions, their union began to unravel.

This divorce distinguishes Elizabeth Tuttle's life from that of most colonial goodwives. Because the Massachusetts and Connecticut colonies considered marriage to be a civil contract, not a religious sacrament, divorces were on occasion granted for cause. This unconventional end to her marriage is commonly paired with the early baby that damaged her union from its outset. These two experiences can tell us much about who Elizabeth Tuttle was, but whether they identify her as a rebellious woman, as biographers of Jonathan Edwards have commonly assumed, is a principal question driving this work.

Richard Edwards attributed the breakdown of his marriage to the willful and unsubmissive behavior of his wife. This figure of Elizabeth Tuttle, the only one preserved in the historical record, has a weight that is difficult to escape. In both the seventeenth and the twenty-first centuries, the conviction that women are by nature deceitful, untrustworthy, and prone to sexual sin undermines more positive images. Puritan divines directly challenged this threatening figure by constructing an image of woman as man's domestic "helpmeet" and spiritual companion. They "mounted the most cogent, most sustained, and most enduring attack on the contemporary wisdom concerning women's inherent evil." However, the older image of woman as a "necessary evil" persisted, ready to be deployed whenever she strayed from her God-ordained place in submission to men.[8] At one and possibly two moments in her life, Elizabeth Tuttle failed—or refused—to serve the man to whom she was yoked. Predictably, when she stepped out of place she morphed into the menacing figure of the unsubmissive woman. This image has endured for three centuries, acquiring new force as it appeared in new historical contexts.

My construction of a new figure of Elizabeth Tuttle is, therefore, an attempt to peel away this well-worn veneer and recover the fragments of lost humanity that lie beneath. To give this effort narrative coherence, I have structured it as a search not only for who Elizabeth Tuttle was but also for how she explained the breakdown of her marriage. Her husband's explanation has been preserved in his divorce petitions. But the disintegration of a marriage of almost twenty-five years seldom has only one explanation. Rarely is either party wholly innocent; both probably failed in some ways in their roles as husband, wife, and parent. I use the search for a thicker description of the cause of this divorce as a plot device that unifies the discrete elements of Elizabeth's experience into one sustained narrative. Like the uranium in Alfred Hitchcock's classic film *Notorious*, this cause is my "MacGuffin," a small mystery that sets the plot in motion.[9]

This narrative is constrained by Elizabeth Tuttle's absence. A conventional linear account of her activities in each successive stage of her life is impossible. Adjusting for this lack of biographical detail, I have assembled a series of interlocking episodes, each focused on a defining moment in the lives of the people to whom she was closely related. At times, my protagonist makes an appearance in these smaller stories. More often, she stands on the periphery of events, a participant whose part is unknown. These tales cumulatively form a larger narrative tracing an alternative explanation for the divorce. Although Elizabeth Tuttle has a leading role in this drama, her presence remains shadowy and ill defined. My narrative of the divorce exists on the boundary "between what we can know and what we can't know" about the past.[10] This is an exciting, but frustrating, place to be, always pointing to realities just beyond my grasp. In this location no complete explanation of any past event, including the divorce, can be discovered. But the lack of a complete explanation does not mean that all explanations are equally valid. Although the "evidence is uneven, various, and will generally support many interpretations," the historian Richard D. Brown observes, it "will not support *any* interpretation we may imagine."[11] Likely stories must be measured against what can be known to suggest the shape of the unknown.

Why does this small story matter? Why reconstruct the sources of unhappiness that caused the marriage of one ordinary puritan couple to fail? Why care about Elizabeth Tuttle at all? Microhistorians, who intensively study the lives of ordinary people from the past, have been accused of loving their subjects too much. This sin is, however, redeemed by larger motives. Microhistories commonly aim to solve small mysteries by tracing obscure subjects through meager records. But this exercise in historical detection is, as the historian Jill Lepore observes, a "means to an end—and that end is always explaining the culture."[12] One thing Elizabeth Tuttle's divorce helps to explain is the complex reality of puritan family life. Looking through this lens magnifies the sorrows endured by colonial men and women in their daily lives. Traditional studies of the puritan family emphasize factors contributing to its formation and flourishing, because they are representative of the normative family. Aberrations from the ideal, while recognized, are not the principal object of investigation. Events promoting family failure, such as mental instability, sexual indiscretion, death, violence, and financial loss, recede from view, creating the impression that each "little church" and "little commonwealth," to use the well-known seventeenth-century descriptors, modeled the ideal.[13] The Tuttle and Edwards families in their early generations reveal that not all colonists succeeded in their most important earthly task, the creation of an orderly household. The sorts of frustrations these men and women encountered while struggling to form families and to meet their domestic responsibilities, although more intense than most, were an ordinary part of daily life.

The story of Elizabeth Tuttle's divorce brings these frustrations into focus by capturing moments when they exploded into violence or caused marriages to break down. It shows that "conflict was central to family experience and that intersections of gender, sexuality, and violence were essential to both family and community in early America."[14] Although a unique conjunction of small misfortunes and shocking crimes constitute her story of family failure, the characters in this drama are ordinary people who experienced extraordinary events. An intensive study of the forces that ruptured the bonds tying these interlocking families together, therefore, exposes an underexplored dimension of the domestic lives of the colonists. It brings us one step closer to understanding the lived experience of ordinary people of the past.

This story also brings a second ideal a bit closer to the real. In the study of early American history, Jonathan Edwards has been loved too much. This inordinate love has exaggerated the singularity of the great theologian's work and distorted our understanding of his past. Modern scholars of Edwards have noted the domestic difficulties of his paternal grandparents, but like the friends and family of a divorcing couple, they have taken sides. Representing Elizabeth Tuttle as the guilty party preserves Richard Edwards's virtue. He has been presumed innocent on account of his grandson's accomplishments, and she has been condemned through her association with the image of the rebellious woman. Reconstructing the sources of this couple's unhappiness complicates this neat apportionment of praise and blame. Victim and villain cannot neatly be identified. As with most failed marriages, there is plenty of blame to share.

Passionate lovers of Edwards may read this narrative as a sort of betrayal. Microhistorians commonly do commit this sin, for their method, as Lepore observes, leads them "to betray people who have left abundant records in order to resurrect those who did not."[15] My story, however, is disloyal only to the disembodied image of Edwards first constructed by Perry Miller, the most important twentieth-century scholar of the colonial theologian's work. "The real life of Jonathan Edwards was the life of his mind," Miller announces in the opening line of his influential biography.[16] This approach constitutes its own act of betrayal. By equating "life" with intellectual production, Miller renders lifeless the ordinary men and women, like Elizabeth Tuttle, who have historically been denied elite expressions of agency. By idealizing Edwards's mind, he neglects the embodied world that produced this brilliant intellect.

The bodies of Edwards's seventeenth-century ancestors are impossible to ignore. Some had sex with unsanctioned partners and neglected their marital duties. Others defaulted on their creditors because they could not manage their money. And two committed brutal murders in fits of violent rage or uncontrolled madness. These all-too-physical acts forcibly situate Edwards in the social history of colonial New England. They embed his mind in the fleshy particulars that constituted the daily lives of the colonists. That he was a product of this world, and that he engaged this world throughout his ministry, does not, as Miller believed, trap his thought in the eighteenth century, nor does it negate his literary and philosophical accomplishments.[17] But it does challenge us to integrate his mind with his body and attend to how images of the ordinary people who inhabited his physical world have been constructed.

The women who played supporting characters in the drama of Edwards's ideas have predictably been represented by two sharply contrasting figures. His wife is depicted as the model mate for a great theologian, while his grandmother is cast as her opposite. By flaunting her infidelities and delighting in her disobedience, she appears just the sort of woman to make a man miserable. This representation of Elizabeth Tuttle, however, itself has a history. Tracing the construction of this image forms the sequel to our reconstruction of the divorce. This narrative of remembrance and forgetting begins in the years following the divorce. Like most voiceless women of the past, Elizabeth quickly disappears, taking with her all traces of the divorce. By the beginning of the nineteenth century, this unpleasant episode had been so effectively forgotten that Edwards's early biographers claimed his grandfather had remarried following his wife's death, not a messy divorce. Only as America began fashioning a new relation to its puritan past did the memory of Elizabeth Tuttle return.

These memories first reawakened during the colonial revival period of the latter nineteenth century. As the historian Joseph Conforti has shown, Edwards's theological writings were in the century following his death forged into an influential religious tradition. This Edwardsian tradition, in turn, laid the groundwork for his emergence as a "totemic figure in heavily nativist colonial revival narratives explaining the Anglo-Puritan origins of American culture."[18] This cultural appropriation of Edwards gradually revived memories of Elizabeth Tuttle and led her to reappear in a surprising new location. Because of Edwards's iconic status in American culture, his illustrious line of descendants was cast as the exemplar of a eugenically superior bloodline, illustrating the heritability of such traits as intellectual ability, moral character, and leadership. Searching for the font of this hereditary genius, eugenics promoters discovered the figure of Elizabeth Tuttle. Critics, however, deployed a more menacing image to discredit the campaign to limit reproduction of the "unfit." My protagonist emerges from this debate with an identity fashioned from two of the eugenics movement's central preoccupations: hereditary insanity and sexual deviancy. And this identity persisted throughout the twentieth century. Adopted by early American historians, the crazy-grandmother story became a regular feature of the Edwards myth.

. . .

So, who was Elizabeth Tuttle, and what was her story of the divorce? Taking these questions as my starting point, I have uncovered two new narratives, bound together by the figure of Elizabeth Tuttle. The first section of the book reconstructs the circumstances contributing to the breakdown of her marriage. Spanning three generations, the story of this one marriage's failure comprises many families. In this dense web of domestic relations, multiple households were damaged or destroyed by the same things that cause marital crises today—economic instability, sexual indiscretion, violent death, and mental illness. By telling these small stories, each chapter illustrates how difficult the puritan family ideal was to achieve and how easily it could be shattered. Together, they trace the slow accumulation of stressors that contributed to the collapse of Elizabeth's marriage.

Chapter 1 explores the factors that may have led Elizabeth's father, William Tuttle, to leave his ancestral home in the English Midlands and migrate with his large and flourishing family to the New Haven colony, where our female protagonist was born. Chapter 2 similarly traces the migration of William Edwards and his mother, Anne, from their modest east London home to Hartford, Connecticut, where our male protagonist was born. Although raised in a dysfunctional household, Richard Edwards married a girl from a prominent family; his union with Elizabeth was, however, damaged from the outset by the domestic crisis caused by the arrival of an early baby. Chapters 3 and 4 focus on the two murders that bookend the disintegration of their marriage. Nine years after the wedding, Elizabeth's younger brother Benjamin murdered their sister Sarah in a moment of uncontrolled rage. This awful providence shattered the large Tuttle family, and in its aftermath Elizabeth, as well as two of her siblings, began to break down. Her older brother David was eventually placed in a guardian's care, while her younger sister Mercy, in a shocking repetition of her brother's crime, was driven to kill her eldest son. Chapter 5 brings all these threads together to reconstruct the long train of tragedies that eventually led Richard Edwards to file for divorce.

This book, however, is not simply about telling stories of ordinary people from the past; it is also about how the stories of great men are remembered and retold. The second section of the book traces Elizabeth Tuttle's contested memory. Chapter 6 considers how in the years after the divorce the Edwards family waged an extended campaign to refashion the past. Richard quickly erased his troublesome first wife by remarrying and starting a new, more prestigious career. Although plagued by anxious doubts, Timothy

Edwards continued his father's makeover. By the third generation, all troubling memories had been forgotten, leaving Jonathan Edwards free to fight his own battles. Chapter 7 examines the complex of factors leading to the reemergence of the figure of Elizabeth Tuttle. The search for the source of the crazy-grandmother story, which appears repeatedly in modern scholarship on Edwards, eventually leads to the eugenics movement. Documenting the prominent role an image of the Edwards family played in this popular social reform program reveals an unexplored dimension of the puritan theologian's nineteenth-century legacy.

These two narratives intersect in the figure of Elizabeth Tuttle. She is the plot device joining the original story to its sequel, but the sequel in turn reveals why her image has dominated the telling of the original tale. By deconstructing the source of the crazy-grandmother story, we open a quiet space in which to listen for Elizabeth Tuttle's voice. Her representation as a rebellious woman has, however, an ineluctable narrative power. Even as we strain to catch a few words from our protagonist, this familiar image will likely be heard muttering mad threats and taunting her poor husband with her extramarital escapades. But there is another way to tell the story of the divorce, and we will now begin teasing it out from the historical records.

PROLOGUE

On the morning of the last Tuesday in May 1690, Richard Edwards was perhaps carefully planing the edge of a pipe stave or tamping a hoop into place around a finished cask. He would not, however, spend this day working in his cooper's shop. Having more important business, he took off his apron, set aside his mallet and driver, picked up a thick bundle of papers, and set out for Sandford's Inn, where the Connecticut Court of Assistants met for its twice-yearly sessions.[1] As he entered the court chamber, Edwards likely felt confident that his case was strong. He had obtained two witnesses to substantiate his charges, having persuaded his oldest children to testify in a sworn deposition to their mother's "great obstinacy and averseness against our Father." He had also solicited the support of several local divines, who judged that the "Scriptures seem to allow a Husband Some (limited) personal power in putting away his wife."[2] His petition, which had been composed almost a year earlier, filled more than eight closely written quarto-sized pages. When his case was called to the bench, he submitted this lengthy document to the Assistants and presented his argument. In the petition he describes a long train of abuse that he claims his wife began in the early days of their marriage and continued with only a few periods of remission for almost twenty-three years. He also includes an extended exegesis of several New Testament texts to demonstrate that scripture permits divorce for "Any Esencyall Breech of the marage Bond."[3] Despite these weighty evidences and arguments, however, the court postponed its ruling.

This delay gave the Assistants additional time to consider the defendant's response to her husband's allegations. As a young woman, Elizabeth Tuttle had married and moved from New Haven to Hartford, where the Edwards family lived, so she had no close kin in town to testify in her defense. The court, accordingly, ordered that notice be given to the "brethren and sister of Said Edwards his wife" to attend its fall session and "Object what they have to Say in the Case." The Assistants also wanted to hear Elizabeth's side of the story. Although women regularly appeared in colonial courtrooms, she had not been present to witness Richard argue his plea or to issue a rejoinder. To obtain her testimony, the court formed a committee and ordered it "to Inform the Said Edwards his wife, of her husbands desires, and to make report of what She Shall Say unto them, unto this Court."[4]

No record exists of what Elizabeth said when she learned of "her husbands desires." If the committee made a written record of her response, the document has not survived. More likely, the findings were reported orally to the Assistants at the next hearing of the case. Either way, Elizabeth's side of the story has been erased, leaving only the sound of Richard's powerful voice. This small gap in the historical record is hard to see and even harder to fill. But if we listen closely, Elizabeth's silence becomes a clue pointing to a more complex narrative. Pursuing this clue uncovers a hidden world of murder and madness, hasty marriage and thwarted ambition. We cannot know what Elizabeth said to the men who visited her home on their unpleasant errand, but searching for her answer is a reminder that, despite the basic stability of the puritan family during the first century of settlement, individual families did not always flourish. All was not right in these little peaceable kingdoms.

HARDY PURITAN PIONEERS

The story of Elizabeth Tuttle's unhappy marriage has several possible beginnings. This telling starts with the *Planter*, which in April 1635 was moored in the Port of London awaiting its second voyage to the Massachusetts Bay colony.[1] England in the seventeenth century had a flourishing river life, and the River Thames was constantly congested with traffic. The *Planter* was but one of a bewildering variety of watercraft—pinnaces, ketches, lighters, wherries, barks, shallops, pinks, and sloops, to cite just a few—that sailed its waters at any one time. Although boats were free to moor as they liked, large merchant vessels generally dropped anchor in the pool below London Bridge and discharged their cargo at Billingsgate and the other legal quays, for the bridge's narrow arches and rapid waters made passage treacherous even with the drawbridge raised.[2] Skilled watermen piloted barges and other small craft upriver to unload their goods at Queenhithe and the many wharves and landing places that crowded the north bank of the river. And along the waterfront from Westminster to the Tower, boats also picked up and discharged passengers who found water travel more convenient than navigating the dirty cobblestone streets of the capital city.[3]

The ship that transported Elizabeth's family to the New World had been built the previous year in Wapping, through the investment of two puritan merchants and its master, Nicholas Trerise. At 170 tons, the *Planter* was a medium-sized vessel, likely having two decks in its main hull to accommodate the crew, cargo, and provisions necessary for the long voyage. In March 1634, just prior to the ship's first sailing to Massachusetts Bay, its owners had obtained a certificate permitting them "to furnish their ship with ordnance out of the founder's store," for like other sea-going ships, the *Planter* could

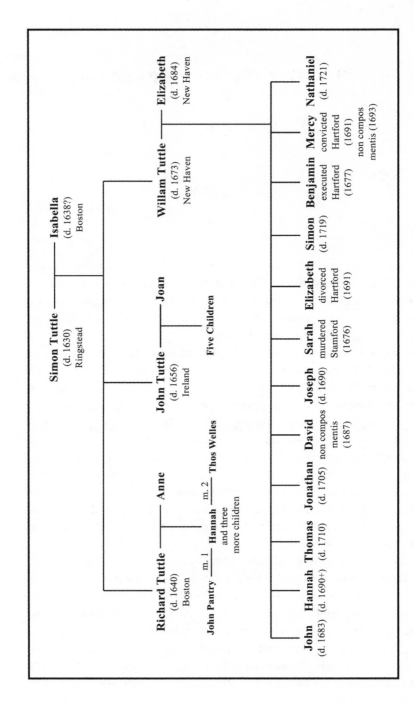

Tuttle genealogy. Illustrated by John Luchin.

not venture from port without the arms to protect itself from privateers.[4] The following spring it was boarding passengers for a second trip to New England, as one of five ships that sailed from London to Boston in April 1635 at the height of the puritan migration.[5]

The *Planter* transported 118 English colonists on this second voyage, considerably more than the average of 69 passengers that sailed on New England–bound ships in 1635. The "closeness" of the ship would have been mitigated, however, by the near-relation of many on board. The composition of its passengers clearly illustrates that "travelers organized themselves so as to brave the uncertainty of an Atlantic crossing with relatives and neighbors." The historian Allison Games estimates that at least 35 of the passengers traveled from St. Albans, Hertfordshire, to board the *Planter* together, and approximately 40 percent of the ship's passengers whose county of origin can be identified were residents of Hertfordshire. Another roughly 22 percent came from the county of Suffolk, with smaller percentages from Northamptonshire and Middlesex.[6] And within these geographical groupings most passengers traveled in the company of family members. The New England migration comprised primarily families. Although estimates vary, the number of family cohorts was high, ranging between 60 and 90 percent depending on the sample.[7] Commonly a married couple and their children made the voyage together, but a significant number of "extended families of sometimes extraordinary complexity" relocated to New England as one company.[8]

The Tuttle clan was certainly the largest family company on the *Planter* and one of the largest extended families to emigrate as a group in 1635. Three Tuttle brothers were the group's core household heads. Richard Tuttle, who at forty-two was the eldest, sailed with his wife, Anne, and their three children, ranging in age from six to twelve years. John Tuttle and his wife, Joan, ages thirty-nine and forty-two respectively, traveled not only with their four young children but also with four older children from Joan's previous marriage and her eldest daughter's new husband. William Tuttle, the youngest brother, was twenty-six years old when he boarded the *Planter*. He and his wife, Elizabeth—future parents of the Elizabeth Tuttle who is our story's protagonist—brought with them three children less than four years of age, including a three-month-old infant. In addition to this horizontal sibling network, the company of Tuttles also extended vertically to include Isabella Tuttle, the brothers' seventy-year-old mother, and John Tuttle's sixty-five-year-old mother-in-law.[9] Counting servants, who were considered part of their masters' households, the large company traveling with the Tuttles to Massachusetts Bay reached a total of twenty-seven members, and possibly more.[10]

Debate about the motivations for migration has focused on the economic and religious factors that pushed and pulled so many English men and women to leave their homeland between 1620 and 1640. Most historians, however, agree that "[m]onocausal explanations of motivation are simplistic and unhistorical," arguing instead that "a number of factors intersected to form a matrix of migration."[11] To more effectively map this matrix, recent work on the migration has focused on an analysis of the regional and local conditions of life in early Stuart England, where such data is available.[12] But if the migration "had as much to do with private hopes and frustrations, and opportunities of the moment, as with assessments of the comparative religious and economic prospects of England and America," then individual explanations will ultimately remain opaque to us.[13] Because the emigrants left few traces of their decision-making processes, "historians of the Great Migration must live in a world of the plausible, not the conclusive."[14]

The "plausible" story of the Tuttles' migration begins in the English Midlands. They were a Northamptonshire family that hailed from the village of Ringstead, located in the northeastern part of the county about twenty miles from the county town of Northampton. By 1635, the year of their migration, John had moved to Hertfordshire to pursue a career in the cloth trade, while Richard and William were raising families of their own in Ringstead. These three brothers, and their wives and children, must have spent long hours debating the merits of migration. What did not lead them out of England is, however, easier to identify than what did. The Tuttles may have been pushed by financial worries or pulled by hopes for greater gain, but like most migrants they did not flee England to escape poverty or financial ruin.[15]

The Tuttles were a family of middling status, neither gentry nor landless poor but prosperous landowners who made a living farming and raising sheep. The brothers' father described himself as a "yeoman."[16] One step on the rural social ladder below the gentry, yeomen traditionally held land in freehold having an annual value of 40 shillings or more. In practice, however, yeomen were substantial farmers who earned incomes that could range anywhere from £40 to £200 a year, trading surplus agricultural products on the growing English commodities market.[17] That the Tuttle patriarch was a freeholder is confirmed by a 1605 list that named him one of seven men of this status in the village of Ringstead.[18] Given that this village had no resident gentry, Simon Tuttle and his fellow yeomen would have occupied a position at the top of the local hierarchy, the "cocks of their parish."[19]

The Midlands was England's principal grain-producing region. Its yeomen typically raised crops of wheat, barley, and peas and supplemented their

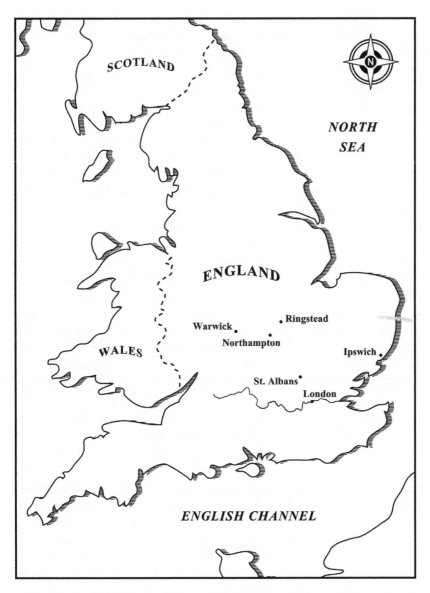

England, 1600s. Illustrated by John Luchin.

income through other rural pursuits, such as cattle and sheep grazing, in a practice known as mixed husbandry.[20] The Tuttles, for example, owned a malt mill, which suggests that they, like many Midlands families, grew barley and brewed their own ale, and they raised sheep to take advantage of the expanding market for wool, which had by the early seventeenth century become one of Northamptonshire's main cash crops.[21] These commodities would have cushioned the Tuttles against the volatile market that troubled early modern England, allowing the family to withstand times of dearth and profit from shortages and rising prices. Like other well-positioned yeomen, Simon Tuttle used his profits to expand his land holdings.[22] While small farmers floundered in the marketplace and lost their land to enclosure, his family's standard of living improved.

Despite this economic success, the Tuttles were undoubtedly affected by the general social upheaval that accompanied the enclosure of common farmland in their region. By the end of the fifteenth century almost half the arable land in England had been fenced.[23] The Midlands in general and Northamptonshire in particular were hit hard by the adoption of this new method of land management, which ended the customary right of peasants and small landowners to farm open fields. According to the enclosure commissions of 1517 and 1607, the total acres enclosed was far higher in this county than in others investigated.[24] In response, Rockingham Forest, which occupied much of the region north of Ringstead, experienced a surge in population as displaced small farmers and unemployed rural wage earners were attracted to its ample common lands and forest industries.[25] The incidence of enclosure riots also increased in the area, climaxing in the Midland Revolt of 1607, the largest of the riots during James I's reign. Violence began in several villages just west of Ringstead, near the market town of Kettering, before spreading to the neighboring counties of Warwick and Leicester.[26] Desperate agricultural workers, according to one contemporary observer, "violently cut and broke down hedges, filled up ditches, and laid open all such inclosures of commons and grounds as they found enclosed." The rioting continued for several weeks, until the ringleaders were hanged and their quarters publicly displayed in various Northamptonshire towns, including Thrapston, located only a few miles north of Ringstead.[27]

Although these changes were often disastrous for small farmers, yeomen, whose interests largely coincided with those of large gentlemen landowners, recognized their advantages and actively implemented enclosure on their lands. The Tuttles likely profited from such uncertain economic times, but they were also surely aware of the risks. The volatility of the agricultural market may have encouraged the second son to abandon rural life and pursue a career in the cloth trade. Internal migration was commonplace in early-seventeenth-century England, "a part of the life cycle for most young men and women."[28] Many moved to escape poverty and starvation, others for economic betterment. Such betterment migrants were commonly children of rural landowners who had the resources to start a son in an urban trade. Because wealthy townsmen occupied a social status higher than that of rural yeomanry, such a move could be a step up.[29]

The Tuttles established their son in St. Albans, located about fifty miles southeast of Ringstead in Hertfordshire. Travelers from nearby London regularly lodged in the many inns that lined this ancient abbey town's central thoroughfare, as did farmers and merchants coming from East Anglia to trade at its twice-weekly market.[30] In this likely location John Tuttle set up business, paying £6 "freedom money" to gain admission into the Mercers' Guild, one of the four companies that dominated the town's local economy.[31] Mercers, who traditionally dealt in such luxury fabrics as silk, linen, and fustian, faced during this period increased competition from unlicensed tradesmen and suffered from the depression that crippled the cloth trade in the early seventeenth century, as it shifted from dealing in broadcloth to "New Draperies."[32] Despite such challenging economic times, John appears to have flourished in St. Albans; he married a wealthy widow with an £800 estate and joined the town elite.[33]

The Tuttle brothers also benefited from their father's skillful financial management. When he died in 1630, Simon Tuttle left all three of his sons with sufficient means to be independent householders. The eldest, who had already obtained his portion of the estate, received only a modest inheritance, consisting of a few acres of pastureland and "half a dusson sheepe."[34] The second son was given "a dwelling house" in Ringstead, "with all the houses thereunto belonginge and the yard and orchard thereunto adjoyning." William, the son of principal interest to this story, was unmarried when his father died and, unlike his older brothers, had not yet been set up in a career. He accordingly was granted the bulk of the estate, but his father ensured a comfortable maintenance for his widow by stipulating that his youngest son would inherit only after his mother's death. Isabella's life estate included the "house, messuage, or tenement wherein I now dwell, togither with all the houses, landes, yardes, meadowes, pastures, commons, profits, commodities, and appurtenaunces whatsoever thereunto belonging." William was directed to "husband his mother's busines to the best of his power," knowing that, upon her death, he would inherit not only this property in its entirety but also most of the movable goods within the house, his father's flock of sheep, and additional meadowlands.[35]

Lacking the inventory of the Tuttle estate, we cannot now estimate the full extent and value of this property. One clue is provided by a deed of sale the Tuttles executed in November 1634, undoubtedly in preparation for their voyage. At the height of the migration, costs for a modest migrant family were around £50, including ship fare, baggage charges, and foodstuffs for the trip.[36] Transport for the large company of Tuttles would have required an outlay of several hundred pounds minimum, and substantially more if the family made the journey in some comfort. Five months before their departure, the eldest son sold his homestead and lands in Ringstead for £760.[37] This substantial sum, a part of which was surely used to cover the costs of his family's passage, indicates that on the eve of migration Richard Tuttle, like his brother John, was a prosperous member of his local community. Young William had not yet come into his inheritance, but given the size of his mother's estate he could anticipate receiving in the future considerable real and personal property.[38] Neither he, therefore, nor his two older brothers boarded the *Planter* in a state of economic distress.

The Tuttle family migration was also not a flight from religious persecution. Only a minority of the New England colonists had experienced persecution or imprisonment for their beliefs. According to the historian David Cressy, some felt the demand for religious "uniformity to be intolerable, and anticipated worse to come, but few were direct victims of its wrath."[39] Even if the Tuttles never had to answer for their faith before a magistrate, however, they likely were troubled by religious concerns. Although no clear statement of religious commitment remains, evidence suggests they were members of Northamptonshire's godly, or puritan, community, which in the early seventeenth century was forced to conform its habits of worship to the Crown's demands.

The Tuttle patriarch's will contains several signs of the family's puritan sympathies. Appended to its standard preamble, which commits the dead man's "soule into the handes of Allmightye god my Creator," is the more explicitly Calvinist hope "through the onely meritts of Jesus Christe my Saviour to be made partaker of Everlasting life."[40] Stronger clues are found in its burial instructions.[41] Instead of requesting a sacramental burial in the churchyard, Simon Tuttle directs his wife to give him a "Christen burialls," a phrasing that indicates a more nonconformist stance, and he voices the distinctive Pauline hope to receive "at the general resurrection, not a mortall, but an immortall and glorious bodye."[42] Finally, as a last bequest he leaves twenty shillings "to be distributed amongst the poorest sorte" of his village of Ringstead, a common expression of the social concern of the godly.[43] Although wills must be read with caution for hints of the testator's religious beliefs, this accumulation of strong Protestant sentiment clearly reflects a commitment to the puritan cause.[44]

Another indication the Tuttles were a puritan family is found in the bill of sale for the eldest brother's Ringstead property, which identifies the purchaser as "John Bellamy, citizen and stationer of London."[45] Bellamy came from a prominent Northamptonshire family that lived just north of Ringstead, and the Tuttle brothers had probably known him before he left home to take up the book trade. But they likely would not have maintained their association with this London radical for more than twenty years had they not shared his religious beliefs. A member of a separatist congregation with ties to the community of English Protestant exiles that founded Plymouth Colony, Bellamy became a leading publisher of puritan writings on both sides of the Atlantic. His bookshop "at the three Golden Lyons in Cornhill" printed treatises by such leaders of the migration as John Robinson, John Cotton, William Bradford, and John Winthrop. He also published important tracts promoting colonial settlement. The Tuttles may have read several Bellamy imprints as they prepared for migration. *Good News from New England*, for example, chronicled the settlement of Plymouth, while *New England's Prospect*, which appeared the year before they sailed, praised the abundant natural resources in the colonies.[46] Bellamy fueled puritan migration to New England by publishing these popular promotional tracts, and by purchasing Richard Tuttle's estate he provided a family of hardy puritan pioneers the means to escape the campaign to enforce religious conformity in their home diocese.

Peterborough, which included the counties of Northampton and Rutland, "was a diocese of sharp contrasts, wherein representatives of a wide range of the religious opinions available in the early seventeenth century existed side by side."[47] A robust puritan tradition flourished alongside a persistent conservatism supported by the local aristocracy, which included several old Catholic families. Protestant ideas first took root in the Nene River valley, which stretched along the eastern border of the county and included Ringstead. Powerful puritan gentry, who dominated the western highlands, worked with widespread cooperation of the laity to support puritan clergy through the patronage system.[48] Ringstead itself was a chapel annexed to the parish of Denford, whose advowson was owned in the seventeenth century by a Northamptonshire

Catholic family.[49] Nevertheless, in the 1630s a group of godly Londoners salaried at Ringstead a curate named Henry Raymond, who quickly developed a reputation as a leading nonconformist by preaching openly against the *Book of Sports*. This controversial tract, which promoted recreation and leisure activities on the Sabbath, discouraged strict puritan worship.[50]

The Tuttle family likely relished the rich diet of godly sermons available in parishes spread throughout their diocese.[51] Familiar with the journey downriver to the large Northampton market, they surely on occasion heard the preachers at All Saints, a center for radical puritanism that brought many neighboring parishes into its orbit.[52] As early as 1570, ministers had begun meeting for religious "exercises" and "prophesying" in Northampton, the largest urban area in the diocese.[53] Despite suppression of these activities, godly clergy again began to gather regularly at Northampton during the reign of James I, and by the mid-1630s a combination lecture, in which several ministers preached in rotation, had been established there.[54] The county town was not, however, the only preaching center in the diocese. Combination lectures were established in at least seven other large market towns.[55] Ten miles upriver from Ringstead a combination operated at Oundle, where a scandalous group of millenarian separatists had formed in the late sixteenth century.[56] And at Kettering a lecture survived for more than twenty years, making the market town closest to Ringstead "one of the county's most vigorous evangelical centres" until the lecture's suppression around 1636.[57]

The campaign to enforce ceremonial conformity in worship began in the Peterborough diocese in 1601, when a staunch anti-Calvinist, Thomas Dove, was appointed bishop. During his long tenure the "enforcement of conformity in the diocese [was] more vigorous than was typical nationally at this date."[58] In 1604 twenty-nine diocesan clergy were suspended from their posts for nonconformity, and sixteen of the most uncompromising were deprived of their livings, a number larger than that found in any other diocese.[59] Additional clergy were suspended in 1611, a clear signal that the occasional conformity commonly practiced by moderate puritans in the diocese would no longer be tolerated. In 1615, the newly appointed chancellor of the diocese, Sir John Lambe, began a sustained campaign against nonconformists in the county town of Northampton. Clergy were presented for such offenses as refusing to wear vestments or to use the Book of Common Prayer, and even more provocatively, laity were required to conform in such matters as kneeling for communion and observance of saints' days.[60]

When Charles I acceded to the throne, Arminianism, which rejected the Calvinist doctrine of predestination, became the official policy of the

Church of England, and the campaign against nonconformity in Peterborough acquired the Crown's full support.[61] Diocesan bishops who served in the 1630s worked in concert with Archbishop William Laud to suppress the word-centered piety of the puritans and replace it with a new sacramentalism, which asserted that grace was available to all who participated in the ceremonies of the Church. The material expression of this sacramentalism was a rigorous altar policy that shifted the locus of grace in the Church from pulpit to table, preaching ministry to sacramental priesthood. Each parish was required to fix its communion table, which had been placed at the center of the congregation during communion, at the east end of the chancel and to rail it in to prevent wandering animals from profaning the sacred space. In this new position the table became an altar whose inherent holiness was emphasized by kneeling and bowing requirements, the use of elaborate communion utensils, and the consecration of the church and its yard.[62]

In the years preceding the implementation of this new altar policy, the Tuttle family, like other Northamptonshire puritans, probably tensely debated the changes occurring in their diocese. "Peterborough was particularly polarized, perhaps owing to an entrenched puritan community clashing with an anti-Calvinist episcopal administration of unusual longevity."[63] The oldest brother, who served as a churchwarden in Ringstead, could not have avoided entanglement in the debate over the growing strength of Arminianism in his diocese.[64] During the early 1630s parishes throughout Peterborough began actively to resist compliance with Laud's altar policy. "[N]o church or chapel, however insignificant," the historian John Fielding observes, "escaped the repercussions of the policy." Ringstead, for example, was ordered in 1631 to repair its chancel screen, designed to separate clergy from laity, and in 1634 it was cited for allowing swine and cattle into the churchyard.[65] To explain the lack of a railed-in altar, the church, in carefully chosen words, noted that the position of the pulpit had caused "Inconveniencies."[66]

When word of these disturbing developments reached St. Albans, the second brother likely responded with his own religious grievances. Like the county of Northampton, Hertfordshire had a long history of nonconformity. St. Albans' proximity to London, the center of Elizabethan puritanism, encouraged the growth of a godly community in the borough's four parishes. During the latter sixteenth century, a lecture was established at St. Michaels, sponsored by local puritan gentry, and the pastor at the Abbey church presided over a largely puritan congregation. However, because St. Albans was an archdeaconry in the diocese of London, its godly clergy were closely watched and frequently disciplined, and by the time John Tuttle began establishing his business in the borough, strict conformist ministers had been installed in each of the parish churches.[67] He probably found St. Albans' religious climate as hostile as that constricting his brothers in Ringstead.

As this reconstruction suggests, in the years preceding their migration to New England the extended Tuttle family likely experienced both economic uncertainties and religious frustrations. These factors should be included in the accumulation of hopes and grievances that ultimately tipped the scales in favor of migration, but neither seems to have had sufficient weight on its own. Among the many members of the Tuttle clan, moreover, each "active decision maker" undoubtedly "had his or her personal mix of reasons for leaving."[68] While these individual pushes and pulls have been lost, religious motives surely predominated for some, while others were drawn by the hope of economic gain. The historian Virginia Anderson argues that without religious motivation successful farmers and tradesmen like the Tuttles would never have "exchanged an economically viable present for a most uncertain future." "[R]eligious motivation is the only factor," she concludes, "with sufficient power to explain the departure of so many otherwise ordinary families."[69] The migration of the large company of Tuttles, however, reveals another powerful motivation. The only factor sufficient to explain the movement of the entire family, including two elderly widows, several servants, and a three-month-old infant, is the family itself. Yeoman emigrants were typically characterized by their "kin-connectedness."[70] What carried the Tuttles together to New England was the strength of their family ties.

John Tuttle may have provided the first push. Having relocated to St. Albans, he had already broken the family's deep roots in the Northamptonshire soil. Frequent travel to buy and sell cloth at distant markets would have further accustomed him to travel. The opportunity for a second migration, always less difficult than the first, appears to have presented itself when a group of investors formed in St. Albans to finance a voyage to New England. The large number of passengers from this town on the *Planter* suggests it was a center of organization and recruitment for this voyage.[71] What tied this central Hertfordshire group to passengers from other counties is uncertain, but the link with the Northamptonshire cohort is clear. Kinship bound the extended family John Tuttle had formed in St. Albans to that of his two brothers in Ringstead. If he did make the first decision to move, Richard and William may have joined him not only to escape economic uncertainty or religious distress but perhaps, more important, to keep their already fragmented family together. Certainly, this was the effect of their group migration, for it appears that no significant member of the family remained behind.

The *Planter* began taking on passengers in March 1635. Before boarding, each prospective migrant was required to submit to a rigorous examination in order to obtain formal permission to depart. The Privy Council had the previous year stayed the *Planter* and "divers Shipps now in the River of Thames" until its passengers had taken the oaths of supremacy and allegiance and its master had posted a £100 bond guaranteeing his compliance with this order.[72] By the time his ship again sailed, its passengers were also required to obtain a certificate of orthodoxy from a minister and an attestation of financial solvency from two justices of the peace.[73] Having cleared these hurdles, the first group of passengers boarded the *Planter* on 22 March 1635. Over the next few weeks the ship gradually filled. The St. Albans company arrived on the 2nd of April and were joined in a few days by the remaining Tuttle family from Ringstead, whose journey to London was longer and more difficult than that of their brother. The final passenger boarded a week later, and if the winds cooperated Master Trerise piloted his ship out of the Port of London on the next tide.[74]

Spring was the favored time for migration.[75] Making their passage before the height of the hurricane season, colonists had time to settle into their new homes before the New England winter began. Furthermore, travel on poorly maintained English roads and waterways ground to a halt during the winter.[76] The winter before the Tuttles sailed to New England had been so hard that, according to one contemporary observer, "the Thames was frozen and men went and rode over it."[77] Until the thaw, no ship could have sailed from port. Passage to New England took on average between six and twelve weeks.[78] The hardships of the voyage are well known: cramped quarters, seasickness, scurvy, infectious diseases, and the ever-present possibility of privateers, shipwreck, and death. While few travelers actually drowned and most arrived safely in New England, ships were occasionally lost.[79] Two years earlier the *Planter*'s master had captained a ship that began leaking so badly he was forced to return to port.[80] More commonly, however, passengers perished from accident and disease, and only the rare ship made it across the Atlantic without any loss of life. The Tuttles likely prepared to die before boarding by drafting wills and seeking signs of assurance of salvation. But perhaps their best preparation for the voyage lay in the large network of relations, servants, and neighbors they had assembled as traveling companions. Once the ship had set sail, these familiar faces would have lightened the "enormous emotional, physical, and psychological strain that long Atlantic voyages put on passengers."[81] And because most ships traveled in convoys with other migrant vessels, the *Planter* itself also probably did not make the journey alone.[82] Together with the *Hopewell*, the *Elizabeth*, and several other New England–bound vessels that departed the Port of London in April 1635, it apparently sailed safely into Boston Bay on the 7th of June, when John Winthrop recorded the arrival of seven ships.[83]

The New World that the Tuttles encountered when they disembarked from the *Planter* was both familiar and strange. By 1635, the "howling wilderness" had receded as increasing numbers of immigrants arrived in the colony, built homes, cleared farmland, and planted new towns and settlements. Having a population of around 600 inhabitants principally engaged in agriculture, Boston resembled in size and occupation the small village that had been the Tuttle home.[84] The three brothers probably gasped at the cramped and hastily built houses in which even the town's elites lived, but they likely welcomed several other features of their new homeland. Godly ministers regularly preached at the Boston meetinghouse. Land ownership was liberally, if unequally, spread throughout the population. And the franchise was broad, making participation in government affairs more accessible than in England.

The two older brothers quickly established social positions comparable to those which they had occupied prior to their Atlantic passage. Richard and his wife were admitted as members in the Boston church only a few months after their arrival, just as the qualifications for admission were becoming more rigorous.[85] Beginning in 1635, prospective members had not only to profess their faith and exhibit a Christian way of life but also to relate a convincing narrative of their conversion experiences to the congregation, who subsequently voted on their admission.[86] Only thirty of the 1635 migrants qualified for admission in the year of their arrival.[87] That two of the Tuttles earned this distinction further demonstrates that at least some members of the family boarded the *Planter* with strong religious commitments.

Because church membership was a prerequisite for freemanship and, for a time, land ownership in Boston, early admission paved the way for additional advancements.[88] Richard Tuttle was granted a home lot in town and 161 acres of farmland on the North Shore, and through additional purchases he soon owned a total of 344 acres.[89] Only days after taking the freeman's oath, he was elected to serve as one of the first group of selectmen, overseeing land allotment and other matters of business for Boston.[90] And in 1638 he was elected constable, a court officer who served as "the right arm of the magistrates." These distinctions placed the eldest brother in the lower ranks of Boston's gentry, comprising a coterie of 27 men who dominated the social, political, and economic life of the town. Identified as one of Boston's "richer inhabitants," he quickly built a solid foundation for a successful career in the Bay Colony.[91]

The second brother likewise became a leading member of the new town of Ipswich, located about 30 miles north of Boston on the coast above Cape Ann. Having convenient access to the sea, Ipswich promoted its commercial economy from the outset by fostering business and trade. Many of its early settlers were artisans and tradesmen from industrial towns in East Anglia and the neighboring county of Hertford, which had been John Tuttle's adopted home.[92] The wealthy cloth merchant was granted a home lot in the village and several parcels of land. Quickly acquiring substantial additional property, he had land holdings totaling on average 300 acres, including the hundred-acre "farm" that the town granted him in 1643.[93] He took the freeman's oath in March 1639, indicating that by that time he had qualified as a member of the Ipswich Church.[94] Over the next 15 years he served on a variety of committees, joined the prestigious Massachusetts Military Company, and was elected representative to the General Court.[95] As a commercial trader who bought and sold goods on the overseas market, he soon enjoyed a place among the five wealthiest men in his new hometown.[96]

For the youngest of the brothers, the Bay Colony was less welcoming. In the months after his arrival, William Tuttle was accepted as an inhabitant of Charlestown, conveniently connected by a short ferry ride to Boston's North End.[97] Settling near his brother Richard's home, he maintained the family residence pattern established in England, particularly important perhaps while the Tuttles' aging mother was alive. But Charlestown, one of the seven original Bay Colony towns, was by 1635 dominated by a well-established and wealthy gentry class that had amassed large land holdings. Although his older brother was able to penetrate a comparably closed social elite in Boston, William apparently did not command the necessary resources. Younger than the average Charlestown resident, he did not bring to the community proven experience in business, trade, politics, or religion. And despite good family connections, he did not achieve what was perhaps the most important prerequisite for social advancement in Charlestown, church membership.[98] His wife quickly qualified for admission, joining in 1636 the Boston church attended by her brother-in-law's family. But no record indicates that William Tuttle joined either the Boston or the Charlestown church during his time in the Bay Colony.[99] This failure hurt his prospects. In 1637 Charlestown's elites solidified their town dominance by limiting land ownership to church members. In a year's time "18 percent of the population controlled over 70 percent of the land."[100]

Soon after William Tuttle settled into Charlestown, the town allowed him "to erect a windmill on the Town Hill" and appointed him to a minor committee. He also received a piece of hay ground and a share of common lands on which to graze cattle.[101] No record, however, states that he was granted a home lot or that he obtained property through purchase.[102] The only indication of his involvement in a land transaction dates from April 1638, when "Mr. Tuttell of Ipswich, and Mr. Tuttell of Charlestowne" acquired a house in Boston as payment for a debt. William and his growing family may have moved out of Charlestown at this point, but their daughter Elizabeth was not to be born in the Bay.[103] The female lead in our domestic drama was to make her home in the newly established colony of New Haven, after her family had endured the rigors of a second migration.

The internal migration of the New England colonists mirrored English patterns of mobility. Accustomed to looking for greener pastures in times of adversity, dissatisfied settlers frequently moved from older, well-established towns to smaller outlying villages, or they swarmed in groups to plant a new settlement.[104] By migrating within and between the New England colonies, settlers "sorted themselves out into the communities in which they would remain for the rest of their lives."[105] A variety of forces propelled this movement, but, as with internal migration in England, the strongest impetus was economic betterment. Newly formed towns offered household heads not only the opportunity to purchase land but, more important, the benefits of proprietorship. A town's original proprietors received an allotment of land proportional to their social status. They also received the right to shares in future distributions of the town's common lands, which offered economic security for generations to come. For many colonists this lucrative benefit was worth the price of a second migration.

The Tuttles' move to New Haven did entail some losses. By leaving the Bay, William ruptured the family ties that the brothers had worked so hard to preserve by their mass movement to New England, and he lost the companionship and support of the two older brothers who had watched over him in the years since their father's death. His wife left behind the church that had embraced her as a sister and had baptized two of her children. In the years since she had joined, however, the Boston church had been in turmoil, split into contentious factions by the Antinomian Controversy. Their family, moreover, was rapidly increasing. This young couple settled in Charlestown with the typical immigrant "family-in-progress," that is, a family that was "*complete*—composed of husband, wife, and children—but not yet *completed*."[106] Having sailed on the *Planter* with three young children, Goodwife Tuttle continued in her new home to give birth at the expected rate. By 1639 she had delivered two more babies, and at age twenty-seven she had every prospect of producing many more.[107] The land shortage in the Boston area compromised her husband's ability to provide for this rapidly growing family. To improve his prospects, the family packed their belongings a second time.[108]

New Haven was founded by John Davenport, pastor of St. Stephen's, Coleman Street, and one of his godly parishioners, the wealthy London merchant Theophilus Eaton. Accompanied by a group of investors who had agreed to plant a town together, they arrived in Boston in June 1637. When the Bay offered no suitable site for the commercial town this company envisioned, they scouted for an alternative within the territory covered by the patent of the Earl of Warwick, finally choosing a coastal site located at the mouth of the Quinnipiac River that had not only rich farmlands but also the "best harbor between the Connecticut River and New Amsterdam." The Tuttles were not, however, among the first company of settlers, who had arrived at the Quinnipiac by the middle of April 1638.[109] Perhaps they remained behind because Goodwife Tuttle was again pregnant, but soon after the Boston church baptized their fifth child the family made their move.[110] Arriving in New Haven by early summer, William Tuttle was one of sixty-three men who gathered on 4 June 1639 to sign the "Fundamental Agreement" establishing the framework for the town's civic and religious order.[111]

Once they were in New Haven, the Tuttles' economic fortunes rapidly improved. Unlike the long-settled towns of Boston and Charlestown, land was plentiful along the shores of the Quinnipiac. The planters had laid out their town in a half-mile square bounded on two sides by waterways. This town plot was subdivided into a grid of nine squares; with the center reserved for the town green, land in the remaining portions was distributed as house lots for the town's proprietors.[112] Allotments were determined "according to a ratio depending partly on the number of persons in the family, and partly on the amount the family had invested in the common stock of the proprietors." The Tuttle family lot was located in the northeast square, called Eaton's quarter or the Governor's quarter because the colony's first governor and several members of his extended family resided in this square.[113] That Tuttle acquired this prestigious location for his residence reflected not only the increasing size of his family but also the substantial estate he brought to

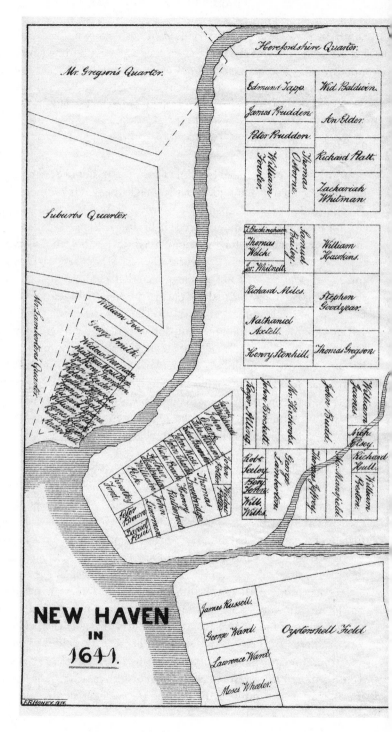

Mr. Gregson's Quarter.

Herefordshire Quarter.

Edmund Tapp. | Wid. Baldwin.

James Prudden. | An Elder.

Peter Prudden.

William Fowler. | Thomas Osborne. | Richard Platt.

Zachariah Whitman.

Suburbs Quarter.

T. Buckingham | Samuel Bailey. | William Hawkins.

Thomas Welch.

Jer. Whitnell.

Richard Miles. | Stephen Goodyear.

Nathaniel Axtell.

Henry Stonhill. | Thomas Gregson.

Mr. Lamberton's Quarter.

William Ives.

George Smith.

Nadaw Thurman. Matthew Moulthrop. Anthony Thompson. Peter Reeder. Robert Cogswell. Samuel Blackley. Richard Beach. William Ives. Francis Hall. Andrew Hull.

Jarvis. Peter Clerkson. John Charles. John Nash. John Brocket. Richard Beckley. William Peck. Timothy Ford. Peter Brown. Daniel Paul.

John Wigg. Luke Atkinson. Thomas Kimberly. Henry Rutherford. John Clemmens.

Roger Alling.

John Brockett.

Robt Seeley. Benj Fenn. Will Wilks.

Mr. Hickocks.

George Lamberton.

John Budd.

Thomas Jeffrey. | Mr. Mansfield.

William Tuttle.

Nich. Elsey.

Richard Hull.

William Peaton.

James Russell.

George Ward.

Lawrence Ward.

Moses Wheeler.

Oystershell Field.

NEW HAVEN
IN
1641.

E.R.HONEY. N.H.

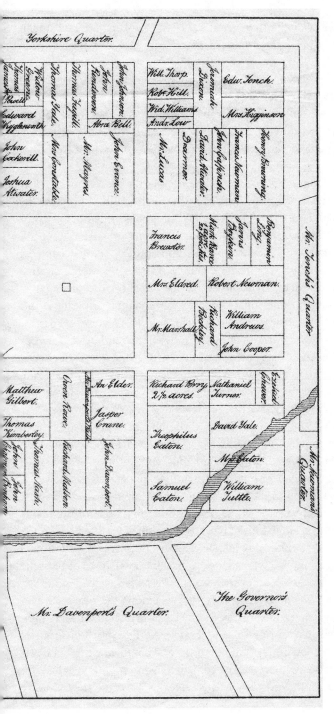

Original Nine-Square Plan of New Haven, 1641. Courtesy of The Whitney Library of the New Haven Museum.

the new settlement, valued originally at £400. In October 1640 he contributed an additional £50, an inheritance perhaps from his oldest brother, who had died earlier that year. Because of this second investment, his estate was assessed at £450 on New Haven's first tax roll, completed around 1641. He also by this date owned 178 acres of land.[114] This second migration, therefore, quickly transformed William Tuttle from a virtually landless inhabitant of Charlestown into a wealthy proprietor of a new and promising port town that numbered among its residents several of the most prominent New England merchants.

Governor Eaton, boasting an estate of £3,000, was the town's most wealthy proprietor, and on his home lot, which bordered the Tuttles' property, he constructed a lavish house that reputedly had 19 fireplaces. Nine other proprietors had £1,000 estates, including Pastor Davenport, whose 13-fireplace home stood just across the street from the Eaton house.[115] Tuttle occupied a place firmly within the town's mid-level gentry. Although 30 of the original proprietors were wealthier than he, his estate was well above the £180 median for the 123 inhabitants included on the 1641 tax roll. Likely contributing to this sudden elevation in status was the death of his mother. When she boarded the *Planter*, Isabella Tuttle had a life estate in her deceased husband's property. As the designated heir, William would have inherited the remainder of this estate upon his mother's death. Although no record exists of her death, this young settler's contrasting fortunes in Charlestown and New Haven suggest he came into this inheritance before moving to the Quinnipiac.

Like many of his neighbors, William Tuttle hoped to improve his economic fortune by moving into trade. New Haven had quickly established trade with New Amsterdam, Virginia, Barbados, and, through Boston, with England and the European continent. As a commercial enterprise, however, the colony never lived up to the expectations of its founders, and investors reeled from one failed venture to the next. Tuttle joined one of the town's most dramatic failures, an ill-considered project to plant a settlement on the Delaware River. In December 1650, the inhabitants decided "that some part of the towne should remove" to this beaver-rich territory claimed by both the Dutch and the French, which appeared "a place fitt to receive plantations."[116] Eager to cash in on this new venture, Tuttle was among the fifty men who sailed from New Haven the next spring for the Delaware. On their way south, however, the Dutch governor of Manhattan arrested the expedition's leaders and several of their company, including Tuttle, and confined them "in a private house." To secure their release, the company had to promise to abandon the project and return to New Haven. This setback was costly. The following

September, Tuttle and another member of the company petitioned for "sat-isfaction for their unjust Imprisonment" and "for the due Repair of theire loses," which they estimated, likely with some exaggeration, to total more than £300, but no record remains of their reimbursement.[117] Most likely, the Commissioners forced the adventurers to absorb their losses.[118]

Another obstacle thwarting William Tuttle's ambitions was his failure, once again, to obtain church membership. His wife had quickly qualified in Boston, and in September 1639 this congregation voted to recommend "Our Sister Elizabeth Tuttle" for membership in the newly gathered church in New Haven.[119] In his first public act as a New Haven proprietor, William affirmed his "purp[ose,] resolution and desire" to "be admitted into church fellow-ship according to Christ as soon [as] God shall fitt [him] thereunto."[120] But only a minority of the New Haven population ever achieved this distinction. According to Cotton Mather, John Davenport's standards were even more rigorous than those imposed in Boston. "[H]e used," writes Mather, "a more than ordinary exactness in trying, those that were admitted unto the com-munion of the church," for "church purity" was "one his greatest concern-ments and endeavors."[121] During the first 30 years of the church's existence, therefore, the church brethren accepted into their fellowship only 267 New Haven residents, most in the early years of settlement.[122] Tuttle failed to demonstrate his conversion during this formative period, and thereafter his chances dropped precipitously.

Lack of church membership kept William Tuttle from advancing in town or colony government. The colony's "Fundamental Agreement" affirmed that "church members only shall be free burgesses," the term used in New Haven for those persons qualified to vote and hold elective office. Tuttle's uncon-verted state did not, however, wholly disqualify him from serving the town. Because both free planters and free burgesses attended town meetings, he was able to participate in public affairs, and in August 1644, he readily swore to "submitt both my person and my whole estate" to the "lawfull authority" by taking the colony's newly instituted "Oath of Fidelity." To prove himself a responsible public servant, he regularly served on committees formed for such tasks as surveying outlying lands, building a sheep pen, repairing the mill and the meetinghouse, and recovering outstanding debts.[123] Moreover, in the first seating of the meetinghouse, introduced in March 1647, he was granted a prestigious position, on the first "cross seat" at the upper end of the house to the left of the pulpit, next to a church member whose estate was val-ued at £800. His wife took her place on the fifth bench in the center section, among the sisters of the church.[124] At the monthly celebration of the Lord's

Supper, she would partake of the sacrament after he exited the church with other inhabitants deemed unworthy to join the communion of saints.

This mixed record of both success and failure suggests that William Tuttle did not realize all the ambitions that led him as a young man, just starting a family, to leave his Northamptonshire home and sail with his brothers to a new land. But he did find a community that embraced his wife as one of the saints and that provided a secure economic future for his children. In fact, Tuttle probably found his greatest sense of accomplishment in his family. The family was a colonial man's most important sphere of responsibility, and evidence suggests that this patriarch ably fulfilled his role as household head. Following the Delaware River setback, he skillfully managed the family economy and governed his lively brood of twelve children with a firm hand. And although barred from the upper ranks of New Haven society, he achieved over the years a significant record of accomplishment in both town and church.

Elizabeth Tuttle, the seventh child and the protagonist of our family story, was therefore born into a large and prosperous puritan household, which had built upon its sturdy yeoman heritage a respectable place in colonial society. Mistress Tuttle's church membership qualified her children for baptism in the New Haven church, and Elizabeth, who was named for her mother, received the sacrament in November 1645, bringing her soon after birth into this godly congregation's watch and care.[125] Unlike several of her siblings, whose adolescent misbehaviors at times attracted the attention of town authorities, no evidence suggests she had a penchant for rebellion as a girl. Growing into womanhood, she likely looked to her mother's example and planned to assume in due time her place as the goodwife of her own flourishing household. At twenty-two, however, this dream was shattered when marriage to a young Hartford cooper entangled her in an ugly sex scandal. But after this rocky start to adult life, she seemed to settle down with her new husband, Richard Edwards, who as we shall see had a much different colonial beginning. His family—on both sides of the Atlantic—struggled to achieve the patriarchal ideal that his wife's family so clearly displayed. The legacy of this failed manhood overshadowed their union from the start, and while not the last straw, it was one of many burdens that ultimately caused their marriage to break apart.

[2]

THREE STRUGGLING PATRIARCHS

Elizabeth Tuttle's prosperous family was likely drawn from their Northamptonshire home by the lure of New World opportunities and freedoms. By contrast, Richard Edwards's story begins with a family in crisis. The crisis was a common one for families living in London's sprawling eastern suburbs, where poverty, disease, and death were the ordinary worries of everyday life. In the mid–sixteenth century rural wage laborers had begun flooding into the capital city, and its population had exploded. Much of this growth occurred in suburban areas outside the city walls, especially the eastern parishes where low-wage jobs for dockhands, weavers, and unlicensed tradesmen were in plentiful supply.[1] The laborers who crowded into the "filthy Cottages" that "pestered" this area lived hard lives and suffered early deaths, often from the many infectious diseases that were endemic throughout the East End in the seventeenth century.[2] Influenza, typhus, and smallpox outbreaks were common, but the biggest killer was bubonic plague.[3] In 1625, one of the hardest-hit years, more than 33,000 people died of this terrifying disease in the London metropolitan area, mostly children and youths under 20 years of age.[4]

Domestic life was fragile for families living in these poor and densely populated parishes. The struggles of Anne Edwards Cole, the grandmother of our male protagonist, and her husband to provide a home for their children were shared by many suburban households. On the eve of her migration, this godly young woman lived in Whitechapel, a notoriously squalid parish. During the past decade, her fortunes had steadily declined. She had been raised in East Smithfield, a parish just south of Whitechapel, in the household of a prosperous urban tradesman who was a member of the Coopers' Company.

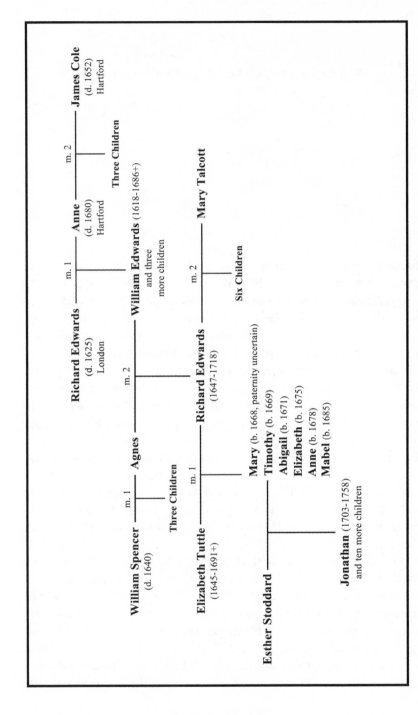

Edwards genealogy. Illustrated by John Luchin.

Coopers were in high demand in London's eastern suburbs. Barrels were the universal shipping containers of their day, and the maritime trade, which dominated the suburban waterfront from Limehouse to the Tower, used them to transport everything from meat and fish to grain, nails, and gunpowder. The brewing industry, which supplied beer and ale to taverns and ships, likewise required a steady supply of pins, pipes, butts, and firkins to store and transport its products.[5] The makers of these early modern necessities accordingly took in a middling income, and some, like Anne's stepfather, did quite well. He proudly displayed his company membership by wearing a "seale Ringe of gould whereuppon the Coopers' Armeoure [was] engraven." Other luxury items in his household, including a "silver gilt" cup and bowl and a "Jewel Ringe of gould," further testify that barrel making could be a lucrative trade.[6]

Reflecting her family's respectable position in London society, Anne's first husband was a university-educated man who pursued a genteel career. Richard Edwards, according to Jonathan Edwards's earliest biographer, was a "minister of the gospel in London," who "lived in Queen Elizabeth's day." This characterization is only partially accurate.[7] Dying the same year Charles I took the throne, the English progenitor of the Edwards family was a Stuart subject for most of his adult life and, although he was educated as a minister, no record confirms that he ever obtained a regular living.[8] He and Anne likely married sometime in 1614, for their first child was baptized in July of the following year.[9] And probably through her family connections, he secured a post as schoolmaster—a common occupation for unemployed clergymen—in Ratcliffe in London's East End.

"Richard Edwards, B.A." was in October 1620 "admitted Master of the Free-School at Ratcliffe, county Middlesex, having subscribed to the Thirty-nine Articles."[10] This school, which had been founded in 1536, was owned and run by the Coopers' Company of London as part of a charity that in addition to the school contained six almshouses for impoverished coopers.[11] Free schools gave boys of the middling classes the education commonly available only to the aristocracy.[12] At Ratcliffe Free School, an endowment provided tuition for thirty scholars; and the sons of successful merchants, tradesmen, and artisans, for whom a superior education would ensure social advancement, probably filled Richard Edwards's classroom.[13] In compensation, he received a salary of more than £23 a year, which he could supplement by taking on additional tuition-paying pupils.[14] For five years this income provided an adequate, if not lavish, living for his wife and four young children. Enjoying the status that came with a polite profession, the couple probably began preparing their second child, a son named William, to follow in his father's footsteps.[15]

The plague of 1625 brought this comfortable living to a ghastly end. Stepney parish, which bordered Ratcliffe, was hit hard by the epidemic that ravaged east London in this year. Beginning in March, more than 3,500 people died in this poor and overcrowded area before cold weather could end the devastation.[16] Anne's husband died in August, at the height of the epidemic, and was buried hastily in St. Dunstan's overflowing parish yard, if the churchwardens were able to find room for his grave.[17] She likely also buried other members of her household during this difficult time, for deaths tended to cluster in family groups.[18] Her four young children, particularly the two babies she had delivered since moving to Ratcliffe, would have been especially vulnerable to the disease.[19] By September little may have remained of the Edwards household besides the mother and her seven-year-old son, William, the only other family member known to have escaped death in this year.[20] Suddenly losing her husband and thus his income, Anne faced homelessness and financial ruin. Like many widows in her precarious situation, she chose remarriage as her best survival strategy.[21]

With infant mortality high and life expectancy low, London's suburban families lacked the permanence and stability found in more healthy rural areas, like Northamptonshire, where the Tuttles lived.[22] Marriages were frequently interrupted by death, and family composition was constantly changing as husbands and wives rapidly remarried after the sudden death of a spouse. Plague epidemics in particular were "catalysts of an active remarriage market," as broken families scrambled to reconfigure economically viable living arrangements.[23] For the newly widowed Anne, who had no independent means of support, marriage was a necessity, and about three months after her husband's death, on 6 December 1625, she remarried at the Stepney parish church. Her new husband was also well acquainted with loss, having buried his first two wives in quick succession. Together, she and James Cole hoped to start domestic life over again.[24]

A London turner named Nehemiah Wallington may have brought the couple together.[25] Wallington was James Cole's close friend and a trusted acquaintance of Anne's parents, especially her mother, who named Wallington as an overseer of her will.[26] These three families were bound together by a common religious commitment. As members of London's well-established godly community, all lived in parishes with long traditions of nonconformity. At St. Dunstan's Stepney, where Richard Edwards was buried, religious radicalism dated back to the reign of Henry VIII, when its rector was burned for heresy.[27] At St. Mary Whitechapel, James Cole's home parish, a leader of the London nonconformist movement lectured for almost fifty years, despite his presentation for maladministration of the sacraments. After their marriage, the Coles may have visited the chapel at Wapping-Whitechapel where the curate had a long history of controversy and lost church-livings.[28] They probably also on occasion heard the Wallingtons' pastor address the congregation at St. Leonard Eastcheap and attended lectures at St. Katherine by the Tower, Anne's parents' home parish.[29] Henry and Julian Munter probably approved of their daughter's second match because he was a godly man.

Another connection was the coopering trade itself. Like Anne's stepfather, James Cole was a barrel maker, who probably ran a shop in the back of his small Whitechapel home. Coopers commonly lived in areas like Whitechapel, clustered together in particular neighborhoods with other artisans pursuing the same trade.[30] Cole did not have the status enjoyed by Anne's first husband, but in this crisis her primary need was for financial support. Having made a good first match to a university-educated man, she took refuge with a godly craftsman who worked in the family profession. And for several years this reconstituted household seems to have flourished. Their Whitechapel home filled with children, and young William Edwards, apparently the only surviving child from Anne's first marriage, began training in the cooper's trade.[31] By 1634, however, another crisis had overtaken the family, leaving Anne and her children once again alone with no ready means of support. A rare collection of letters that Cole's friend Nehemiah Wallington preserved in his voluminous diary allows us to witness James and Anne's desperate struggle to overcome this next threat to their domestic happiness, which, as we shall see, eventually led them to seek another new beginning in the New World.

"O my deere wife and my tender and sweet children," James Cole wrote from Ipswich in June 1634, "the thoughts of you and of my children doth pench my heart and weaken my strength."[32] Located about eighty miles from London on the Suffolk coast, Ipswich had an economy that was, like east London's, dominated by the maritime trades.[33] Perhaps because it resembled home, Cole first looked for work in this growing borough town when financial ruin forced him to flee Whitechapel. The cause of his undoing was a common one for families living in London's eastern suburbs. The early modern economy operated within what the historian Craig Muldrew has called a "culture of credit." Every English family "was to some degree enmeshed within the increasingly complicated webs of credit and obligation with which transactions were communicated."[34] These entanglements left even the most scrupulous trader vulnerable to failure and made business particularly risky for independent craftsmen like Cole, who made many small daily transactions on credit. Increasing the financial confusion, he probably kept no account book and had little sense of his true financial worth.[35] Keeping credits above debts was a constant struggle and source of anxiety. Wallington, also a woodworker, frequently reported "being much troubled with thoughts how to pay my deats."[36] Cole likewise lamented that his "great debts and dangers" had "Lien heavily upon mee many years" and caused "inward temptations" and "outward miseryes." To cope with such daily uncertainty, these godly craftsmen placed their financial fortunes in the hands of the Lord, who "Casteth down and raiseth up againe at his pleasure."[37]

When providence frowned on James Cole he, like many desperate debtors, fled London to escape the debtor's law. Debt litigation increased in the early seventeenth century as the economy grew and defaults became more frequent. Many informally contracted debts went unpaid for years, but sealed bonds often contained penal clauses to ensure payment by a particular date. If Cole had broken a bond his creditors may have begun the process of arrest and attachment, which would have led to his imprisonment if his goods proved insufficient to cover the debt.[38] He claimed, however, not to be afraid of prison. "[I]n this extremity," he wrote, "if I had [been] so Limnited to imprisonment I could not much have wanted, neither did I much feare it."[39] Such boasting masked the fact that London's prisons were fearful places. While aristocratic debtors kept comfortable accommodations in Ludgate or the Fleet, insolvent businessmen like Cole who could not pay the warden's fees lived in hopeless and squalid conditions. Unable to work from prison, but unqualified for release until their creditors were satisfied, they effectively served life sentences, until death from jail fever or even starvation discharged their debt.[40]

English reformers, who advocated amending or reforming the debtor's law, often cited its injustice and irrationality.[41] As the author of *Imprisonment of Men's Bodyes for Debt* asserted, "[I]mprisonment no way enableth the means for payment of Debts, but doth absolutely consume the Debtor and his estate to the enriching of Lawyers, Keepers of Prisons, Bayliffs and others."[42] Cole echoed this argument to justify his flight from London. In prison, he wrote, he would have had "Littel hope either to have reli[e]ved my family or to have paid my deats." To maintain "some hope of both," he had to get out of town. Regretting "the Great Losses of my Creditors," he prayed that God would then "put into my hands Such imployment" that "I may make them restitution."[43]

Even without the threat of imprisonment, Cole's ability to pay off his debts would have been jeopardized by his loss of credit. In early modern England credit was a moral virtue, signifying trust, honesty, and character. "To have credit in a community meant that your character was respected because you could be trusted to keep your promises and contracts, to pay back your debts and to perform your tasks." Once Cole's default became public through gossip or litigation, his reputation would have been ruined and the credit he had worked to acquire over years of trustworthy dealing would have been lost. Merchants, shopkeepers, and chapmen would have refused him trade, knowing that one unreliable party made the whole chain of credit insecure. Cole, therefore, would have been hard pressed to rebuild his credit in the same community in which he had lost it, and without credit he had no means to repay his debts.[44] To persuade him to return to London, Wallington reassured his "Loving and deere Friend" that his situation was not yet this grave. "It is not yet much spread abroad," he wrote. "It is no shame to Come Hoame again; It was a Shame to goe from home." Cole prays to "obtain such strength of Faith that it might make poverty, shame, persecution, Banishment, Debts, and all troubles not dreadfull and harmfull, but usefull and serviceable to mee." But his humiliation was too great. "[I]f I mite winne the whole world," he cries, "I cannot come to London again."[45]

The threat of prison and the humiliating inability to pay his debts kept Cole from London, but as an "Ancient Christian" and "valliant Champion in the Lord's quarrel" he incurred an even greater disgrace by his absence.[46] His fellow godly householders sharply condemned his desertion and demanded he come back to his family. "I intreat you, in the Name of God, Returne! Returne!" wrote Nehemiah Wallington, "with Teares in mine eyes."[47] John Wallington, Nehemiah's father, likewise wrote to his "Christian Friend and beloved brother in Christ Jesus," begging him "to make hast and prolonge not the time to settle your selfe in your place."[48] But Anne's stepfather issued the harshest rebuke. "Father Monter" has "dashed in peeces all my Comfort" and "take[n] part with my grand enemy against me," Cole complained to his more sympathetic mother-in-law. "He reproaches me with running from my Country" and "doth accuse mee that I have no care of my wife and Children." The wealthy cooper's authority for this uncompromising censure of his son-in-law was scripture. "[M]y Father minds me of that place," Cole reports, "That he [who] Cares not for his family is worse than an infidel and deneys the faith" (I Tim. 5:8). This text communicated a clear message. As long as Cole lived in separation from his wife, he violated God's law.[49]

These three successful male householders interpreted Cole's absence as a failure of his Christian duty. As husband and father, Cole had the responsibility to provide a sufficiency for his wife and children. When he defaulted on his debts, he failed in his duty to provide and placed in question his status as a man of credit and honor in his community. The humiliation that drove him from London was, therefore, gender related, generated by his inability to sustain the masculine ideal of economic self-sufficiency. Moving to the provinces did not, however, remove Cole's shame or restore his manliness. Finding wage work outside London preserved his economic competence, but deserting his wife and children violated the ideal of Christian manhood, which viewed male headship as a calling from God.[50] For the men in Cole's godly network, such irresponsibility jeopardized his family's spiritual well-being, and they censured him for placing his dependents in grave peril. "Now Brother Cole," chided John Wallington, "Consider where you be and then Consider where you should be." As a Christian householder, "[Y]ou should be at White Chapell with your wife," he reminded the younger man, fulfilling your duty to "dwell with her as a man of knowledg, and [to] instruct her and your Children and Sarvants in the wayes of God." Without a family head, he warned, they were left "in a mournfull maze, and know not what to doe till you Come that should direct them all."[51]

Nehemiah Wallington was similarly confounded by his godly friend's absence. "O, I intreat you," he begged, "Consider how many ways you doe dishonour your good God which you doe most desier to glorifie." He even traveled to Suffolk to impress upon Cole the urgency of his return, and once in Ipswich he convinced Cole to go to "God's faithful ministers, and powre out your mind to them and Aske their Advise." The two men visited the town's lecturer, Samuel Ward, who was soon to appear before the High Commission, charged with forty-three nonconformist offenses. This radical puritan directed Cole to return home.[52] "You knowe," he told the errant husband, "the cheefe care of a child of God is and must be still to glorifye God in the place and calling wherein God hath sett him." This weighty council apparently convinced Cole to journey home, but his resolve failed him just as he was entering London. He stopped outside the city, at a place called Barking, where "his wife came to him."[53] Although duty pulled him this far, fear and humiliation kept him from going back with Anne to White Chapel. Abandoning her once again, Cole fled to Warwick, a Midlands market town whose economy was dominated by agriculture and trade, where he worked for several years to rebuild his reputation and to repay his debts.[54]

How Anne provided for her family in the years of her husband's absence is unknown, but her condition was a common cause of poverty in London's eastern suburbs. Seamen's wives managed on their own for years while their husbands sailed on long voyages or were impressed into the royal navy.[55] Like them, Anne probably worried that her family would break up when her husband left home. "The process of seeking work," the historian Joanne Bailey notes, "made it all too easy for husbands to fail to return home or contribute to their families' support when communication broke down or they failed to find employment."[56] Ten years earlier Anne had been left in a similarly precarious position by the sudden death of her first husband, but this new crisis was potentially more severe. Because remarriage was not an option, she had to shoulder alone the household responsibilities in her husband's absence.

James delegated to her the duties he could no longer fulfill. He ceded his position of religious authority to his "good wife," instructing her to "catechise my Children and nurter them in the feare of God." He also placed on her the more burdensome responsibility of negotiating with creditors. He asked her to determine "who is most sufferable unto you," so that "they of all other shall be sounest discharged." And counseling her "to dell with my Credettors in faire words and not in bad terms," he instructed her to divide his estate "amongst them equally as it will rech to the uttermost."[57] Like many wives of urban artisans, Anne was likely accustomed to dealing with suppliers and customers as she helped out in her husband's shop. Some wives even learned the rudiments of their husbands' crafts and kept the family businesses running after their deaths.[58] But with the household credit ruined and much of its furnishings sold to satisfy impatient creditors, she would have been hard pressed to manage the shop on her own.

Cole's plan was to reunite his family once he had found work. In a letter from Ipswich, he asked his wife "to come unto mee, wherein by a letter you shall here I am settled." Writing from Warwick several months later, he insisted to the Munters that "I desier to have my family with mee," and "do hope that God will so provid that ere Long for to send for them to abide with mee where now I am."[59] The oldest son did eventually join his stepfather in Warwick. At sixteen, William Edwards likely earned wages of his own and could have helped his mother weather the family's financial crisis had he remained in London. But when Cole requested "to have the biggest Child with mee," a neighbor paid for his transportation and gave him a shilling for the journey.[60] Anne and the two younger children, however, apparently remained in Whitechapel.[61] Unwilling to exchange the support of parents, friends, and neighbors for an uncertain life in the provinces, she chose to stay in London, at least for a time. But this choice was no solution, for without her husband she had no reliable means of providing for her family.

Financial ruin, therefore, painfully narrowed the options available to this east London cooper's family and forced its head to choose between two types of shame. By returning to London as his religious duty required, James Cole risked prison and the humiliating inability to pay his debts; by remaining in the provinces, he incurred the godly community's reproach. In this tight spot, he began to dream of an even more radical escape. Migration was a way out. This new door may have first opened during Cole's stay in Ipswich, for the city was located in the "geographic center" of the puritan migration.[62] Between 1630 and 1640, more residents of Suffolk left for New England than did residents of any other English county, many swarming onto ships moored in the Ipswich harbor. While working in this maritime center, Cole may have heard Samuel Ward promote colonization in his lectures and seen companies set sail for Massachusetts Bay from the town docks.[63] But it was not until he was working in Warwick that he informed his wife of his plan. "My Lord's desier," he wrote in November 1634, "is to imploy me for New England."[64]

Like Ipswich, Warwick was a nonconformist stronghold. Its robust puritan gentry had supported godly preachers since early in Elizabeth's reign. Robert Rich, the second earl of Warwick, and Robert Greville, the second baron Brooke, were important puritan patrons in the seventeenth century and prominent opposition leaders in Parliament. Lord Brooke, who sheltered a series of nonconformist ministers at Warwick Castle, regularly invited members of the godly brotherhood to preach in its chapel. Cole may have heard these powerful preachers, for he attended nonconformist services sponsored by puritan noblemen in Warwick.[65] "Where I do now sojou[rn]," he wrote with amazement,

> there be two Congregations that is in two grat men's hands, where there is neither Crosses, nor Surpl[us]es, nor kneeling at the Sacrament, nor the booke of Common prayer, nor any other behaviour but reading the word, Singing of psalms, prayr before and after sarmon, with catechisme.

He had joined these worshippers "in the use of God's ordinances," Cole reported to his in-laws. "[I]f I have not a competency and good means from my Lord," he observed with satisfaction, "I should content my selfe with poore meanes So I might injoy such Christian Liberty."[66]

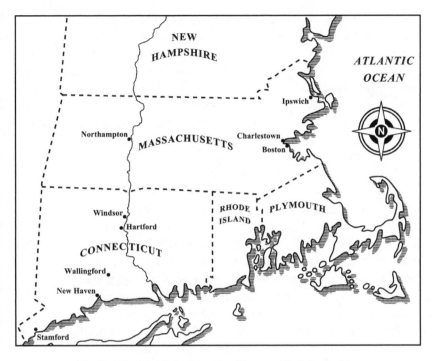

The New England Colonies, 1600s. Illustrated by John Luchin.

New England offered Cole both financial competency and Christian liberty. Craftsmen of all sorts had skills needed in the new settlements, and woodworkers like Cole were in high demand.[67] In *New England's Prospect*, William Wood puts "the handy cooper," who "can make strong ware for the use of the country," on his list of "what men be most fit for these plantations."[68] Hartford, whose investors planned to develop a maritime economy, was a likely home for a cooper. Both James Cole, a skilled cask maker used to working around the docks, and his stepson, William Edwards, who was learning the trade, had something to provide this newly planted village. In turn, it could give them a fresh start. Anne, too, may have viewed migration as the best means of reconstituting her family, but when and where she reunited with her husband is unknown. Perhaps James eventually paid his debts and returned to London for the voyage to New England. More likely, she joined her husband and son in Warwick, and the family sailed from a west coast port like Bristol to the new village of Hartford.[69]

Hartford's settlement began in the summer of 1634 when six men from the Massachusetts Bay town of Cambridge, then called Newtown, sailed around Cape Cod "to discover Connecticut River, intending to remove their town thither."[70] Two years earlier the Earl of Warwick, who had helped secure patents for the Plymouth and Massachusetts Bay colonies, granted a group of investors that included Lord Brooke and several other puritan aristocrats a deed of conveyance for the lands along the Connecticut.[71] Traveling upriver, the Cambridge scouts chose as a likely location for their new settlement a place the local Indians called Suckiaug, where several years earlier the Dutch had built a fort and trading post.[72] Its ample meadows, forests, and farmlands were an attractive alternative to the cramped allotments available in Cambridge, whose residents had been complaining about the "want of accommodation for their cattle."[73] At the confluence of two waterways, the site was also favorable for commerce, for what the settlers called the Great River afforded merchant ships a passage to the Atlantic while the Little River, flowing in from the west, opened a channel for trade with the region's native inhabitants.[74] Encouraged by these prospects, a small group of pioneers migrated from Cambridge the following year, and in June 1636 pastor Thomas Hooker arrived, having traveled by foot on the "Indian path" to Connecticut with 160 head of cattle and the majority of the families in his Cambridge congregation.[75] These overland migrants were soon joined by travelers sailing directly from England, including a number of prominent Warwickshire families who may have recruited James Cole to settle in the colony.[76] By 1639, when this struggling cooper and his family arrived, about 150 men and their families populated the new village of Hartford.[77]

No passenger list records the family's voyage, so neither the date of their departure nor the ship on which they sailed can be identified. They likely remained in England until at least September 1638, when Henry Munter, the family patriarch, died. For New England–bound migrants, a death in the family at times provided the opportunity for departure.[78] The Tuttle brothers had waited until the death of their father, and Anne Cole may also have hesitated until this important family tie had been broken. In addition, Munter's will provided a small inheritance that probably helped this financially challenged family start a new life. She received "thirtie shillinges sterlinge" from her stepfather, as did her son William and the younger Cole children, while James obtained a lesser sum of twenty shillings.[79] To supplement these funds he may have found a benefactor in Warwick willing to subsidize the costs of his family's passage, or he may have signed on as a ship's cooper.[80] However the journey was financed, the family began settling into their humble

Hartford home sometime in 1639, for in this year he appears on the list of the village's original ninety-five proprietors.[81] This new status restored to Cole the competency he had lost in the east London suburbs and allowed him to resume his godly calling as household head. On this small but stable foundation, he and his family began building their new colonial lives.

As a town proprietor, Cole received a house lot and the right to a share in future distributions of the town's land. His family lot, located on the south side of the Little River, was of average size, approximately three-and-a-half acres, sufficient for the "outhouses, yards, and gardens" colonial life required.[82] Because land was allotted in proportion to social status, he obtained only ten acres in the first distribution of the town's "undivided lands" and another twelve acres a year later.[83] Soon after arrival, however, he purchased a small quarter-acre lot "lying by the meetinge house" on the town green.[84] This central location, across from the town's twice-weekly market, was ideal for trade. Both the taverns operating on the green and the ships moored nearby at the landing place would have required a steady supply of casks. Barrels and pipe staves were also in high demand for export to the West Indies.[85] With a ready market for his product, Cole prospered in his business. He acquired several additional parcels of land, allowing him to supplement his income by raising cattle and corn, and at his death in 1652 he left his family a middling estate of more than £116.[86] For the man who had once fled London to escape prison and the humiliating inability to pay his debts, this sum probably represented a kind of new birth.

William Edwards's colonial career followed a longer and more tortured path. A young unmarried man of twenty-one when he migrated with his family to Hartford, he was ineligible to receive the proprietor's rights generally reserved for male household heads.[87] To acquire full manhood status he had to marry and establish himself as an independent householder, and for six years he likely made barrels alongside his stepfather as he worked to achieve this goal.[88] Among early Connecticut pioneers more than half the adult men were single, and most were young and propertyless. Without enough women to go around, finding a mate was often a struggle. Young men, therefore, waited on average until the age of thirty to marry, nine years after reaching the age of legal majority.[89] Despite these obstacles, William Edwards made an unlikely match to a high-status Hartford widow in 1645, when he was twenty-seven years old.[90]

Agnes Spencer had migrated to Hartford in 1639 with her husband and their three young children. William Spencer had first settled in Cambridge, where, as one of the town's most prominent residents, he held numerous public offices, including town clerk and representative to the Massachusetts General Court.[91] An officer in the Cambridge trainband, he had also served as a founding member of the Massachusetts Military Company.[92] Lt. Spencer quickly assumed among the Hartford town proprietors an elite position comparable to that which he had occupied in the Bay. During his brief residence, he kept the town book, served as townsman and representative to the Connecticut General Court, and helped draft the colony's early code of laws.[93] Dying suddenly in the summer of 1640, he left his wife and children a respectable estate totaling more than £231.[94]

For five years following her husband's death Agnes Spencer acted as her family's household head, caring for her three children and improving her husband's estate. Widows of status and means had a measure of power in colonial society generally unavailable to married women. Governing a household alone, a widow had not only "unquestioned primacy over her children and servants" but also "precedence over all low-ranking men."[95] The widow Spencer's authority was enhanced by her inheritance, which gave her the freedom to postpone or forgo remarriage. Unlike most colonial widows, who received a life estate in one-third of their husbands' real and personal property, she inherited full title to her third, with the remaining estate distributed to her son and two daughters.[96] Even with these advantages, however, caring for her children alone was likely a heavy burden.[97] But why this middle-aged woman chose to forfeit her property and independence to a young man, who had neither land nor a well-established livelihood, is uncertain. For William Edwards, the match was quite a step up.

A man who followed the normal life course married after obtaining the financial "competence" to provide for a wife and children without dependency or debt. As his family and property grew, he gradually became a "full member in the community of adult males," a group limited to independent householders and heads of families.[98] William Edwards's union to Agnes Spencer placed him on the path to manhood, but following a shorter route. For a young man who stood to inherit none of his stepfather's realty, marrying a wealthy widow was a shrewd choice.[99] The town apparently awarded the newlywed a small home lot, located across the town green from his stepfather's shop.[100] From his wife's estate, however, he received more substantial land holdings. Married women in seventeenth-century Connecticut had no property rights. The "real property a woman brought to her husband in marriage became his absolutely, to sell or mortgage as he saw fit." Edwards accordingly acquired full title to his wife's realty, and he took possession quickly.[101] Only three days after the wedding he sold a strip of land through the Spencer property, which he calls "my home lott" in the deed of sale, and received from the town thirty shillings in property damages.[102]

In addition to property, Edwards acquired through his wife a ready-made family. By marriage he became the stepfather of Agnes's three children, having the responsibility to provide for them and direct their education and spiritual development.[103] He could not, however, look forward to the full display of manhood that came through fathering a succession of children over an extended period of time. At forty-one, Agnes Spencer Edwards had only a few childbearing years remaining to her. When she gave birth to a son two years after the marriage, the colonial branch of the Edwards family began to take root. They named the boy Richard after his paternal grandfather, the schoolmaster who had died in east London of the plague.[104] This new American Richard Edwards, Elizabeth Tuttle's future husband, was his father's sole offspring.

Although marriage quickly conferred upon William Edwards all the external signifiers of the patriarchal ideal, it did not make him a man. Manliness in colonial New England was primarily an internal moral attribute characterized by such qualities as "maturity, rationality, responsibility, self-control, and courage." A man displayed his possession of these virtues by firmly governing the subordinate members of his household and wisely managing the family economy.[105] For Edwards, this moral dimension of manhood was more difficult to acquire than its corresponding external attributes. Young and accustomed to dependency when he obtained his ready-made family, he struggled throughout adulthood to govern his household with the rationality and self-control required for the task.

Fourteen years younger than his wife, Edwards occupied a position of ambiguous authority in the household he had joined. Most widows who remarried chose men older than they who were mature household heads experienced in family governance.[106] At twenty-seven, Edwards had no marital experience to guide him in his new position of authority. His wife, however, had established her authority in the family by serving as its head for five years. Marriage made him her governor and required her to submit to him. Separated by age and experience, both Agnes and William may have found this sudden power reversal awkward. While her adjustment was probably facilitated by a habit of subordination developed over a lifetime, evidence suggests he struggled as a patriarch. Unable to manage the family economy prudently, he repeated in the second generation the financial failings of his stepfather. Fiscal irresponsibility never drove him to abandon his wife and children, but it damaged his financial position and ultimately forced him to forfeit his manhood to his more competent wife.

William Edwards's battle to keep credits above debts is clearly displayed in the Connecticut court records. Most colonists, both male and female, appeared in court at various moments in their lives, if only to execute a will or settle an account.[107] Craftsmen, who sold their products on credit, used the judicial system with perhaps greater frequency than most to collect overdue debts. Even for a cooper, however, Edwards was an unusually active litigant. Between June 1644 and September 1670 he was named party in at least sixty-three civil actions and five criminal complaints. He had periods of inactivity—in seven of these twenty-six years he engaged in no lawsuits—but in each of the remaining nineteen years he appeared on the court's docket almost four times on average. A range of actions brought him to the bar, but his most common contests were about debt. Almost a third of his civil suits were identified as debt actions, a higher percentage than any other category of action, and those involving such issues as attached goods, accounts, and breach of trust were also debt related. Several others, labeled simply "actions of the case," the most common civil action in colonial Connecticut, also likely concerned debt.[108] Despite this frequent recourse to the court, however, Edwards was seldom a successful litigant. Although he joined suit as plaintiff as frequently as he did as defendant, he lost three times more often than he won, and his financial losses were even higher. Excluding court costs, his liability from negative judgments totaled more than five times the amount he gained from lawsuits decided in his favor.[109] More often than not, therefore, he left the Hartford courtroom in a worse financial position than when he walked in.

This man of poor credit had difficulty resolving privately the disputes that commonly pitted neighbor against neighbor in colonial Connecticut. The New England economy, like that of the mother country, operated within a culture of credit, in which commercial relations between creditors and debtors depended upon trust. In east London or Hartford, a man's reputation for fairness and dependability in his dealings determined his creditworthiness. Because the local economy involved regular face-to-face transactions, colonists preferred to settle disputes privately, using litigation as a last resort.[110] Simply threatening to sue often produced a private settlement.[111] Arbitration preserved the bonds of trust integral to the colonial credit market and allowed community members "to resume their normal neighborly relations" once a dispute was resolved.[112] Edwards at times negotiated a settlement—a quarter of the cases to which he was party were withdrawn before proceeding to trial.[113] Most of his suits, however, went to the jury. In these cases Edwards's bad credit may have foreclosed a settlement, but his hot temper also probably made private arbitration difficult.

This Hartford cooper appears to have had as much difficulty controlling his tongue as his money. Charged with speech offenses on at least four occasions, he was convicted once for slander and once for the more serious charge of "defamation in a high degree."[114] The rulings in two additional suits suggest the court believed the accusations had some merit. Although charges of "profane swearing, Lyeing, drunkenness, Wanton Loose Laciviouse carriages, Besides Intolerable Bawdy Language" were not legally proved, the judges cautioned that they would "seveerly deale" with him if such charges were substantiated in the future.[115] And when the Wethersfield minister charged Edwards with slanderously accusing him of making a "false oath," they likewise cautioned him to cease such "clamors."[116] Nevertheless, on a subsequent occasion he successfully presented Daniel Clark, a member of the General Court, for "breach of his oath."[117]

These lawsuits were part of a complex web of interpersonal contact and conflict common in small settlements like Hartford.[118] For example, a year before Edwards brought a defamation charge against a wealthy tavern owner with whom he served in the Hartford dragoons, the man had complained against Edwards for "uncivill cariage towards his wife," and six months later he sued him for "unjust molestation." Perhaps Edwards offended his fellow trooper while enjoying the hospitality of his public house, a common setting for loose words and careless actions. The conflict could also have been debt related, for Edwards twice brought this likely purchaser of his casks to court on a debt action.[119] Men most commonly found actionable words that expressed economic disability, like "rogue" or "thief," and sued to protect their reputations for creditworthiness.[120] Being a man of poor credit, Edwards was apparently eager to lash out at higher-status men with either his tongue or a legal suit. But given his poor litigation record, these desperate actions likely did his reputation more harm than good.

The portrait of William Edwards that emerges from this quarter-century of litigation is clearly drawn. Quick to swear out a suit or speak out in anger, he was a man prone to interpersonal conflict. His disorderly tongue, like his disordered household economy, were signs that he lacked the inner self-restraint that manhood required. This contentious character likely explains his brief entanglement in the witch-hunt that inflamed Hartford in the mid–seventeenth century and resulted in at least three executions. A middle-aged woman named Elizabeth Seager was convicted in 1665 and would have been hanged if the governor had not intervened. To support the charge that Seager had made a pact with the devil, one witness repeated a conversation she had overheard between the accused and Edwards. When he "told Goodwife Seager that she did fly," the witness recalled, the accused witch replied, "if I did fly William Edwards made me fly."[121] This testimony implicated Edwards in the diabolical conspiracy Hartford residents believed was threatening their town. He was the perfect target for such a provocative accusation, for persons with abrasive personalities were particularly vulnerable to witchcraft charges. Like Edwards, they commonly had a history of speech offenses and small conflicts with neighbors, and the few men charged with witchcraft also shared his record of unusual litigiousness.[122] No formal charges of witchcraft were ever brought against Edwards.[123] He could not, however, wholly escape the destructive effects of his contentious nature, for under his ineffectual guidance the family's financial standing steadily declined.

Edwards lost much of the property his wife had brought to their marriage. A mortgage on his home lot and a parcel of Spencer pastureland paid for a shipment of wheat and peas bought from a Cambridge businessman.[124] Perhaps to redeem this mortgage, he sold off most of Spencer's east side division, and ninety acres his wife received in a subsequent division was also sold. Only the Spencer home lot and two small parcels remained for his stepchildren's inheritance.[125] The most significant sign of financial failure, however, occurred in 1663 when Edwards was forty-five years old. Full manhood was for colonial householders an achievement of middle age.[126] In an unusual admission of his inability to achieve this patriarchal ideal, Edwards relinquished his independence and reclaimed the dependent status he had occupied as a young, unmarried man in his stepfather's family. Overturning the domestic hierarchy, he restored to his wife the place she had occupied as a widow prior to her remarriage and forfeited to her his position as household head.

Edwards accomplished this inversion by deeding to Agnes full title to all his possessions. He transferred to her all his real property, including "his dwelling house and Shopp together with his Home lott, it now Standeth upon, as allso a parcell of land In the North Meadowe Containing by estimation fower Acres." He also gave his personal property to her, both his "Cowe and all his Swine" and "all the moveables, household Stuff, Goods and apparell what Soever which are in the dwelling house." This conveyance left him literally only the clothes on his back and his "workeing Tooles," the source of his livelihood, which he had in part received as an inheritance from his step-father.[127] Like most colonial goodwives, Agnes Edwards was probably accustomed to exercising a measure of informal economic agency in the household.[128] And once, acting as agent to her husband, she had traveled to Boston and hired an attorney to collect a legacy he had inherited from his English grandmother.[129] But the legal doctrine of coverture specified that a wife stand under the "wing, protection, and cover" of her husband. Her "very being or legal existence," states Blackstone's *Commentaries on the Laws of England*, "is suspended during the marriage," or is "consolidated into that of the husband."[130] At marriage, William acquired under this doctrine full ownership of his wife's property; with this transfer of property he reversed coverture and relinquished to Agnes the legal right to act independently regarding the family holdings. He established for her a separate estate in the family property and ceded to her the power to act as a *feme sole* within marriage, an anomalous position under colonial Connecticut law.[131]

The inheritance Edwards received at the death of his mother reaffirmed his financial impotence. The death of her husband had left Anne Edwards Cole, for the third time in her life, to rely on her own resources. Purchasing a small lot on the Hartford green, she lived independently for almost thirty years, until her death in 1680.[132] On her deathbed she bequeathed all her property, valued at more than £100 at probate, to her only living child, William Edwards. She did not, however, grant him ownership outright but declared him "only to have the use and improvement for himself and his wife during their natural life." This life estate once again placed Edwards in a subordinate position usually reserved for women. Like a husband trying to ensure that his widow would not squander his children's inheritance, Anne Cole gave her son the right to use but not sell her house, land, and personal property. This arrangement protected the inheritance of "her grandson Richard Edwards and his heirs forever," who, she stipulated, would take full possession of the property after his father's death.[133]

Richard Edwards, the male lead in our family drama, had a good start in life. He had acquired at birth the social advantage of property and status and was trained in a profitable trade that would eventually allow him to become an independent craftsman. But he was raised in a disorderly household, governed ineffectively by a failed patriarch. His father had struggled as a boy to acquire the habit of manly self-control from a flawed role model. Richard, in turn, could not wholly escape this intergenerational history of family failure.

While both his half-sisters made good matches at young ages, he and his half-brother were settled with more difficulty.

The Spencer children were insulated from their stepfather's financial mismanagement by their family inheritances. In 1650 Hartford magistrates "sequestered" £30 of the Spencer family estate "for the use of the children."[134] The three also inherited from a London uncle £50 "to be divided between them equally."[135] These legacies provided modest dowers for Agnes Edwards's two daughters, and both easily embraced the role of colonial goodwife.[136] Her first son also eventually established himself as a householder of some prominence in Hartford, but he did not make it to adulthood without incident.[137] When almost thirty years old and still unmarried, Samuel Spencer was presented in Hartford County Court for "lascivious practices" with two local girls, a charge that "involved a range of acts between unmarried and unbetrothed couples that fell short of proven intercourse." They may simply have been caught kissing and embracing, but the fact that he alone was charged with and convicted of a misdemeanor suggests a more aggravated offense.[138] The punishment was proportionately severe. Judged "deeply guilty," he was fined £10 and ordered "to be kept in durance at the Common goale one month" on "Hard labor and co[a]rse diet."[139] While Samuel served out this harsh sentence, his parents were likely cleaning up another sex scandal that had disrupted the family. Less than a month after his step-brother's conviction, on 19 November 1667, Richard Edwards married a New Haven girl named Elizabeth Tuttle, who apparently was already pregnant with his child.[140]

Both age and status made Richard Edwards an unlikely mate for Elizabeth Tuttle. Twenty-two years old, she married at a common age for colonial women in the seventeenth century. The man she chose as her husband was, however, rather young to take a wife. Because men could not fulfill their duties as household head without property and an established livelihood, few married before twenty-one years of age. Such prudence, however, did not characterize Richard Edwards's marriage. He was only twenty when he set up a family, two years younger than his new wife and almost eight years younger than the average newlywed man in neighboring Wethersfield.[141] And although his cooper's training was likely complete by this time, he would not have been well established in his trade. Nothing indicated this seemingly unsettled youth could fulfill a householder's duty to provide.

Elizabeth Tuttle also married beneath her. She came from a prominent New Haven family whose social position was clearly superior to that of her in-laws, and she had good family connections in Hartford. Elizabeth likely met her future husband at the home of her first cousin, who had moved from Boston to Hartford around 1649 to marry the son of one of the wealthiest of the town's original proprietors. Following his death she married the son of a Connecticut governor, bringing from her first husband's estate an inheritance valued at more than £1,200 at probate.[142] Richard may have thought an alliance with this prominent family an advantageous match—marrying up, after all, ran in the Edwards family—but Elizabeth's motive is less clear. A clue as to why this mismatched couple wed appears a year after their marriage in the Hartford County Court records.

On 5 November 1668 "Richard Edwards and Elizebeth his wife" were "called to an account for Incontenancy before Marriage" by the Hartford magistrates and were fined £5, the court's standard penalty for this offense at the time.[143] Couples were presented for incontinence before marriage when the delivery of an early baby provided evidence of premarital sex. Sometime prior to her appearance in court, Elizabeth had given birth to a daughter named Mary, and although the birth date was not entered with the town clerk, the baby probably appeared sometime before June 1668, because a full-term child born within seven months of the wedding was assumed to have been conceived before the union.[144] Although premarital sex was for puritan New Englanders a serious sin, it was a sin easily remedied. Public repentance and punishment allowed the couple to reenter the godly community without stigma, and a hasty marriage ensured both mother and child a means of financial support. The Edwardses' fornication conviction suggests the couple made the godly choice. Like most seventeenth-century men in a similar situation, Richard apparently took responsibility for his transgression by accepting paternity and marrying his lover.[145] Pregnant with his child, Elizabeth likewise chose to marry the father of her baby, despite his youth and inexperience. In a society that valued deliberation over passion as the foundation for marriage, pregnancy was perhaps not the best reason to form a household.[146] But Richard Edwards and Elizabeth Tuttle, like the five other couples convicted of premarital fornication in Hartford County Court between 1668 and 1670, had no reason to believe it would undermine their union from the outset.

In colonial New England, "marriage usually followed, if it did not always precede, pregnancy."[147] English popular culture sanctioned premarital sex between courting couples. "[P]remarital intercourse did not represent a wanton rejection of moral propriety by ordinary people. Instead, it arose from a common belief that the boundary between illicit and licit sex was crossed once a couple became committed to each other."[148] Puritan officials in New

England rejected this longstanding practice, attempting instead through both legal and religious sanctions to confine sex to marriage. During the first few decades of settlement, colonists cooperated in this effort, but increasing convictions for fornication and bridal pregnancy suggest that compliance waned in the latter seventeenth century. The study of New Haven County conducted by the historian Cornelia Dayton indicates that the shift began in the 1690s, but in Hartford County it may have started somewhat earlier.[149] The Edwardses' fornication case occurred at the outset of this upsurge, and the magistrates handled their misdemeanor in a routine manner. Payment of the fine should have allowed them to get on with their lives.

On this interpretation Elizabeth Tuttle's marriage to Richard Edwards looks like a simple story of bridal pregnancy. A closer reading of the court record indicates, however, that this simple explanation of the marriage was only part of the story. Unlike most bridal pregnancy cases, the record of the Edwardses' fornication conviction is not just a brief notation of their confession and punishment. The case was complicated by a controversy that the magistrates attempted to resolve by examining Richard about his premarital sexual activities. When questioned in court, he did not contest the substance of the fornication charge, for he readily confessed to having had intercourse with his wife twice before their wedding. According to his testimony, on one occasion "he was Upon Bed with her at Mr. Wells his house before marriadge the best part of one Night." Was Thomas Welles, the husband of Elizabeth's wealthy Hartford cousin, supervising the courting of his young relation by permitting bundling in his household? If so, this was an early example of a practice that became common in New England a century later.[150] Or perhaps the couple met clandestinely at the Welleses' home, as they apparently did on at least one other occasion, when, according to Richard's testimony, he was "in Company with her at New Haven."[151] By his own admission, therefore, he had ample opportunity to father the child his wife was carrying when they wed. Nevertheless, after their marriage he stubbornly refused to acknowledge the infant girl as his own. This refusal transformed a simple case of bridal pregnancy into a contested paternity suit.

Despite the couple's recent marriage, the magistrates approached the Edwardses' fornication case as if Elizabeth had given birth to a "bastard" child. The "bastardy" statue adopted by Connecticut in 1672 codified existing procedure for providing relief to women who had out-of-wedlock births. It stipulated that the man identified by the mother's "constant" accusation, especially when made "in the time of her trav[ai]l," was legally the "reputed Father" of the child and was liable for its maintenance.[152] When

Hannah Payne, for example, accused Thomas Burr of "begetting her with child" the court found through questioning that the child had been conceived when "she lay in the house of the father of the Sayd Burr, none being in the house but the Sayd Thomes," and they noted that she was "allwayes constant in Charging him to be the father of the Child." It accordingly ruled that Thomas Burr "is to be accounted the reputed Father of the Child" and ordered him to pay child support for four years. This case was heard two years after Connecticut adopted the bastardy statute, but in 1666 the Hartford Court had disposed of an earlier paternity suit in a similar fashion.[153] By the time Richard Edwards and Elizabeth Tuttle had married, therefore, the procedure for addressing such disputes had been established in fact, if not in law.

The Hartford magistrates followed this procedure when trying the Edwardses' case. Whom Elizabeth named as the father is not noted in the records. However, Richard was questioned to determine that he had had the opportunity to father the child, and he confessed to his "incontinency," which strengthened the evidence against him. The court accordingly judged that on one specific occasion—when he had traveled to New Haven to "keep company" with Elizabeth—the child had been conceived. The language of the decision is also that of a contested paternity suit. Having established time, place, and opportunity, the magistrates ruled that they "cannot but Judg and declare the Child born of the sayd Elizabeth to be the *reputed* child of the sayd Richard Edwards."[154] The use of the term "reputed" in this context indicates that Richard denied his paternity. His confession to fornication before marriage, however, undercut the foundation for this contention and led the court to rule that the infant was his "reputed" child. This judgment should have settled the case; nevertheless, Edwards persisted in his denial, claiming apparently with his father's encouragement that another man had fathered the child.

William Edwards addressed this family crisis in the same ineffectual way he had repeatedly attempted to settle conflicts throughout his adult life. Litigious by nature, he again looked to the law to provide relief for the injury he believed his son had suffered. The action he brought in New Haven County Court on behalf of his son against one Joseph Preston provides the identity of the alleged "other lover." Joseph Preston was the son of William Preston, one of New Haven's original proprietors. His parents were members of the New Haven church, and he undoubtedly had been raised in a godly home.[155] Nevertheless, his reputation made him a likely candidate for a paternity charge. Given to drink and disruptive behavior, he repeatedly aggravated his offenses by refusing to confess or take responsibility for his actions. When accused of disorderly conduct on militia-training day he had "lobed out his tongue" and run away; when charged with the same offense in court he was placed in the stocks for failing to admit his fault. And three years before the Edwardses' marriage, he had been whipped and fined forty shillings for denying a fornication charge and again fleeing the courtroom.[156] Despite this rebellious nature, he cooperated fully in the Edwardses' lawsuit.

This suit, which was brought about seven months after the wedding, resembled what would come to be called an action for criminal conversation. The criminal conversation suit was devised in the latter seventeenth century, as English common law courts "extended the range of the action of trespass, which had previously been used as a remedy for mayhem, battery, or wounding." Part of a more general expansion of the idea of property, a criminal conversation action was grounded in the claim that the husband had a property right over his wife's body. A cuckolded husband could, therefore, bring a civil action against his wife's alleged lover, demanding monetary damages in compensation for trespass upon his property—that is, the body of his wife. More commonly, he threatened an action to force a private financial settlement that avoided the scandal of prosecution in open court. By 1692, the year of the first high-profile criminal conversation trial, the action was a well-established tort in English common law.[157]

Unlike the standard criminal conversation suit, the action against Joseph Preston was brought not by the party claiming injury but by his father. Furthermore, because the injury had allegedly occurred prior to the formal solemnization of the marriage, Richard Edwards had only a tenuous claim, perhaps grounded in an informal espousal or promise to marry, that Elizabeth Tuttle's body was his possession at the time in question. Despite these weaknesses, William Edwards brought "an action of trespass" against Joseph Preston "for abuseing his son's wife" and demanded £50 in damages. Because Elizabeth failed to appear and present evidence, the court did not test the merit of this claim. When Preston asserted his right to confront his accuser "face to face," the magistrates deferred the action to the next court session. At this second hearing, William Edwards withdrew the civil action and made a criminal complaint. He "accused the said Preston unto authority that hee had comitted fornication with his daughter-in-law before marriage to his Sonne Richard." Once again, however, Elizabeth failed to appear, and he was forced to withdraw. When the case was next placed on the court docket, Edwards's chief witness against Preston was for the third time absent from the courtroom. Being already again pregnant, she was likely reluctant to suffer the humiliation of a public trial in her hometown. Or perhaps she refused to cooperate because she knew the defendant was innocent. Without her testimony, however, the plaintiff had no choice but to abandon his case. The magistrates accordingly dismissed it and discharged Preston.[158]

Why did Richard Edwards doubt his fatherhood? This question is central to our story of this marriage—both its beginning and its end—but contemporaneous sources provide no answers. Even if Elizabeth Tuttle had two premarital lovers, neither man could likely have denied paternity with absolute certainty. Determining both the time an infant was conceived and its probable delivery date were matters of much medical debate in the seventeenth century.[159] The Hartford magistrates judged that conception had occurred when Richard and Elizabeth had sex in New Haven, apparently ruling out her other illicit couplings, if such existed. But no court decision could overcome the lingering uncertainty that likely clouded Richard Edwards's judgment. Wounded manhood transformed his doubts into the poisonous conviction that he was not the father of her child. Nursing this wound for more than twenty years, he would retell his version of the early-baby story in his plea for divorce, and we will revisit the event when our narrative reaches this climactic moment. One thing, however, is now clear: Richard Edwards began his career as household head believing he had been cuckolded by the humiliating behavior of an unchaste woman.

Elizabeth Tuttle likewise began domestic life disgraced by a potent and gendered shame. In puritan New England, virtuous women lived chaste lives. While marital fidelity and premarital purity were valued in both sexes, a woman's honor was dependent on her sexual restraint. "For a woman," notes the historian Laurel Thatcher Ulrich, "sexual reputation was everything; for a man, it was part of a larger pattern of responsibility."[160] Elizabeth's fornication conviction placed her virtue in question. Like most women in this humiliating situation, she tried to repair the damage by confessing her sin and marrying her child's father. But rumors of a second premarital lover—uncorroborated in court but supported by her husband's unwillingness to take legal responsibility for the child—likely perpetuated the stain. Certainly, her husband's actions expressed to the community his belief that his wife was a "lying whore" or a "filthy slut," terms commonly used in the seventeenth century to describe women of questionable virtue.[161] By refusing either to keep the contested infant under his roof or maintain her with his income, he clearly displayed his claim that the child was a bastard. Elizabeth would have seen her daughter from time to time when she visited her parents' home in New Haven, where Mary was raised, but she likely experienced a deep anger at the loss of her child.[162] Unable to gain her husband's trust, she began her career as goodwife feeling unjustly shamed by his intractable doubts.

Like Richard Edwards, we cannot finally know what to believe or whom to blame. The records preserve only frustratingly incomplete fragments of a story, the full complexity of which is forever lost to us. Without Elizabeth's voice, her side of the story is particularly difficult to hear, especially over the roar of her husband's angry accusations. Even an incomplete reconstruction of likely events reveals, however, that Richard Edwards and Elizabeth Tuttle began their marriage in a mess. He brought to the union a heavy weight. As sole male heir, he bore alone the expectation that he would finally free the Edwardses from their intergenerational history of family failure. Coming from a large and flourishing puritan family, Elizabeth carried the opposite burden of perpetuating in the second generation her parents' successful colonial career. For both, therefore, marriage was the foundation of future hope, quickly shattered by the crisis that erupted soon after the wedding. Each had cause to feel angry and betrayed by the other. Each probably said things difficult for the other to forget and did things difficult for the other to forgive. "Paternity uncertainty" damaged their relationship from the outset and created deep wounds that never fully healed.[163] In these early moments, the puritan ideal of companionate union between a husband and his willing helpmeet may have been irretrievably lost. For a time our unhappy couple seemed to have put the past behind them, as they worked together to manage their household and raise several more children. But during the next, even more damaging family crisis, this uneasy equilibrium again came undone.

A BRUTAL MURDER

Elizabeth Tuttle and Richard Edwards were married for more than two decades. Following their rocky start, whatever equilibrium the couple established in their domestic partnership was eventually lost. He began building a case for divorce almost twenty-two years after their wedding, and the petition was granted about two years later. What caused this marriage to break down? Having traced the stories of our protagonists' colonial beginnings and considered the messy circumstances in which they started married life, we can now begin to piece together a fragmentary answer to this question.

As with most failed marriages, the story of the collapse of the Edwardses' union has several intertwining subplots. Many factors, both internal and external to the relationship, probably contributed to its breakdown. Richard's version of the story has been preserved in his two divorce petitions. He identifies events internal to the marriage—specifically Elizabeth's own faults as a goodwife—as causing the failure. While the inside story will be the subject of the fifth chapter, this chapter and the one following consider external events that Elizabeth might have cited had her story been preserved. But because she cannot speak for herself, her version must be told using the meager clues available to us. Several such clues are found in her large extended family. The first, and most telling, is a murder. In 1676, the flourishing Tuttle family was struck by a sudden act of brutal violence. This tragedy raised many troubling, and ultimately unanswerable, questions. Why does evil exist? How dark is sin? Is all hope of salvation lost? The Tuttles surely struggled with these questions in the aftermath of the murder. Some likely found solace in their families and their religious faith. For Elizabeth and two of her siblings, however, this event seems to have precipitated a protracted crisis that neither family nor faith could resolve.

To tell this story we must return to William Tuttle, the family patriarch, who settled in New Haven in 1639 with his growing family. Unlike William Edwards's disorderly domestic relations, William Tuttle embodied in his large household and substantial estate the patriarchal ideal of manhood. With his wife of more than thirty years he fathered eight sons and four daughters, all of whom lived to adulthood. This large brood of children was not only an index of William Tuttle's manliness; it also helped him to achieve financial competency, or household independence, an even more important source of colonial manhood. His sons provided crucial labor in the fields, as did his daughters in the home. All helped him maintain an orderly household and established his reputation as a responsible household head, capable of providing a sufficiency for his family. He managed his resources well, only rarely appearing in the New Haven courtroom as party to a debt action. As a town proprietor, he steadily increased his land holdings with each distribution of the common lands, meadows, and wastes within New Haven's jurisdiction. He also acquired additional lands through purchase and assumed responsibility for the care and nurture of two more children—daughter Elizabeth's first child and a five-year-old boy who was an orphaned family relation.[1]

Because the matriarch of this flourishing family was a member of the New Haven church, each of her children was baptized after birth and was subject to the church's watch and care. The church cooperated with the family in the common task of raising the young to live disciplined and pious lives. William and Elizabeth likely taught their children to read the Bible and to recite the catechism and the Ten Commandments. Daily devotions and prayers also probably instilled in them the virtuous habits necessary to restrain the power of sin and lead them to salvation.[2] Despite these advantages, however, the Tuttle family government at times failed. Young Elizabeth was not the only child in the family to go astray, nor was she alone in her conviction for a sex-related offense.

In colonial New England, the godly lifestyle promoted by the twin institutions of church and state competed with an alternative value system, expressed in such profane activities as dancing, drinking, swearing, and card playing. Public flirting, kissing, and petting were further evidence of popular disagreement with the official position that sex should be confined to marriage. Young people were drawn to this lifestyle as a temporary rebellion against the norms and values of adulthood. Often having to endure a protracted period of adolescence between puberty and marriage, they "traditionally enjoyed greater freedom to indulge in the profane activities of the wider popular culture before they settled into the responsibilities of forming proper family governments."[3] Groups of young men and women would gather clandestinely at night in defiance of their parents to frolic in barns, drink in taverns, and walk through the woods and fields on the outskirts of town. These illicit meetings also allowed colonial youths to pursue their interest in members of the opposite sex. Loose talk about sex was common and at times led to more serious forms of illicit sexual behavior.[4]

The variety of minor offenses committed by the Tuttle children clearly reveals the presence of a flourishing youth culture in colonial New England. The eldest was accused of attending a "disorderly" meeting, where a group of young men drank "strong watter," smoked tobacco, and were "heard to singe filthy corrupting songs." Three younger brothers were fined for being "inviters and Entertainers" at a corn husking; one of them was again fined the following year for participating in a "disorderly meeting" of young people "at the shop" of a local craftsman. Sister Sarah's flirtatious banter earned her a conviction for "imodest, uncivell, wanton, lascivious" behavior at age eighteen. When a local boy snatched her gloves and teased that he would return them only if she kissed him, "they sate downe together, his arme being about her, and her arm upon his shoulder or abut his neck, and he kissed her and shee him, or they kissed one another, continuing in this posture about half an houre." At the same age, brother Thomas was whipped when he and "sundrie youthes" were convicted of committing "much wickedness in a filthy corrupting way one with another." Two years later, when again implicated in a scandalous incident involving a servant girl and a young man visiting from nearby Stratford, he avoided whipping only by confessing "he spake very sinful words to her" and showing "himself most penitent for his fault."[5]

Elizabeth Tuttle's premarital sexual experimentation with Richard Edwards—and perhaps Joseph Preston—should be viewed in the context of the colonial youth culture revealed by these incidents. When she and her future husband "kept company" in New Haven, their behavior differed only by degree from that of her siblings. The harsh punishment of Richard's older stepbrother for "lascivious carriage" provides further evidence of the pervasiveness of such practices. These youths were typical colonial adolescents. Although raised in diverse family circumstances, they all shared a youthful penchant for rebellion. That the Edwardses struggled to maintain economic order in their household likely promoted their boys' misconduct. But the children in the Tuttles' large, orderly family also enjoyed activities that expressed values "subversive of adult, puritan standards."[6] Having twelve children was a blessing, but it multiplied the opportunities for misbehavior.

This adolescent counterculture, although enthusiastically embraced by many colonial youths, was for most a transitional phase. For a few, the profane lifestyle became a permanent habit. But most young men and women ended this time of youthful indulgence with marriage, when they assumed the economic and religious responsibilities of mature household heads having property and children of their own.[7] The majority of the twelve Tuttle children followed this developmental pattern. Prior to their father's death, all but four had married and begun governing families of their own. Three of the daughters had moved from New Haven to settle with their husbands in outlying Connecticut towns. The sons, however, preferred to establish households closer to home.

William Tuttle facilitated his sons' smooth transition to adulthood by setting them up with homes of their own. The historian Philip Greven has documented that in colonial New England a "fundamental characteristic of most first-generation families was the prolonged exercise of paternal authority and influence over sons." Fathers maintained their authority by controlling the family property. Although sons moved out of the household when they married and often built homes of their own on family property, fathers were commonly unwilling to grant their sons full title to this land prior to their deaths. The uncertainty of this inheritance ensured that sons would remain "dutiful, obedient, and in some measure dependent" upon their fathers for many years after assuming all the responsibilities of household head. As a result, second-generation men frequently postponed marriage until their late twenties and achieved full economic independence only after their fathers had died.[8]

The Tuttle boys did not have to wait until their father's death to obtain at least a portion of his estate. Following a pattern more characteristic of second-generation patriarchs than of those of the first generation, William Tuttle enabled several of his sons to achieve full autonomy and independence by distributing to them part, if not all, of their inheritances during his lifetime.[9] Through these financial transfers he eliminated a major source of intergenerational conflict within colonial families. As a result, most of his sons appear to have maintained strong bonds with their father as they grew to adulthood. In 1656 William moved the family homestead to the Yorkshire quarter, and this New Haven neighborhood then became the center of Tuttle family life. His second son acquired the lot next door, and his eldest son moved with his wife and children into a house neighboring both his father's and his younger brother's properties. Jonathan and Joseph, although living in other parts of town, likewise remained in the New Haven area.[10] The Tuttle patriarch's skillful apportionment of his estate, therefore, kept his older sons near at hand while promoting their independence. By the year of his death, four had taken their places within the community of household heads that formed the core of colonial life.

William Tuttle died suddenly in the spring of 1673.[11] The life expectancy of men and women in colonial New England was high. Although deaths from accident and infectious disease were common, first-generation men lived on average at least thirty years after migration, with a substantial portion surviving well into their seventies.[12] At sixty-five, William Tuttle had lived for thirty-eight years in his adopted home, but he died before the completion of his parental responsibilities. As was customary, the court named "Elizabeth Tuttle, widow, the relict of the said deceased" the administrator of his substantial estate, valued at almost £500 at probate.[13] Sixty-one years old when her husband died, Mistress Tuttle also assumed the duties of household head, responsible for the welfare of her four unsettled sons. Unlike their older brothers, these young men struggled to marry and establish themselves as independent householders. The lack of paternal guidance likely made it harder for them to settle down, but the absence of a firm hand cannot fully explain the crisis that would soon shatter this well-ordered puritan family.

The first sign of trouble occurred about a year after the patriarch's death. Young Nathaniel was the only child still living at home when the family governor died, and evidence suggests that this twenty-year-old was poorly prepared for the sudden loss of paternal guidance. He was at the age when many of his older siblings had found the lure of youthful rebellion irresistible. That he was caught in an offense was, therefore, not unusual, but his reaction to the charges displayed a contempt for authority more extreme than that of his rowdy brothers and sisters.

When a local native with a reputation for inebriation was presented for breaking down the ferry house door, he was "called and questioned where he had his drink." Selling alcohol to Indians was forbidden by Connecticut law, and "Rum Tom" named Nathaniel Tuttle as one source of his supply. Unlike his siblings, who eagerly confessed and repented their sins in court, Nathaniel denied the charge. Even when "cautioned to speake the truth," he refused to confess and demanded proof that he had committed the crime. After "much debate" with the magistrates, he finally "owned that he had sold him both Cydar and liquor" and was fined £5. This cooperation was, however, short-lived, for the following session he failed to appear in court when presented "for his challenging and tumultuous carriage before the authorities." When he finally arrived late that evening, the court fined him ten shillings for his absence. Several years later, he was again presented for a conduct-related offense when he assaulted the miller "in a forcible and tumultuous manner." For this breach of peace the court fined him forty shillings and "committed [him] to the Marshall until the same be payd."[14]

Contempt for authority was part of the profane lifestyle that characterized colonial youth culture.[15] Nathaniel's "tumultuous scuffling" with the miller and his "tumultuous carriage" toward the magistrates suggest, however, a more profound failure of self-control. As youths, his brothers and sisters had been charged with social and sexual offenses—drinking, company keeping, kissing, and teasing. Unlike his siblings, this youngest Tuttle, who came of age after his father died, was prone to acts of verbal and physical aggression that did not dissipate until he married and gained his independence, a milestone he failed to achieve until age twenty-nine.[16]

Simon and David Tuttle likewise postponed establishing households of their own. Both had before their father's death invested in the new satellite village of Wallingford, planted in 1670 on the Quinnipiac River about fifteen miles north of New Haven.[17] The benefits of settling in a new town must have been clear to these men, whose father had made two migrations. David's plans to marry and settle in Wallingford were, however, never realized, while Simon postponed marriage for almost a decade. Although the older Tuttle brothers had wed at an average age of twenty-five, Simon waited at least until thirty-one and did not move his family to Wallingford for several years after the union.[18] The family patriarch's passing disrupted these men's smooth transition to adulthood. This death, however, was but a minor source of confusion compared with the sudden chaos caused by brother Benjamin's cold-blooded murder of their sister Sarah.

Benjamin Tuttle, the next-to-youngest son in the family, was twenty-five when his father died. He too was unmarried, but unlike his brothers, he had moved away from New Haven. Connecticut law stipulated that all persons who were not independent householders must be subject to family government. Benjamin was, then, obliged to live with another family, either as a servant or a lodger, whose head ensured that he "walk[ed] diligently in a constant lawful imployment, attending both Family duties, and the publick worship of God, and keeping good order day and night."[19] He first apparently boarded with the large family of his older sister Hannah, who had married and moved to Stratford when he was only six.[20] By 1676, however, he was living with his sister Sarah, who had moved to Stamford when she married John Slauson, the oldest son of a prominent town leader. By the time Benjamin joined this household, she had given birth to at least two sons and two daughters.[21]

The factors that pushed and pulled Benjamin Tuttle away from New Haven are unknown. One common motive for migration was land. Both Stratford and Stamford had in the 1670s small populations and plentiful lands. The previous decade Stratford had significantly increased its territory by purchasing additional lands from neighboring Indian tribes, and Stamford had begun privatizing its common land by distributing it to the town's proprietors and selling it to new inhabitants.[22] Benjamin may have been working to establish himself as an inhabitant and landowner in one of these two towns, but by the time of his father's death he was far from this goal. In 1673, he had received only £3.5 of his inheritance; three years later he had obtained substantially more—slightly more than £33 by his mother's accounting—but had little to show for it.[23] By 1677 his small estate, valued at £38 at probate, was spread out over three towns. Although he had received a few parcels of land from his father's estate, his personal property was meager. In addition to his "chest and armes and ammunition and Apparell," he owned two sheep, two oxen, and a "parsell of Indian Corn upon the grownd at Stamford."[24] Slowly acquiring the resources needed to marry and establish himself as an independent householder, Benjamin Tuttle was, like his brothers, forced to endure a protracted period of dependence.

Children also left home to escape the annoying restrictions of parental control. Sons who moved away acquired a degree of autonomy denied their siblings who remained at home. Benjamin did not, however, choose to break completely with his family. Although leaving behind parents and friends, he kept within the orbit of the extended kinship network the Tuttles had established since settling in New Haven. Internal migrants commonly "chose to settle in places where they had members of their families living also, maintaining some degree of family connection both in their new communities and with their families" back home.[25] Benjamin's sisters' households mitigated some of the difficulties of migration by providing him a place to live and work, but a profound sense of isolation probably remained. Unlike in New Haven, where every man and woman had a familiar face, most people he encountered in Stratford and Stamford would have been relative strangers. That he stayed only a few years in each town also prevented him from putting down roots. Estranged from the larger community, he likely grew more dependent on his few remaining intimate relationships.

As the years passed, Benjamin likely found this dependency increasingly difficult to bear. Living within his sister Sarah's household was probably particularly trying. Although only six years his senior, Sarah, along with her husband, had enjoyed the status of independent household heads for many years. As a Stamford proprietor, John Slauson had achieved the patriarchal ideal of manliness that his younger brother-in-law was still struggling to obtain.[26] For Benjamin to submit to his government may have been a daily reminder of his own personal failure. By 1676 his father had been dead three years, but he was not free of patriarchal control. Because autonomy was a common reason sons moved away from home, this slow path to manhood may have been particularly frustrating. But personal disappointment and thwarted ambition alone are insufficient to explain why this young man committed a sudden act of brutal violence.

Murder is an opaque crime. Even the most detailed motive cannot finally close the gap that separates act from explanation. The distance grows wider when the murder is committed with great ferocity, for the horror of the crime itself impedes understanding. Likewise, acts of intimate violence are particularly unintelligible and frightening. Violence between family members "juxtaposes two antithetical images[,] that of a loving and nurturing family with that of repetitive violence, pain, sexual abuse, fear, and even murder."[27] Although victims, witnesses, and neighbors may struggle to reconcile these images, what transforms the bonds of affection into engines of suffering and death remains elusive. No coherent narrative can finally be constructed to satisfy the human quest for an explanation.

Benjamin Tuttle's murder of his sister Sarah defied understanding. He shattered a moment of ordinary family intimacy with a shocking act of uncontrolled rage. The incident occurred on the evening of 17 November 1676 at his sister's small Stamford home. Seventeenth-century colonial New England houses were modest structures, commonly comprising a hall and parlor on the ground floor and a low loft or storage chamber upstairs. At the center of the structure stood a large chimney with a cavernous fireplace used for both heating and cooking. This hearth formed the heart of the colonial goodwife's domestic domain. Sarah undoubtedly spent hours every day standing at her fireplace, tending the fire and preparing her family's simple daily meals.[28] On the night of her death, she was sitting in what was probably her most familiar and secure spot in the house, her chair by the fire. Her husband, who was serving on night watch, was absent from home, but she was not left alone.[29] Also snuggled into the chimney corner were her four young children and her brother Benjamin. Had this evening passed like any other, Goodwife Slauson would perhaps have spent the time mending clothes or listening to her children recite their lessons. But this night, events took a horrifying turn. A quarrel broke out between Sarah and Benjamin, and he stalked out of the house in a rage. Quickly returning with an axe in his hand, he struck his sister a savage blow on the right side of her head. The neighbors who answered the cries of alarm found her "laying dead across the hearth with hur head In the cornar of the chimney." The axe was resting in a pool of blood at her side, where Benjamin had dropped it. When she was "barbrusley Slayen In her one hous" by her own brother, Sarah Tuttle Slauson was thirty-four years old.[30]

Murders were rare in colonial New England. Prior to 1660 only three English colonists had been tried for homicide in Connecticut, and none had been convicted.[31] The first execution for murder in the colony occurred in 1667, and between 1667 and 1711, when the Court of Assistants was replaced by the Connecticut Superior Court, only six English colonists went to the gallows on a homicide conviction. Benjamin Tuttle was the third white man found guilty of capital murder in the colony.[32] His crime was, therefore, not totally unprecedented, but it was a shocking aberration from the normal patterns of daily life. Such an uncommon occurrence was newsworthy. John Bishop, who had pastored the Stamford church for more than thirty years, lived just across the meetinghouse lot from the Slauson home.[33] When he learned of the murder, he, like many of his neighbors, probably raced to the scene of the crime to view the bloody corpse, and he subsequently reported his shock to his Boston correspondent Increase Mather. Knowing his colleague's eagerness to hear of "illustrious providences," he described to Mather the "horrid murther committed among us, here at Stamford." "A brother kill[ed] his own dear sister," he related. She was "a very good woman that loved him dearly, but was ill requited, killed her with an ax, maulling and mashing her head to many pieces, in a barbarous and bloudy manner." Offering a fitting improvement, Bishop observed, "The Lord is proceeding stil to humble his poor wilderness people . . . by stroke upon stroke, correction upon correction . . . to teach us instruction."[34]

Despite its singularity, when this homicide is compared with other early Connecticut murders it appears remarkably ordinary. Of the conditions conducive to violence in this period, intimacy was the most lethal. Large households shared small spaces, and neighbors were almost constantly in and out of one another's homes.[35] "With little privacy in the home or at the work place and no place else to go, people lived constantly in the same small group."[36] Such frequent contact caused conflict, which on occasion escalated to murder. Each of the six English colonists sentenced to death for murder by the Connecticut Court of Assistants was convicted of an intimate homicide. In addition to an infanticide that occurred in New Haven in 1668, Peter Abbott slit the throats of his wife and child in Fairfield in 1667, and Henry Green "knockt" a neighbor's child "on the head with an ax" in Farmington in 1675. The following year Benjamin Tuttle murdered his sister in Stamford, and in 1678 John Stoddard "Knocked" his infant stepbrother "on the head with a hatchet" and then murdered his New London neighbor and two of her children by "knocking them in the head" with an axe. Finally, in 1706 Abigail Thompson of Farmington killed her husband by "striking him on the head or face" with a "pair of Taylors Shears." The one murder committed by an African in this period also conforms to this parade of horribles. The year before Benjamin Tuttle murdered his sister, Cloyes Negro had "knoct his wife In the head with an ax" in Stamford. Even Squampum used an axe to murder two Indians in the Wethersfield home of Samuell Wright in 1685.[37]

Each of these murders was a household crime. Each occurred in a domestic setting and involved persons who commonly shared the same domestic space. The three spousal murders clearly illustrate the potential for intimate violence, but the marriage bond was not the only relation ruptured by homicidal rage. Siblings and neighbors, whose daily lives were intimately intertwined, also resorted to violence to resolve conflict. The greatest act of carnage was triggered by a rejection. When young Stoddard asked his neighbor if he could stay the night in her house, she "bid him be gone . . . and thrust him oute of Dores over the threshold and . . . gave him A blowe with her hand and shut the Dore." Denied entry into the sanctuary of the home, he burst through the door and slaughtered his neighbor and her two children, sparing her infant only because it was too young to speak.[38] Like this multiple homicide, each of the other killings appears to have occurred in a moment of explosive violence. With the possible exception of Abbott's attempted familicide, none was the consequence of extended premeditation.[39] Acting in an uncontrollable rage, these colonists struck out at the objects of their frustration. And to communicate their fury, they grasped whatever ordinary domestic instrument was near at hand; a knife or a pair of shears would suffice, but the most common instrument of death was the axe.

This weapon resembled the tomahawk or war club that native peoples frequently employed in battle with the English.[40] Acting as if the Slauson home had been raided by Indians, Benjamin Tuttle gave out the hue and cry after the murder. According to subsequent testimony, he shouted "Arm! Arm!" as he ran out of the house, and the neighbors probably seized their weapons on hearing this alert.[41] Throughout its history, Stamford had been dangerously exposed to Indian attack. In 1642, the town hired Captain John Underhill, who had fought in the Pequot War, to command its defense, and in the 1640s he worked to contain the Indian threat. Native homicides did, however, on occasion occur. In 1648 the body of a Stamford deputy who had disappeared from his farm was later located by one of the local natives, who identified a Mohawk as the killer. Four years earlier another Indian had entered a Stamford home and killed a woman with a hammer.[42] Although hostilities between Indians and English declined in subsequent decades, with the outbreak of King Philip's War in 1675 the old anxieties returned and rumors began circulating that the "Sta[m]ford Indyans are in Armes."[43] By the time Sarah Slauson was murdered in November 1676, the war was over in southern New England, but memories of the bloody conflict would still have been fresh. When Stoddard slaughtered his neighbor's family in New London, which had served as a main base of supply for Connecticut's troops during the war, two Indians were initially suspected.[44] Had Tuttle also killed the eyewitnesses to his crime, his ruse might have been more credible. The Slauson children, however, lived to tell of the murder, and they said their uncle, not an Indian, had savagely killed their mother with an axe.

Every colonial household required an axe, and most probably had several of differing sizes and weights. Because the household fire needed continual care, wielding an axe was a skill everyone learned at an early age. Hatchets were used to make kindling, while larger axes split logs and felled trees. Because the distinctive American axe, with its heavy poll and shorter blade, was not produced until the late eighteenth century, Tuttle's murder weapon was probably of European design.[45] The jury of inquest described it as a "narro ax," suggesting it was felling axe, a tool usually used with a "two-handed overhead, over-the-shoulder, or side-swinging action, to deliver chopping strokes," instead of a broad axe, which was used with "short, two-handed strokes as a shaping tool."[46] The axe was, however, not simply used for woodworking; it was an all-purpose implement employed in a variety of household tasks, including, quite commonly, killing.

For an example of the axe as an instrument of death, New England colonists needed only to look to their local butcher. Until the late eighteenth century, the traditional means of slaughtering larger livestock, like cattle or oxen, employed an axe.[47] "The most general method of killing oxen in England," noted *The Experienced Butcher*, "is by knocking them down first, by

Early-seventeenth-century broad axe and narrow, felling axe heads excavated at Historic Jamestowne. Courtesy of Preservation Virginia.

striking them with a pole-axe on the forehead, and then cutting the throat."[48] Butchers had used this method of slaughter for centuries. A seventeenth-century text, *The Academy of Armory*, observed that the axe, which it called the "Butchers Knocker Down," is used "to strike down great Beasts when the Butcher is to Blood them and tickle them out of their Lives." The repeated use of the phrase "knocked on the head" in accounts of colonial homicides clearly links axe murder to this method of animal slaughter. As the butcher knocked an animal down "by giving him a blow or two on the Forehead with the round end of the Ax," so domestic killers in colonial Connecticut similarly dispatched their victims.[49] A single stroke of the axe transformed a loved one into a hapless beast, lying on the killing floor as the blood drained from its lifeless body.

What forces transformed Benjamin Tuttle into an axe-wielding butcher who viciously killed his older sister? Lacking the manly virtues of rationality and self-control, young, single men were thought to be prone to violence, but nothing in Tuttle's past suggests he had been a hot-tempered youth.[50] Existing court records contain no evidence of pre-existing conflicts with authority. If he had been accustomed to youthful carousing, he did not attract the attention of the New Haven magistrates. Unlike his brothers, he was never charged with a conduct-related offense as a young man.[51] The records of his murder trial likewise contain no testimony to a bad character. Colonial courts commonly heard testimony concerning a defendant's character in their proceedings. Michael Dalton, the author of the popular judicial guidebook *The Countrey Justice*, recommended that magistrates consider a suspect's "company," "course of life," and "evill fame or report" when determining whether to indict.[52] At Stoddard's murder trial, for example, the court heard an affidavit made by four of his neighbors certifying that "hee hath Allwayes bin a Most terrible wicked boy" whose parents "offten said they thought he wold Com to the gallows."[53] The evidence submitted in Abigail Thompson's murder trial likewise included numerous testimonies from neighbors and relations alleging that she had engaged in a pattern of violent behavior toward her husband.[54] In contrast, if a chain of lesser crimes led to a great crime, as colonists commonly thought, no evidence of a vicious life course for Tuttle was apparently presented to the court.[55] All witness statements entered in his case solely addressed events immediately preceding the murder.

This testimony was presented on two occasions. The day after the murder, a jury of inquest was held in Stamford to inquire into cause of the "very suddain, untimely," and "un-natural Death" of Sarah Slauson.[56] After viewing the body and examining the wounds and the weapon, the jurors questioned the eyewitnesses to the incident. The four Slauson children, who had watched in horror as their uncle Benjamin shattered their mother's skull, were qualified to provide evidence in judicial proceedings. As the historian Holly Brewer asserts, "It was only during the late seventeenth century that the rule that children should not testify was introduced—for the first time." The English jurist Matthew Hale first recommended that the minimum age for witness testimony in felony cases be fourteen, but he maintained that the "testimony of those between nine and thirteen should be allowed 'in some cases.'"[57]

Young John Slauson, who the jurors note was "aged abought twelve years" when his mother died, provided the most detailed description of the incident, and his account was corroborated by his nine-year-old sister, Sarah.[58] The two younger children, who were but four and six years old, apparently did not testify.

The case came to trial some six months later, when the Court of Assistants met in Hartford in May 1677. Although the children's testimony would probably have been sufficient for conviction, several additional statements by Connecticut magistrates who had questioned Benjamin Tuttle following the crime and urged him to confess were also entered into evidence. Because colonists considered every violation of the law to be both a crime and a sin, confession was encouraged. Confession eliminated the element of doubt; it also demonstrated repentance and contrition for sin, especially important in capital cases. Tuttle's behavior after the murder conformed to this expected narrative. When during pre-trial examination a magistrate "labor[ed] to remember him of the greatness and horror of his sin," Tuttle "plainly owne[d] his killing his sister" and "hoped God wold grant him Repentance."[59] But he did not repeat his confession in court. After the reading of the indictment, he pleaded not guilty and asked for a jury trial. Given the overwhelming evidence of guilt, however, the jury easily reached a verdict, and the twenty-nine-year-old man was sentenced to hang.[60]

Because no real question of fact or responsibility was presented in this case, the Crown's burden was easily met. Tuttle's motive for the crime did not need to be addressed by the court. Having readily established who, what, when, and where, the court deemed the why to be extraneous. The witness statements, therefore, contain only a few fragmentary clues to the murder's motive or cause, allowing us to reconstruct at best only a partial and unsatisfying answer to the story's most salient question: Why did Benjamin Tuttle murder his sister Sarah? Certainly, rage was the proximate cause of the attack. It occurred in a heat of frenzied violence. According to young John, at the first blow of the axe, his mother "fell and nevar spock nor gron more." One stroke from such a lethal weapon was probably sufficient to kill; it was, however, insufficient to satiate Tuttle's passion. Standing over his senseless sister, he "followd with sevrall bloos aftar she fell." These final blows crushed the dead woman's skull. Her "scull an[d] Jau [was] exstremly brock from the Jau to her neack and soo to the crown of the heed," noted the jury of inquest, and "part of hur brayens" oozed from a "hool wich was struck through hur head behind the eare." Such gratuitous violence suggests a deeply entrenched rage.

The trigger that ignited this rage was a petty quarrel, the kind of quarrel most colonial households surely endured on a regular basis. Sitting by the fire with her brother and her children on a cold November night, Sarah began to fret about her husband's welfare. After visiting the local pastor's home, he was apparently scheduled to attend the town watch, a duty that would keep him out all night. He had, however, left the house without eating his evening meal, and this worried Goodwife Slauson. "[S]he was sorry," her son testified, that "hur husband was gone to Mr. bishop's without his suppar, exspexting he was gon to watch." She had the duty to provide her household's daily meals, but on this particular evening she had allowed her husband to go unfed, and she "feard he would be sick for wont of It." Her brother Benjamin took exception to her concern. According to his nephew's account, "he repl[ied] very short: that he might have had It before he went If he would." Sarah objected to the rude and curt manner with which Benjamin dismissed her distress. "[Y]ou ned not be soo short," she chided him. Hearing this rebuke, Benjamin stalked in anger out of the house, leaving the door open in his haste. Sarah then asked her older daughter to shut the door because the draft made the fire smoke. As she pushed it closed, Benjamin burst back into the house—crying "I'll shut the doar for you!"—to do his bloody work.[61]

This brief narrative of the crime leaves much to be explained. There must be more to the story than this. That a small domestic squabble provoked such a disproportionately violent response suggests that this quarrel had a history. During his pre-trial examinations Benjamin admitted that he did not get along with his sister. He confessed "he had never love for his brother and sister" when questioned by the Court of Assistants and explained to a Stamford magistrate that "he kild his sister" because of "som difference that was between them." It "was sad Living," he complained, "always quareling and Chiding." The heated exchange that precipitated the murder was, therefore, the final expression of a long-festering conflict. On their last evening together, Tuttle's pent-up rage exploded into violence.[62]

The disagreement itself contains one small hint pointing to the nature of this more deeply rooted conflict. The dead woman's son reported that "Just as he struck [his] mother the furst blow," his uncle exclaimed, "'I will tech you to scold!'"[63] The word "scold" was a term of abuse commonly used to censure sharp-tongued and loquacious women. Having greater force in the seventeenth century than it does today, "'scold' was a strongly negative term, in destructive impact second only to 'whore' (and its equivalents such as 'drab,' 'jade' and 'quean') as a pejorative label applied to women." In early modern England, women who "disturb[ed] the peace by publicly abusing family members or neighbors" were regularly presented in court and sentenced to such shaming punishments as the "cucking-stool" or the "scold's bridle."[64] In the New England colonies women who nagged or bossed their husbands, criticized their neighbors, or simply talked too much were subject to shaming punishments and community censure.[65] When Benjamin accused his sister of scolding, he, therefore, was reprimanding her for a particularly female failure. Instead of quietly submitting to male authority, she had talked, and in particular she had "chided" or criticized her brother. His response was equally gendered. Like many men, he apparently believed that "scolding shrews could be 'tamed' by (male) physical force."[66] Although an axe to the head was an extreme response, it effectively got his sister to shut up.

The degree of violence may reflect the ambiguity of Benjamin Tuttle's status in the Slauson household. Scolding was a status crime committed by women who had failed to submit to male authority. Tuttle, however, had no real authority in the Slauson family. Although nearly thirty years old, he occupied a subordinate and dependent position in a household governed by his older sister and her husband. She was obliged to submit to her male superiors, and her worry about her husband suggests she knew her place. It was, after all, concern for his well-being which sparked the argument that led to her death. But as her family's female head, Sarah Slauson had the authority to discipline her younger unmarried brother, especially in her husband's absence. Benjamin Tuttle, although a dependent, may have resented her attention to her husband's needs and craved to command the authority of household head. "I will tech you to scold!" he shouted as he bashed in his sister's head. But Benjamin Tuttle was neither Sarah's teacher nor her governor. Discontent with his dependency, he destroyed this constant reminder of his powerlessness, and for this crime he was sentenced to death.

Benjamin Tuttle's heinous crime demanded both punishment and explanation. On the day of an execution both needs were addressed if all participants played their appointed parts in the elaborate civic and religious ritual that attended capital punishment in colonial New England. The role of the civil authorities was to restore the social fabric that had been rent by Tuttle's shocking crime.[67] By definition, felonies were malicious crimes that constituted serious threats to society, but domestic homicides, like that committed by Tuttle, were particularly disquieting. Such intimate crimes "unexpectedly violated the system of trust on which every household, regardless of class and occupation, was founded."[68] To repair this breach, the civil authorities ensured that through the orderly observance of the judicial process Benjamin

Tuttle received a punishment that fit his crime. According to the ancient principle of retributive justice, the only fitting punishment for murder was death. "This sin shall not be satisfied for, with any other punishment, but the death of the Murderer," observed Increase Mather. "Equity requires this; by the law of Retaliation, it is meet that men should be done unto, as they have done to others; and that as limb should go for limb, so Life for Life."[69] Tuttle's hanging was, therefore, an elaborate public display of the power of government to maintain order; it communicated the reassuring message that civil society was secure.

Crimes like Tuttle's also caused a crisis in meaning, precipitated by the pressing need to explain the presence of evil in the world.[70] To address this crisis, the religious authorities provided an explanatory framework within which the community could comprehend such an aberrant deed. This task was accomplished primarily by the sermon preached on the execution day immediately before the hanging, but the interpretative process began long before that climactic event. During Tuttle's seven-month deathwatch in the Hartford jail, the local ministers would have regularly descended to the dungeon beneath the jailhouse to pray with him, hoping he could obtain salvation before the final hour.[71] Tuttle's humble repentance and confession would transform his sin into a revelation of unmerited grace. And if he ascended the scaffold in this same humble frame, thousands would witness this dramatic illustration of God's power to bring good out of evil as both an example and a warning.[72]

Benjamin Tuttle was executed at Hartford on 13 June 1677. The ritual began as he walked slowly, weighted down by chains, across the town green to the overflowing meetinghouse. These curious spectators were eager to see the condemned man take his seat before the pulpit. From this place of shame he could feel the stern looks of the magistrates and other dignitaries who filled the front benches. His aging mother likely sat nearby, surrounded by his many brothers and sisters. Once all participants were in place, the service began. The pastor of the Middletown church, Nathaniel Collins, delivered the execution sermon.[73] Although the text of his discourse has not survived, its purpose was well established. For his rapt audience, Collins would have "sought to integrate extraordinary and perhaps frightening communal events into a familiar theological framework."[74] When this dramatic discourse had concluded, he likely accompanied Tuttle out of the church and walked with him at the head of the large procession that spilled out of the church and proceeded up the road that led to the cow pasture and into the country where the gallows had been erected.[75] If Tuttle played his expected part, he delivered from the scaffold a few last words affirming the justice of his punishment, confessing the wickedness of his sin, and warning the throng of spectators not to follow his example. Although this large crowd had flocked to the gallows to see a gory spectacle, they witnessed a public affirmation of the divine drama of sin and redemption that Collins had surely emphasized in his sermon.[76]

Nathaniel Collins undoubtedly selected a text for his sermon suitable to the occasion. Jesus's comforting words to the penitent thief, that "today shalt thou be with me in Paradise" (Luke 23:43), were popular with execution-day preachers, as was "For the wages of sin is death, but the gift of God is eternal life" (Rom. 6:23). Given the nature of Tuttle's crime, however, Collins may have preached from the same text used by Increase Mather a decade later when addressing a prisoner who had committed murder with an iron spit. "And if he smite him with an instrument of iron, so that he die," warns Numbers 35:16, "he is a murderer; he shall surely be put to death."[77] This passage emphasizes the righteousness of God's wrath over the hope of his infinite mercy, but both themes were integral to the form of an execution sermon and would have been affirmed by Collins.

Voicing the Calvinist theological consensus that still dominated puritan New England in the last quarter of the seventeenth century, the Middletown minister would have examined how Tuttle's wicked crime revealed the universal depravity of human nature.[78] "[I]t is to be presumed," observed Mather, "that a man will not strike another with an Instrument of Iron, except Blood and Murder be in his heart." The heart of the axe murderer was, however, no more sinful than those of his neighbors. "The gross and flagitious practices of the worst of men, are but Comments upon our Nature," explained Samuel Danforth. "Who can say, I have made my heart clean?" Every "heart is the Seed-plot of Murther, Adultery, Fornication, Lasciviousness, and of all manner of iniquity."[79] This doctrine formed the core of the execution sermon's explanatory purpose. It supplied a sufficient cause for even Benjamin Tuttle's savage murder of his sister. Tuttle, like every person in the meetinghouse, had been born with a "Murderer's heart within him."[80] When he brutally struck his sister's head with an axe, he made visible the true depth of his corruption.

The explanatory power of this doctrine was, however, limited. "The problem with universal depravity as an explanation of capital crime," observes the historian Daniel A. Cohen, "was that, in explaining so much, it actually explained very little." If murderers were no more corrupt than their law-abiding neighbors, why did they, and not their neighbors, commit brutal crimes? Why, if all were born with a murderer's heart, did Benjamin Tuttle alone commit a murder? To answer this troubling question, Reverend Collins would likely have employed the concept of restraining grace.[81] "[T]he Children of men bring murderous natures into the world with 'em," Increase Mather explained. "Should not the Lord either by special or common Grace restrain them, how many would soon become guilty of Murder itself!"[82] Cotton Mather echoed his father's words in an execution sermon preached a decade later: "A man would soon Murder his Father & Mother, Destroy his own Wife, and Debauch his Neighbours, Blaspheme God, and Fire the Town, & Run a muck among the people," he proclaimed, "if God should not Lay upon him Restraints." Restraining grace was, however, a gift that God at times withheld. Abandoned to their corrupt natures, people inevitably sinned. Without this "Dam of Restraining Grace," Mather cautioned, "a devouring Flood of Sin will presently carry all before it."[83]

With his finger pointing at Benjamin Tuttle, Collins likely thundered from the Hartford pulpit that he had bludgeoned his sister to death because God had withdrawn his grace. Abandoned to his murderous heart, the wicked desires of his corrupt nature had been unchained—with predictably bloody results. Collins also probably warned the congregation that God had permitted the wretch seated before him to "commit that great and horrendous Sin of Murder" as a punishment for his sins. As another execution-day preacher observed, "it is one of the Lord's most righteous, but withall most tremendous waies of punishing Sin, viz. with Sin, or by Sin. Lesser sins are punished by leaving men to greater sins."[84] This concept of "sin punished by sin" placed heinous crimes like murder within the scope of God's providential government of the world. Benjamin Tuttle's axe murder thereby became not a disruption but an expression of divine order. As his death was fitting punishment for his crime, his crime was just punishment for his sins. Because his sin provoked God's wrath, God had abandoned him to commit even more heinous sins.

This execution-day ritual situated a shocking crime like murder in a common theological framework that made evil intelligible to the larger community. The comprehensiveness of this explanation leads one historian to conclude that there was "no mystery to the crime of murder" in colonial New England.[85] The doctrines of universal depravity and restraining grace did give crime a measure of transparency, but they did not eliminate all mystery. Although all were corrupt and deserving of punishment, only a few were abandoned by God to their sins. Why God visited such an affliction on Benjamin Tuttle was a larger mystery neither Nathaniel Collins nor his ministerial colleagues could resolve. Execution-day sermons regularly catalogued a chain of sins that led to the crime. Given Tuttle's quarrelsome nature, Collins may have identified his "besetting sin" as anger.[86] "Rash sinful Anger is an evil thing," warned Increase Mather; "[m]urder begins there."[87] But in colonial Connecticut many brothers quarreled with their sisters, while only one killed his sister with an axe. The doctrine of restraining grace pushed this mystery back into the inner recesses of the divine sovereignty. Faith demanded submission to God's sovereign will, but it did not penetrate the mystery of his judgment. In this dark core, murder remained an opaque crime.

The many members of the large Tuttle family likely found this mystery particularly difficult to bear. Four years after the patriarch's sudden passing, two traumatic deaths of much greater magnitude had again turned their world upside down.[88] Although death was an ordinary part of colonial life, the Tuttle family loss was monstrous. When Benjamin killed Sarah, their flourishing family was struck a life-threatening blow. Shocked and confused by the sudden emergence of a murderer in their midst, they may have found little comfort in the ordinary rituals for grieving. Like Benjamin, they too may have felt abandoned by God. Sudden death was an awful providence. Persons who died without the opportunity to repent and prepare to meet their maker were "popularly assumed to be under some divine judgment for sin." The loved ones Sarah left behind surely labored to understand what had provoked such a terrible display of God's wrath. Another source of torment was the doctrine of predestination. Although the Stamford pastor believed Sarah to be a "good woman," her family could never know if she had died blessed with a full assurance of her salvation. Benjamin's eternal destiny was even more clouded. When he swung an axe at his sister's head he revealed his murderous heart. During the months he awaited execution in the Hartford jail, he may have repented and received God's mercy. But his wicked deed was likely a sign that God had reserved a place for him in hell. For the remaining Tuttles, such uncertainty would have magnified their despair.[89]

The only theologically sanctioned response to this divine chastisement was repentance. On execution day, ministers commonly admonished the larger community for its collective sin. They "transformed the spectacle of the hanging from a discrete act of communal catharsis to a symbolic demand for more general reformation."[90] Collins may have preached a jeremiad for Tuttle's execution, observing that in the preceding decade God had visited on New England several terrible judgments. Churches had been torn by conflict over the half-way covenant; towns had been ravaged by Indians during King Philip's war, and several Connecticut families had been destroyed from within by murderous rage. In this catalogue of divine wrath, God had singled out the Tuttle family for a particular judgment. This awful providence defied understanding and tested the strength of each family member's faith.

For the ten remaining Tuttle children, life had to go on amidst the confusion. Most had orderly families of their own to support them when the tragedy occurred, and within these households the third generation of Tuttles in America continued to grow, as babies were born at a steady rate. The two youngest sons, who like Benjamin had been single when their father died, finally established households of their own in the years following the murder. Even John Slauson had, within four years of his wife's shocking death, remarried and started a second family. Although he took longer than most widowers in seventeenth-century Connecticut to select a new mother for his children, even he eventually found the strength to start over again.[91]

Whatever equilibrium the family managed to establish following the murder was, however, threatened by continuing troubles and losses. Four months after the murder, the third son was presented in New Haven County Court for three separate offenses: unlicensed liquor sale, illegal leather transport, and breach of peace, for which he was fined a total of £3.5. Two months later the eldest petitioned the New Haven freemen to remit his rates for the past year "in consideration of the afflicting hand of God upon" him. Having also suffered financial strain in the year after the murder, Mistress Tuttle likewise asked the town magistrates to remit a portion of her debts because she had "had grate Loses in my Estate by cattell and other ways."[92]

In the following decade, additional deaths gave rise to new grief. The eldest son died at fifty-two, leaving his wife and eight children a modest £79 estate.[93] The fifth son also died in mid-life, perhaps from complications of an old foot injury. Five years earlier, he had been "freed from watching" because he was "an impotent man, having lost one of his feet." He left behind a widow, nine unmarried children, and a respectable estate of £261.[94] But perhaps the greatest loss came in 1684, when the family matriarch passed away. Having outlived her husband by more than a decade and grieved the unsettling loss of several grown children, Mistress Tuttle died at age seventy-two, in an "aged and infeebeled" condition.[95]

The final passing of the first generation left the remaining Tuttle children in disarray. Clearly displaying this conflict was the estate contest that erupted when their mother's will was probated in New Haven County Court. The contest pitted the youngest son, who had resided in the Tuttle family home

Gravestone of Mrs. Elizabeth Tuttle, now located in Grove Street Cemetery, New Haven.

until his mother died, against his five older brothers. Nathaniel evidently claimed that he should receive a larger portion of the family property, valued at just over £294, because of "his improvement of the said Estate" since his father's death. His brothers, however, maintained that he had exercised undue influence on the disposition of his mother's estate. A witness to the will supported their claim, noting that "Mrs. Tuttle did not declare to him the will as written, but that Nathaniel Tuttle did relate to his mother these things and asked her, if she did not consent to it, that it should bee soe, and then shee did declare her consent." Given these objections, the court refused to approve the will and instructed the brothers "to see if they could agree among themselves about the distribution of the said Estate." When such agreement proved unattainable, it was distributed by court order, thereby circumventing the need for consensus.[96]

Estate contests were not uncommon in colonial New England. As the seventeenth century drew to a close, the Connecticut Court of Assistants was increasingly occupied with adjudicating such family disputes. The cases brought by these squabbling siblings reflect the growing litigiousness of New England society and reveal the difficulty children of the second generation had assuming the positions of authority vacated by their parents' passing. That the Tuttle brothers quarreled over the remains of their mother's estate was, therefore, not surprising, especially considering the extraordinary trial that had afflicted them. Although sickness, death, and financial distress were common hardships, this exemplar of puritan family life had been burdened with a terrifying providence. A brutal murder had shattered the peaceful refuge of their family, stealing two loved ones from them. Following this tragedy, the remaining family members struggled to right their inverted worlds. Most gradually returned to their domestic routines, but for at least three of the siblings the disorder was too hard to bear. In the years following this protracted period of family crisis, David grew increasingly unable to manage his affairs, and his younger sister Mercy began a slow descent into madness. Elizabeth's fragile union with Richard Edwards, which had functioned adequately for about a decade, also began to fall apart.

[4]

A CRIMINAL LUNATIC

A year after Mistress Tuttle's death, the estate contest that had split her family was finally settled. Although her property was "equally divided between the children," the administrators agreed to grant two significant additional bequests. The youngest son was awarded £39 "for his improvement of the said Estate," indicating that his argument had proved persuasive. The court also ruled that David Tuttle "in consideration of *his weakness* is to have four pounds above either of the rest."[1] "Weakness" is an ambiguous word. It suggests that the fourth son suffered from a disability that required extra expense but provides no information about the nature of the affliction. Pursuing this small mystery reveals that in the years following the murder several fresh trials struck the Tuttle family. Benjamin's wicked deed had many victims. His brother David's weakness was not a chronic ailment or physical infirmity but a debilitating mental illness likely exacerbated by his experience of sudden and baffling loss. And the damage did not end there. Two of David's younger sisters also broke down sometime after this tragedy. Mercy's commission of a second shocking murder destroyed her household, while Elizabeth's marriage experienced a lingering decline as she became increasingly unable to fulfill her spousal duties.

David Tuttle's early life appears to have followed an ordinary course of development. As a young man he became a proprietor of the new village of Wallingford, receiving a home lot on its main thoroughfare and the right to shares in future divisions of its outlying lands.[2] This acquisition of property signaled his intention to marry and start a family, but he never achieved this crucial marker of manhood. Because marriage was a prerequisite for household independence in colonial New England, few men failed to find a wife.[3]

Despite the disadvantages of bachelorhood, however, David remained a dependent all his adult life. Perhaps he had first displayed some peculiarities in behavior or temperament in his twenties, reducing his chances in the marriage market. But the Wallingford investment suggests that at thirty-one he was still looking for a mate. If he had managed to marry, his wife would have cared for him in times of illness. By the time his mother died, however, he was an "old bachelor," whose welfare was a source of concern for his family.[4] The extra provision in her estate reflects this need for assistance, but it did not arrest his continuing decline. Two years later he was declared incapable of managing his affairs and placed in his brother Thomas's care.

Madness was an ordinary feature of colonial life. Mentally ill people were not confined or hidden from public view, unless they behaved in an overtly violent or alarming manner. Although such disabilities were rare, men and women suffering from distraction, lunacy, melancholy, and delirium lived in communities scattered throughout New England. Like other dependents, they primarily resided in households that supplied their daily needs, managed their financial affairs, and nursed them during times of illness. The court on occasion appointed a family member to oversee an ill relative's estate, but not until the late eighteenth century were mentally ill persons placed in asylums where medical professionals supervised their treatment.[5] In both large urban areas and smaller rural villages, therefore, colonial men and women were probably far more familiar with the aimless wandering and idle talk of their afflicted neighbors than subsequent generations.[6]

Such incompetent adults fell into two broad categories. Those who suffered mental impairment from birth were judged "idiots" or "natural fools," incapable, as the early modern jurist Matthew Hale explained, of counting twenty shillings or knowing their own age. Those who became incapable later in life were subdivided into two types. Hale identified madness as a "permanent or fixed" condition, in contrast to lunacy, which was "interpolated, and [distinguished] by certain periods and vicissitudes" depending on the phase of the moon.[7] David Tuttle was probably a lunatic, by this definition. That he was not born with a mental disability is indicated by his ability to purchase, sell, and inherit property throughout his life. This financial competence also suggests that as an adult he suffered from an episodic "distraction" that grew increasingly severe as he aged.

The record of David Tuttle's guardianship hearing itself indicates a level of competency on his part. Although family members commonly requested hearings for their incompetent relatives, he initiated the process himself.

Declaring in 1687 that he found "himself very unfitt for the improvement and management either of himself or his estate to advantage," he requested the New Haven Court to "appoint his brother Thomas Tuttell to take care of him and of his estate."[8] Over the next few years he suffered such severe "Sickness or disability" that Hannah Tuttle, the widow of his recently deceased brother Joseph, was paid to care for him. By 1693, however, he was sufficiently competent to sell his Wallingford property, apparently without supervision. That same year, however, he transferred the entirety of his estate to his guardian to compensate him both "for his keeping and maintenance for 6 years past" and "for his maintenance for tyme to Come during Life."[9] An inventory of his property was exhibited in court during this hearing. In addition to several acres of real estate in New Haven, he owned only a few personal items—fitting for a man the court called, using the legal term for insanity, "one non compos mentis." A "smale Gun Barrell or stock" and an "old sword" were markers of the manhood he never achieved, while the "Bedsted" and "old bible" were reminders of the long hours he spent debilitated with illness.[10] Thomas Tuttle took possession of this humble estate when his brother was fifty-four years old. Perhaps dwelling in a small outbuilding on his guardian's land, this aging and incompetent man lived out his days in a reduced and dependent condition.[11]

Did his sister's murder drive David Tuttle over the edge? Psychiatrists generally agree that the incidence of mental illness increases after trauma. Traumatic events do not necessarily cause mental illness. The psychiatric impact of an event is dependent on many factors, including the nature and severity of the trauma, the context in which it occurs, and the personal history and circumstances of the individual experiencing it. While no one who has experienced an "event that is outside the range of usual human experience" can wholly escape its effects, some assimilate the shock more easily than others, and a few break down. As one researcher observes, "[A]lmost all conditions have, at some point, been associated in some way with trauma as a predisposing, precipitating or aggravating factor."[12] Physicians in the seventeenth century also noted this correlation. "Seventeenth-century people," observes the historian Michael MacDonald, "were as convinced as we are that social and psychological stress disturbed the minds and corroded the health of its victims." A common stressor was grief. The troubled men and women who consulted the English physician Richard Napier confirmed that the "loss of family members was so hard to bear that it made some people insane."[13] The author of *The Anatomy of Melancholy* offered a similar diagnosis. The death of kith and kin is "so grievous a torment," he observed, "that it takes away appetite, desire of life, extinguisheth all delights."[14] Unable to adjust to the new world occasioned by the sudden loss of a loved one, the bereaved "fell into" a distracted or melancholy frame of mind.

The cause of David Tuttle's mental illness cannot be known. In 1670 he was preparing to take his place within the community of adult males by investing in the new settlement of Wallingford. By 1685, however, his "weakness" had become so pronounced that special provision was made for him in the distribution of his mother's estate. In the intervening fifteen years, he had experienced a series of catastrophic losses and personal traumas: Two of his siblings had died violent and shocking deaths, both his parents had passed away, and his oldest brother had also suddenly died. "It should not be assumed," warns one physician, "that just because somebody has suffered a catastrophic stressor all of their problems in the immediate or distant future should be attributed to it." Nevertheless, the "possible significance of such events should not be ignored."[15] That David Tuttle's mental state appears to have deteriorated during this extended period of family turmoil was probably not a coincidence. These traumatic events may not have been the primary cause of his breakdown; more likely they aggravated a previously manageable condition. An intractable grief precipitated a lingering decline.

When David Tuttle heard the shocking story of his sister's murder, he, along with the rest of his large family, probably did not know which way to go. Should they race to Stamford to bury sister Sarah or travel with brother Benjamin to the jailhouse in Hartford? Likely they all attended his trial, heard his execution sermon, and stood in shame at the foot of the scaffold as he was "turned off," cut down, and carted away to be buried in an unmarked grave in the wasteland near the gallows.[16] While most members of the Tuttle family seem to have had the strength or the faith to get past this crisis, David, who had no family of his own to support him, apparently had more difficulty making order out of the chaos. This blow to his extended family likely ruptured his already fragile hold on reality. And he was not the only Tuttle sibling whose mental balance was probably disturbed by these ultimately unintelligible events. In 1691, David's youngest sister, Mercy, committed a sudden act of brutal violence even more shocking than that which had shattered the Tuttle family some fifteen years earlier.

Mercy Tuttle, the next-to-youngest of the Tuttle children, was born in New Haven in 1650.[17] At fourteen she was placed in a neighbor's household to work as a servant, a common practice in colonial New England. Boys lived as apprentices in their masters' households while learning a trade, and girls perfected their housekeeping skills by caring for their mistresses' home and children. Without parental oversight, however, young servants had greater freedom to engage in the profane activities of colonial youth culture.[18] Mercy was implicated in a small scandal while a servant. When charged with "gross Pilfring & stealeing several things," her cousin told the court that she and Mercy had drunk "some Liquors" at a neighbor's house. Nevertheless, Mercy was exonerated when the neighbor testified that she had not seen the Tuttle girl that night at her home.[19] Three years after this minor brush with the law, Mercy married and became the mistress of her own family.

In May 1667 the Tuttle household celebrated a double wedding. Mercy likely married Samuel Brown, the son of one of New Haven's original proprietors, at the same ceremony in which her older brother Joseph also tied the knot. The families probably marked these unions with a joint wedding feast, inviting friends and neighbors to join them in celebrating this milestone in their children's lives.[20] At seventeen, Mercy was a bit young to marry, but she and her husband, who at twenty-two was also young to take a mate, appear to have easily assumed their responsibilities as household heads. Although her first child died a month after birth, following this loss she produced the expected succession of children and was the mother of four by the time she was thirty.[21] As the head of this growing household, Samuel Brown began planning for the better provision of his family. In 1670, he joined his brothers-in-law David and Simon Tuttle in their Wallingford investment, perhaps using the settlement Mercy had brought to the union.[22] Connected by family and marriage, these three householders probably planned to settle their families together in this village north of New Haven. None, however, moved to Wallingford for more than a decade.

Samuel and Mercy likely delayed relocating for family reasons. Given the series of shocks the Tuttles experienced in the 1670s, this young couple may have been reluctant to abandon their grieving relations. Simon Tuttle and his family finally moved from New Haven around 1682, but the Browns did not join them until at least 1685. Perhaps they hesitated until the aging Tuttle matriarch passed away, or perhaps Mercy's fragile health delayed the move. Unlike her brother David, no series of court decisions record her increasing mental instability. Marriage would have provided the financial and emotional support her bachelor brother lacked. The only hint of a developing disability lies in the family's childbirth records. For twelve years Mercy regularly gave birth at the expected two- or three-year intervals. After 1679, however, this pattern abruptly ceased. At thirty years of age, she presumably had many fecund years remaining, but during the next decade she produced only one more child, a son who died young.²³ Although a variety of factors could explain this hiatus, subsequent events suggest it marked her decline into madness.

The morning of 23 June 1691 began like any other in the Brown household. Forty-one-year-old Mercy was the first to stir, rising, after a restless night's sleep, at first light if not earlier. As the family goodwife, she had the duty to take care of the early morning chores. While her forty-six-year-old husband slept in the parlor bed, she arose to stoke the fire and begin preparing her family's simple morning meal. The "building and regulating of fires" was the "most basic of the housewife's skills." Experienced housekeepers like Mercy knew to keep a "few brands smoldering, ready to stir into flame as needed."²⁴ On this particular morning, however, the fire had gone out, the first indication that anything was amiss. Instead of trying to kindle a new flame, Mercy walked to her neighbor's house to get some fire from their morning blaze. To carry a burning brand the distance home was itself a challenge, and according to later testimony, she "blowed at [it] as she went and, fearing it wold goo out, turned in to the house again and fetcht more." Once the fire was safely home and burning on the hearth, Mercy attended to the next morning chore. She milked her cows and turned them out into the meadow to graze, but in another deviation from her normal morning routine, she also turned out her daughter's cow. Sarah, who had married the previous year, was living with her husband in her parents' household.²⁵ Although she also had apparently risen early, when Mercy returned from tending the cattle, most of the household was still in bed asleep.

At least two of Mercy's three younger children slept in the chamber located above the ground floor of the house. Such chambers were commonly used for storage, not sleeping, but the Browns had moved a bed upstairs perhaps to give the family's second-best bed, which would have been located in the downstairs hall, to their daughter and her new husband after the couple wed.²⁶ On this June morning, seventeen-year-old Samuel Jr. was asleep in this chamber bed beside one of his younger siblings, presumably his twelve-year-old brother, Francis. Suddenly, the quiet of this ordinary day was fractured by the sounds of horrific violence. Hearing "som Blows" coming from the upstairs chamber, the elder Samuel Brown was startled from his sleep. The scene that assaulted him when he reached the chamber was monstrous. He "found his wife standing by the bedside with an Ax in her hand." The bedclothes must have been red with blood from the two blows she had already given to her son's head. Awakened by the events, young Francis was surely screaming in horror. Mercy delivered a final blow before her husband was able to twist the weapon from her hand. But his wife's murderous passion was not yet spent. When Samuel released her to lift his injured son from the bed, she again snatched up the axe, forcing him to "seize her to prevent further mischiefe to himself or another Child then in the same bed." Once he had subdued his wife, this terrified father must have again rushed to his son, lying wounded in the bed. Young Samuel languished for six days while his family ineffectually tended his broken skull, and he died on 29 June 1691, a victim of his own mother's frenzied assault.[27]

Mercy Brown murdered her son Samuel fifteen years after her brother Benjamin murdered their sister Sarah. The two crimes share some similar elements in terms of both victim and means. Like her brother, Mercy committed a domestic murder, and like her brother, she used an axe as her weapon. These two similarities, however, are not genuinely distinguishing. As we have seen, all the murders for which English colonists were executed in seventeenth-century Connecticut were domestic crimes, and all were committed with ordinary household implements like the axe. These common elements emphasize the ordinariness of Mercy Brown's murder. The singularity of this shocking act of intimate violence emerges from other features of her crime.

Of all the forms of domestic homicide, a mother's killing of her child is perhaps the most alarming. When Benjamin murdered his sister, he violated a family bond, but he acted in conformity with his gender role. Young unmarried men were expected to act on occasion in violent and impulsive ways. Women, in contrast, were viewed as naturally nurturing, inherently tender and loving in the care of their children. Parental love was an affection shared by both sexes. As the puritan moralist William Gouge noted, God has "so fast fixed love in the hearts of parents, as if there be any in whom it aboundeth not, he is counted unnaturall."[28] Mothers and fathers, however, expressed this love in different ways. Although both women and men contributed to the care and nurture of their children, "the affectionate side of child-rearing was symbolically linked with mothers, the authoritarian with fathers."[29] A father who beat his disobedient child to death, although guilty of a failure of self-control, acted within his role as household head, responsible for disciplining his dependent family members. A mother who smothered her newborn with a pillow or threw her toddler down a well acted contrary to the common understanding of female nature. Such a woman was the antithesis of the "Virtuous Mother," whose pure love for her children was extolled by puritan ministers as an image of divine love.[30]

Infanticide prosecutions enhanced this negative stereotype by targeting marginal women. The 1624 statute defining English procedure in infanticide cases was enacted to address the social threat posed by a specific class of women. Of particular concern were "lewd women" who murdered their "bastard children" and hid or buried their bodies "to avoid shame, and to escape punishment." To address the evidentiary difficulties inherent in proving a dead infant had been murdered, not stillborn, the statute made concealment sufficient grounds for conviction.[31] Following this procedure, New England courts regularly convicted of homicide single women who had been charged with the murder of newborn infants. Married women were rarely accused of infanticide, and female defendants in general were seldom charged with any other class of homicide. Of the 68 women indicted for murder in Massachusetts between 1680 and 1779, all but two were accused of infanticide. By contrast, of the 156 men indicted for murder, only ten faced infanticide charges.[32] Both neonaticide, the killing of a newborn less than twenty-four hours old, and infanticide were, therefore, women's crimes. Indictments of women for the killing of an older child, and especially for adult homicide, were uncommon. These types of murder were most often committed by men.[33]

When she split her son's head open with an axe, Mercy Brown violated colonial society's image of the typical female child killer. She was a middle-aged woman who had been married for twenty-four years. Having given birth to at least six children over the course of her marriage, she had reached an age at which her offspring were beginning to establish households of their own. For colonial goodwives, the maturation and flourishing of children was a source of pride that displayed to the community the successful completion of their maternal responsibilities. Instead of rejoicing in the accomplishments of her offspring, however, Mercy murdered her son. As the first-born son, young Samuel occupied a privileged place in the Brown household; he was, in words of scripture, his father's "strength, the excellency of dignity, and the excellency of power" (Gen. 49:3). When Mercy took this child's life, she severed the family's patrimony. And unlike a distraught young mother who clandestinely killed her newborn, she dispatched her husband's namesake in a furious display of uncontrolled violence.

These aberrations made Mercy Brown's murder of her son a particularly opaque crime. Nothing in the colonial understanding of women's nature or women's crimes could provide an explanation for the act. The questions Connecticut authorities addressed to her and her husband on the day following their son's death convey this confusion. Unlike her brother's interrogation,

the search for a motive or explanation for the crime appears to have dominated the questioning. "[W]hat might be the actation, provocation, or temptation of such a Carnall and unnaturall action," they asked the dead boy's
father. "[W]hat moved you soo to doo to your own child," they demanded of
his mother; "what provocation had [you], what temptation were you under?"
Embedded in these questions were two possible causes for the murder.[34]

A "provocation" explained a crime of passion. Benjamin Tuttle's murderous rage, for example, was apparently sparked by his sister's sharp-tongued
rebuke. In Mercy Brown's case, however, such provocation was apparently
lacking. Neither she nor her husband reported that their son had said or
done anything to provoke his mother's anger. "Temptation" likewise provided a cause. Because all crime was a sin, and all sin was provoked by the
devil, who tempted weak and depraved human beings to stray, the "Great
Tempter" was a proximate cause of all violations of God's law. The agency of
the devil was particularly visible in heinous crimes like murder. Even Benjamin stated, when questioned by Stamford magistrates, that he "was over
taken with the temptation" to kill his sister. The language used in felony
indictments reflected the belief that such crimes had a diabolical cause. The
grand jury that indicted Mercy Brown alleged that she had committed her
crime "not having the feare of God before thine eyes and through the instiga-
tion of the divill."[35] Succumbing to these diabolical temptations, people killed
themselves and their near relations, committed adultery and blasphemy, and
engaged in other classes of felony crime. The devil, however, also tempted
people into madness, and this third possible explanation for the murder
dominated the approach to Mercy Brown's case from the outset.[36]

Doubts about Mercy's sanity surfaced first in the initial questioning of her
husband. "What condition as to her understanding or Reason was your wife
in at that tyme, the night and morning before the action was don, and some-
days before, and of late time," the magistrates inquired. This line of questioning gave Samuel Brown an opportunity to mitigate his wife's guilt, but in the
days following the assault, this distraught father appeared not to have questioned Mercy's sanity. He "found [her] to be as Ratonall as he had Knowne
her any other tyme," he responded. To support this assertion, he described
her seemingly ordinary activities on the morning of the murder. He also
identified some particular actions that suggested premeditation. After fetching fire from a neighbor and turning out her cows, he noted, she turned out
her daughter's cow "to get the daughter out of the way." And perhaps most
tellingly, he reported, she "hid her Ax under her apron at night," presumably in preparation for the morning slaughter. John and Mary Beach, the

Browns' neighbors, supported this assessment. When Mercy came to their house for fire, they reported, "she was as rationall in their apprehension then, as at other tymes, not suspecting distraction." The authorities made a similar judgment after their initial questioning of the accused. Although observing that she was "somewhat Crased or under deep Melancholy," they concluded that "she seemed to have her reason."[37] In the coming months, however, this apparent consensus favoring rationality would break down.

Once in custody, Mercy was transported to Hartford and confined in the town jail where her brother had languished while awaiting his trial and execution. Three months passed before the Court of Assistants met to hear her case, and during this time her husband formed a new interpretation of his wife's baffling transformation into a monstrous child killer. When her trial began, he no longer believed that Mercy should be held responsible for her crime. He argued to the court that she "hath been at Sundry times for many years past wholly deprived of the right use of her Reason and understanding, and always vary considerably Disturbed." This alleged history of mental illness suggested her mind was imbalanced at the time of the act. Because the murder was "wholly a fruit and effect of her Distraction," he urged, the court should acquit her of the charge.[38]

Community opinion also shifted in Mercy's favor, as family and neighbors rallied to her support. Several persons submitted testimony to impeach the compromising assessment of her mental state provided by the neighbors. According to two witnesses, John Beach had said on the morning of the murder that "he thot she was destra[ct]ed." After fetching fire at his house, he told them, she "went down the hill towrds the swamp and so stard about as if she was distra[ct]ed." A similar account was reported by Mercy's brother Jonathan, who said he thought his sister was "much out in her head." Another neighbor concurred in this judgment, as did her brother Simon and his wife, who also lived in Wallingford. They testified "that our sister mercye Brown has been a distracted woman," and "was very much out in her understanding" in the days preceding the murder. "[W]e doe believe in our consciences," they said, "that she was a distracted woman when she committed this horid act." Even the two men who first took Mercy into custody believed she "had not the right exercise of her understanding" in the week following the assault, and a Hartford resident who had regularly observed her behavior while in confinement judged "She hass been att Sundry times Distracted" since she "Came to this Gaol att hartford."[39]

The neighbors and kin who testified in Mercy's defense expressed a common assessment of her mental state. Of the variety of terms used to describe her impairment, "distraction" appears most frequently. Distraction was, notes the historian Mary Ann Jimenez, "the most common name for ordinary madness" in colonial New England. Neither a medical nor a legal term, it was used loosely to suggest "a person whose mind is occupied outside present reality."[40] This diagnosis was probably not made through a formal medical evaluation of Mercy's condition. People who interacted with her every day would have been the first to notice any oddity of talk or behavior. Like other Anglo-Americans in the seventeenth century, they "relied on common sense and common knowledge to establish that a person was insane."[41] Mad persons accordingly were identified through the collective judgment of a community—that is, through the activity of the "informal public." Unlike the formal public institutions of church and state, the informal public comprised peers, not elites, and its norms reflected the views of the male heads of household, their wives, and dependents, whose interactions formed the basis of community life in colonial America. Although it had no "formalized regulatory role to perform," the informal public did contribute to the "formation and perpetuation of the social order" in essential ways.[42] One of its roles was to define what constituted normal mental functioning, in contrast to madness.

Prior to the murder, Mercy's distraction was likely local knowledge. In the following weeks, this condition was embraced by members of Wallingford's informal public as the most persuasive explanation for her action. As the men and women of the neighborhood discussed among themselves this shocking death, memories were probably awakened of curious remarks and unnatural actions that she had said and done in the past. From these signs and symptoms of insanity, a narrative appears to have been constructed to explain this shocking disturbance of their peaceful community. Of course, the brutal murder was the most telling sign of insanity. Those who attacked friends and family were in the seventeenth century commonly believed to be lunatics. However, a single "antisocial action by itself, no matter how irrational it seemed, was not proof of lunacy."[43] Although he killed his sister, Benjamin Tuttle's mental state was not an issue at trial. One magistrate noted that "his discourse seemed to be rationall and composed, with out the least signe of Distraction."[44] For an insanity defense to succeed, a person must have exhibited a pattern of madness prior to the alleged criminal act. To demonstrate such a pattern required the support of the informal public. Lacking this support, Benjamin could not claim incapacity as a defense. And even with such support, Mercy's plea proved difficult to establish.

A subsequent infanticide case illustrates the sorts of behavior colonists believed characterized the insane. In 1712 Katherine Wyar, who lived with her husband and six children in Lebanon, Connecticut, stabbed her young son and threw him and his sister down a well. Although the girl was rescued, the boy drowned and his mother was indicted for murder. The numerous depositions submitted in her case reveal a longstanding history of affliction. Most noticeable to neighbors was her apparent incapacity to care for herself. One woman reported meeting her on the "rode, Barfut and bare Le[g}ged, with her Hare hanging downe about her." Several people described how she "would Pull of her Cloths and Run out into the woodes and hide herself for severall Dayes." When the neighbors found her, she was "almost naked, and had Lade till she was almost dead and so benumd that she Could not stand." These accounts reveal a community regularly disrupted by the irrational behavior of one of its members. Katherine Wyar violated social norms by wearing inadequate clothing and endangered herself by wandering off scantily clad into the woods. Her neighbors readily identified such a lack of self-care as a sign of a distracted mind.[45]

Although Mercy Brown had not exhibited such flamboyantly mad behavior, her neighbors and kin were distressed by her irrational actions. Several depositions mention her peculiar movements on the morning of the murder. That on her way home from fetching fire she suddenly "left the path and went to the brow of a hill and looked much about hir" was odd. "Aimless wandering" was considered a common symptom of madness, suggestive of "unchecked passion."[46] According to Mercy's son-in-law, she also had displayed a capacity for violent action. "[S]om times," he reported, "she wold threaten me and wold say that she wold throw scaldin water on me." This menacing behavior led him to conclude that she was "vary moch destracted and out in her had."[47]

In addition to these strange actions, Mercy had also made a number of odd remarks that in retrospect suggested an unbalanced mind. "Idle talk" was considered a common sign of distraction, often revealing a despair of salvation and an inordinate preoccupation with impending judgment.[48] Ordinary puritan piety contained within it a latent tendency to despair generated by the doctrines of predestination and innate depravity. Ministers encouraged prospective saints to strive for grace but also emphasized the impotence of the human will. The morphology of conversion required sinners to recognize that because human nature was corrupt, salvation could come only from God's inscrutable will. Burdened by the mystery of the divine sovereignty, consciousness of human inability declined into spiritual desolation and suicidal despair. The "slough of despond" became a dangerous quicksand from which the tormented sinner struggled ineffectually to escape.[49]

The extraordinary tragedies Mercy Brown and her family had experienced over the years may have left her particularly vulnerable to such predestinarian anxiety. Her speech revealed a deep inner torment and despair. While in prison awaiting trial she reportedly displayed an excessive concern about sin. "[S]he was greived and very much distressed about an offense given In words to a person then present," an observer reported, even though the person "[d]eclared he knew not any such words spoken." Unlike that of most persons suffering from religious melancholy, however, Mercy's distress was not primarily focused on her own spiritual state. It was projected onto her family, especially her children. In the days before the murder, she cautioned her son-in-law that "he must take care of his wife's soul." An elderly neighbor also reported that she came to her house and "sayd that she wold have my husband to look after hur husband."[50] The meaning of this request is unclear. Either Mercy doubted her ability to care for her husband or, more likely, anticipated a time when she would no longer be present to care for him. Such suicidal thoughts are common among filicidal mothers, who kill their children as an "extension of the suicidal act." Unwilling to abandon their children, these desperate mothers take them with them when they die.[51]

The clearest glimpse of Mercy's mental turmoil is provided by a conversation she had with her family the day before the murder. One remark in particular indicates that her melancholy thoughts were combined with apocalyptic fears. "[T]here are dreadfull times a coming," she predicted to her husband. This anticipated upheaval revealed an even more disturbing desire. She offered this ominous forecast to explain why she had earlier declared, "she would fein have her children buryed In the barne." Again, the meaning of this statement is unclear. Mercy wanted her children dead; that desire is unambiguous. But why did she imagine their bodies buried in the barn? Although most corpses were interred in town burial grounds, family plots were not uncommon on larger farms.[52] Mercy's fantasy suggests, however, a clandestine or profane burial, suitable only for persons suffering an unholy death. When young Samuel heard of his mother's dark desire, he bluntly asked, "If she could kill him." To this troubling question she reportedly replied, "[Y]es, If I thought it would not hurt you." This response was not just "idle talk," for the next morning she assaulted her son in his bed as he slept.[53]

Perhaps Mercy wished to have her children buried in the barn to save them from the dreadful times that were coming. In her troubled mind, death seems to have become a means of salvation. Speech moved her from distraction to action. She killed her son, she explained to the authorities, not from "any pro[vo]cation given by him, but from words spoke by him some dayes before." In response to her son's question, she had made a terrible discovery—she could kill. Once she had acknowledged this ability, an irresistible intention began to grow, until "her temptation was soo [great] that she thought it best to dispatch them." How could a mother believe her children better off dead than alive? Mercy apparently imagined that dead and buried in a familiar enclosure like the family barn, they would be safe. Death would protect her children from suffering, but, more important, it would protect them from the sin that tormented her and lead them to salvation. Samuel Brown embraced this motivation for his son's murder. "[H]er understanding being darkened," he argued to the court, "she Conceived it the best way to provide for his eternall benefitt." Mercy may have intended to cast all her children into the protective arms of death, for she wanted them all buried in the barn, or she may have focused on her eldest son as a particular object of concern. At seventeen, he was at an age when the temptations of youth increased, and as he entered adulthood the young man would assume the responsibilities of an independent household head. Death was a means of preserving the innocence of his childhood and ensuring he never reached the age of majority. "[S]hee hoped Hee was Abram's seed," Mercy worried anxiously the day after the assault.[54] Knowledge that Samuel had died before entering the menacing world of adult sin perhaps calmed her predestinarian fears.

These religious delusions classify Mercy Brown's murder of her son as an altruistic filicide. Altruistic filicides are "murders committed out of love."[55] In such killings the parent, most often the mother, believes death to be in her child's best interest. Genuine mercy killings, in which the child is terminally ill or suffering inordinately, are rare. Filicidal mothers motivated by altruism more often kill "to protect or rescue the children from some awful fate that was indicated by their delusional system."[56] The child is not actually in pain but is perceived by the mother to be in imminent danger of suffering that can be avoided only by death. Altruistic filicides, furthermore, have a distinctive profile. While young, single mothers kill newborns who are unwanted and unloved, older children are more frequently murdered by mature married women. These mothers commonly have a history of mental disorder, typically depressive illness, that informs their homicidal choice. Convinced that her child would be better off dead, she kills from a misguided mothering decision.[57]

Mercy Brown's crime appears to have been a typical altruistic filicide. Modern psychological studies of filicide are imperfect instruments through which to view a homicide committed more than three centuries ago. The cultural context in which this murder occurred is, according to most measures, dramatically different from that in which the subjects of these studies lived. The striking resemblance of Mercy's murder to the profile of the altruistic filicide suggests, however, that mothering may not have changed all that much in 300 years. Whether in the seventeenth or the twenty-first century, a mother's murder of her child violates the culturally constructed gender role for women. For an older woman, like Mercy Brown, who had married and formed a family, this gender role had defined her identity for many years. By framing a murder as an act of altruism, she preserved her maternal identity while giving herself a license to kill. This contradiction was clearly displayed by Mercy's response to her son Samuel when he asked his mother if she could kill him. She could, she replied, "if I thought it would not hurt you." Mothers are not supposed to hurt their children. Distracted mothers may, however, murder a child as an act of love. "I Could never Get you to do this," she had reportedly told her husband. Believing she was the only one who could protect her son from a terrible fate, she acted as any loving mother would and split his skull open with an axe.[58]

The Connecticut Court of Assistants convened at Hartford on 1 October 1691 to hear "The Case and Tryall of Mercy Brown of Wallingford." She had been held in the town jail since her son's death and during this three-month confinement had exhibited some signs of distraction. Nevertheless, the court judged her fit to plead when they met for their regular fall session, the first since the murder.[59] The proceedings began with a reading of the indictment, asserting that Brown was guilty of "horribly & most Unnaturally Murthering" her "own son." The grand jurors could have ended the prosecution had they judged her not responsible for her act. When Katherine Wyar, the distracted mother who threw her children down a well, was presented for her crime in New London Superior Court, the grand jury was apparently conflicted about her competency, for they first returned the bill *ignoramus* before reconsidering the facts and voting to indict.[60] Any debate about the facts in Mercy's case was perhaps resolved by her confession. As in Benjamin's prosecution, the matters of fact in this case were uncontested. She had admitted striking her son with an axe when first examined by the authorities, and she had repeated this confession to the grand jury. They, accordingly, returned a *billa vera*, noting that "[t]he Prisoner Mercy Brown in Court did Confess, that she was guilty of Willfull Man Slaughter, or wilfull killing her Sonn."[61]

Once the indictment was returned and read before the court, Mercy Brown was asked to enter a plea. In colonial courts defendants commonly had only two options: confess, or plead the general issue, not guilty. As her brother's plea illustrates, Mercy's prior confession did not rule out a plea of not guilty. A general acquittal on grounds of insanity was, however, a difficult verdict to obtain.[62] To judge a defendant who had indisputably committed a heinous crime "not guilty by reason of insanity," to use the modern terminology, was perhaps as controversial a verdict in the seventeenth century as it is today. When asked, therefore, "whether She was guilty, or not guilty, according to the Indictment," Mercy chose neither option. Instead, she responded that "She was guilty of the Fact but not of Malice in it."[63] This plea acknowledged the harm done but asserted that it was done without the requisite criminal intent.

The doctrine of *mens rea*, or guilty mind, was a well-established principle of English common law. As early as the thirteenth century, the author of the "first comprehensive study of English law" maintained that a "crime is not committed unless the intention to injure exists."[64] This principle was clearly articulated in the text of Brown's indictment. The grand jury charged that she had "willfully and Maliciously" struck with an axe the "body of Samuell Brown thine own Sonn, So wounding him the said Samuell Brown, as that thereby he came to his death." By entering, in effect, a plea of "guilty but mentally ill," she admitted committing the deed but denied the intent.[65]

Once the issue had been joined, Brown put herself "on the Country" and requested a jury trial. Had she pled the general issue, the jury would have weighed all matters of fact in the case. By contrast, an insanity plea placed before the jury the single question of *mens rea*. Pursuing what is now called an affirmative defense, she had to show she lacked this necessary element of criminal responsibility when she committed the homicide. Her burden was to demonstrate that the "late horid fact" was, in her husband's words, "noe other than a fruit or effect of her said distraction."[66] This was a heavy burden, especially for a forty-one-year-old woman unrepresented by counsel. Connecticut denied felony defendants the right to counsel in the seventeenth century.[67] Brown may have received legal advice in preparation for trial, perhaps from her brother-in-law Richard Edwards, who by 1691 was developing a second career as an attorney in Hartford. But once on trial for her life, she faced the bar alone. Although the "presence of women in court was not unusual" in colonial New England, any defendant, and especially a woman, would probably have been unprepared to make an effective argument in such a complex case.[68] For Mercy, whose very competency was in question, mounting a successful insanity defense was even more unlikely.

Also complicating the case was the murky state of the law. Massachusetts insanity law was vague, stipulating only that "Children, Idiots, [and] Distracted persons" shall be granted "such allowances and dispensations in any Cause whether Criminall or other as religion and reason require."[69] Connecticut law acknowledged that children must have "sufficient understanding" to be held criminally liable for their actions, but it made no special provision for mentally impaired adults.[70] In both colonies, courts had little experience assessing criminal competency. According to the historian Edgar McManus, Brown's trial was the "first recorded instance of anything like an insanity defense going to a jury."[71] As a result, the Assistants hearing her case had no local body of law to shape their opinion on the central question in any affirmative defense: what degree of insanity is exculpatory. This "is a matter of great difficulty," Hale astutely observed, because of the "variety of degrees of this infirmity, whereof some are sufficient, and some are insufficient to excuse persons in capital offenses." His treatise *History of the Pleas of the Crown* contained the seventeenth century's most thorough discussion of the "defect of idiocy, madness and lunacy, in reference to criminal offenses and punishments." However, the series of cases that culminated in 1843 with the formulation of the "McNaughton rule," which governs modern jurisprudence on the insanity defense, dates from 1724.[72] No well-established "insanity test" was, therefore, available to the jurors who weighed Brown's mental state.

In *Pleas of the Crown*, Hale made two important points regarding the criminal liability of the mentally impaired. The first concerned periodic madness, or lunacy. A "person that is absolutely mad for a day, killing a man in that distemper," he observed, "is equally not guilty, as if he were mad without intermission." Crimes committed during "lucid intervals" were, however, "subject to the same punishment, as if they had no deficiency." For both madmen and lunatics, therefore, the legally salient question was not the duration of the madness but its degree. Regarding degree, Hale secondly distinguished partial from total madness. Those suffering from a "total alienation of the mind or perfect madness," he asserted, "cannot be guilty ordinarily of capital offenses," for "they act not as reasonable creatures, but their actions are in effect in the condition of brutes." He cited the jurist Edward Coke as precedent for this principle, but unlike Coke, who maintained that only "absolute madness, and a totall deprivation of memorie" is exculpatory, he admitted that "partial insanity" may at times negate guilt. Persons not wholly deprived of the use of reason constituted the difficult case. Hale stated that "this partial insanity seems not to excuse them in the committing of any offense for its matter capital," but he acknowledged that "it is very difficult to define the indivisible line that divides perfect and partial insanity." This question had to be put to the jury, who would determine whether the "incapacity of the prisoner" was "to such a degree, as may excuse him from the guilt of a capital offense."[73]

Neither the judges nor the jury trying Brown's case could have read Hale's discussion of the legal status of the criminally insane, for, although it was written before his death in 1676, *Pleas of the Crown* did not appear in print until 1736. This text represents the "clearest statement of the law and its procedures" in seventeenth-century England, but whether colonial courtrooms followed these procedures is uncertain. The most frequently used guide to common-law procedure was *The Countrey Justice*, a legal handbook first published in 1618. It was widely available in the colonies, and the Connecticut Assistants were undoubtedly familiar with this text, written by an English justice of the peace named Michael Dalton.[74] Like Hale, Dalton accepted the distinction between permanent and periodic insanity, asserting that no felony is committed "if a lunatike person killeth another during his lunacie." He did not, however, address the distinction between partial and total insanity, focusing instead on the doctrine of *mens rea*. "[N]o felonie or murder can be committed," he wrote, "without a felonious intent & purpose." The insane, therefore, could not be held criminally liable, "for they have no knowledge of good and evill, nor can have a felonious intent, nor a will or mind to do harme." As a guide to determining the degree of exculpatory insanity, he compared the legal status of the insane to that of children under the age of discretion. Hale also recommended this analogy as the "best measure I can think of" to assist a jury in its deliberations. Hale, however, following Coke, identified fourteen as the age of discretion, while Dalton set the bar much lower, at eight.[75]

The jury in Brown's case deliberated for two days before returning a guilty verdict. "Mercy Brown, the wife of Samuel Browne of Wallingford," they unanimously agreed, "is guilty of wilfull striking her son, Samuel Brown, on the head with an ax, which was the cause of his death."[76] As the phrase "wilfull striking" indicates, they rejected the defendant's affirmative defense, finding instead that she had intended to harm her son and so should be held criminally liable for the murder. Why the defense failed is unknown. Perhaps the jury judged that she suffered from a partial insanity insufficiently severe to exclude criminal intent. Or perhaps they concluded that, although afflicted with a periodic lunacy, she committed the crime in a lucid interval. Seventeenth-century jurists believed the heavens controlled the phases of a lunatic's madness. Lunatics, Hale observed, "are usually in the height of their distemper" at the "full and change of the moon." On the date of the assault, however, the moon had just reached it first quarter, a lucid period. But the position of the sun would perhaps have lent some support to Brown's defense. Lunacy flared, Hale noted, "especially about the Equinoxes and summer solstice," and in 1691 the twenty-third of June—the day of the murder—fell not long after the solstice.[77]

Brown's actions on the morning of the murder may also have informed the jury's judgment of *mens rea*. Before taking an axe to her son's head, she had not raved like a "brute" beast or one that was "totally depriv'd of the use of reason."[78] She had performed her routine morning chores, tending the fire and turning out the cows. Although witnesses testified that she had exhibited some signs of distraction when fetching fire at her neighbor's home, these momentary lapses did not display the "absolute madness" or "total alienation of the mind" that both Hale and Coke would have considered exculpatory.[79] Samuel Brown's claim that his wife had acted to secure their son's "eternal benefit" argued against the will to harm, for a mother who commits an altruistic filicide is motivated by love, not malice. Nevertheless, he had initially testified that his wife had behaved with both premeditation and consciousness of guilt on the morning of the assault, thereby undercutting his subsequent theory of the crime. Given this evidence, the jurors were faced with a difficult choice. Was she mad or was she bad? Without "pregnant evidence to prove [her] insanity at the time of the fact committed," they voted to convict.[80]

A contemporary observer of the trial placed this verdict in a larger political context. Gershom Bulkeley began public life as a Congregational minister but abandoned the pulpit to pursue a career in both medicine and law. He received a license to practice medicine in 1686 and was appointed justice of the peace for Hartford County by Edmund Andros after the English takeover of Connecticut's government in 1687.[81] By 1691, charter government had been restored and Bulkeley had lost his post, but his position as a learned leader of the colony's Tory faction was secure. In *Will and Doom, Or the Miseries of Connecticut by and Under a Usurped and Arbitrary Power*, he prosecuted his indictment of the reconstituted charter government.[82] Connecticut's rulers, Bulkeley asserted, had from the colony's inception illegitimately exercised sovereign power, assuming rights and privileges unwarranted by its charter. Although Governor Andros had briefly established order, the colony's authorities had resumed their former "usurpation upon the king and supreme authority of the nation" by reviving the charter. "If ever there was or can be a Turkish, French, arbitrary and tyrannical government in Connecticut," Bulkeley shrilly exclaimed, "it is so now."[83] The principal expression of this illegitimate exercise of arbitrary power was the colony's judicial system, particularly its prosecution of capital crimes.

Connecticut's charter empowered its legislature "to Erect Judicatories" and "to Make, Ordain, and Establish all Manner of Wholesome, and Reasonable Laws." It stipulated, however, that no laws should be enacted "Contrary to the Laws of this Realm, of *England*." This restriction had not been observed, especially in the making of capital laws. Like other New England colonies, Connecticut had reduced the number of crimes punishable by death, adopting only those justified by scripture precedent; accordingly, several of its capital crimes had no English equivalent.[84] Bulkeley cited this irregularity as a prime example of excessive governmental power. "The King's subjects are indicted, try'd, judged, and condemned to die," he asserted, "not upon the King's law, or upon the law of the land, but upon the corporation laws call'd the Laws of this Colony." As a consequence, "many have been put to death not by the King's law, but (by pretense at least of) the laws of this Colony." To prevent such a miscarriage of justice, he intervened in Mercy Brown's murder case.[85]

Bulkeley's involvement in the case began when the jury, deadlocked in its deliberations, requested the advice of the former magistrate, whose dual practice of medicine and law made him well qualified as a consultant. He counseled the frustrated jurors "not to meddle in" the case, and perhaps to avoid meddling they tried to return a "special verdict" that would have forced the bench to rule on the central matter of fact in the case, the defendant's competency.[86] Unwilling to render such a ruling, the judges instructed the jury to "bring in a general verdict, either guilty or not guilty."[87] Once a guilty verdict had been returned, however, Bulkeley took Brown's case as an opportunity to promote his charge against the Connecticut judicial system. He submitted a petition to the court outlining several procedural violations he claimed had been committed in the conduct of the case. Each of these alleged violations identified a point at which colonial practice was inconsistent with English law.

Bulkeley first questioned the composition of the trial jury. The jury impaneled to hear Brown's case was apparently drawn from Hartford County, where the Court of Assistants met. Bulkeley argued that using Hartford men on the jury violated a long-established principle of English common law, because Wallingford, Brown's place of residency, was located in New

Haven County. The "Jury ought to come out of the vicinage," or neighbor-hood, of the accused, he asserted, and if it "come out of a wrong place, it is a mystriall and signifies nothing."[88] As originally conceived juries were com-posed of twelve "men of the neighborhood," who entered the "court armed with knowledge of the community's view of the case and of the defendant's reputation."[89] That Brown's jury lacked such local knowledge may have par-ticularly damaged her defense, for madness was a condition established by community judgment, not medical diagnosis or expert testimony. Family and neighbors traveled from Wallingford to Hartford to present evidence of her distraction, but this testimony was an inadequate substitute for a jury long acquainted with her past behavior and therefore prepared to judge her mental state.[90] To convince strangers that the crime had been committed in a moment of madness was a heavy burden.

Bulkeley secondly argued that this burden was wrongly placed. An affir-mative defense shifts the burden of proof from the prosecution to the defense, requiring it to show that the defendant had acted without the requi-site criminal intent. Bulkeley noted that the court explained this distribution of the burden to the jury but asserted that these instructions were contrary to English law. Citing the common-law principle that "the law favors life," he argued that if the defendant "is knowne to be a Lunaticke" who experiences "Lucid Intervalls, there had need be very good and satisfactory P[r]ofe that she was Compos mentis at the time of the fact committed." If the prosecu-tion could not meet this burden, she could not be held responsible for her crime. "If she were not compos mentis at the time of the fact, it is no felony, and consequently no willfull or malicious murder," he reasoned, citing a land-mark insanity case dating from 1604.[91] If the court had applied this principle to Brown's case, Bulkeley concluded, she could not have been held respon-sible for her crime.

The centerpiece of Bulkeley's argument was that the court had exploited this felony prosecution to promote its political agenda. He argued that although the magistrates knew that Brown was a "distracted woman *et non compos mentis*," they were "very forward to have her found guilty" to estab-lish the legitimacy of Connecticut's charter government. Since the restora-tion of the charter, a powerful Tory faction had raised repeated challenges to the legality of this action. Bulkeley, a prominent member of this faction, claimed that the ruling party was using the courtroom as a vehicle to buttress its questionable authority. Capital cases, because they concerned life and death, provided the magistrates with a rare opportunity to exhibit the reach of their judicial power. "[I]f they should presume, for any cause, to put any person to death," Bulkeley charged, "this they think would stop every mouth, and none would dare to deny or contradict their authority any more." The royal agent Edward Randolph had made a similar charge against the Massachusetts government the year prior to the trial. They "have held a Court of Assistants, and have condemned a malefactor for breach of one of their capital laws," Randolph reported from his Boston jail cell. "He was lately put to death, to frighten the people into submission."[92] According to Bulkeley, Connecticut's magistrates intended by Brown's conviction and execution to effect a similar display of judicial power. "No wonder," he wryly remarked, "if their fingers itch to be at that kind of work."[93]

After Bulkeley submitted his petition, the court heard several more witnesses, who testified that Brown was "no other than a distracted woman both in hur words and actions" when she killed her son. Taking these testimonies into consideration, the Assistants decided to "deferr the passing Sentence against her for the present" and ordered her to "be Secured in the Gaol untill further Order be given by this Court about her."[94] Despite this small victory, the Brown family collapsed under the weight of their continuing ordeal. A month before his wife's trial, Samuel Brown had sold all his possessions, including his house, home lot, and farmland in Wallingford, presumably to cover court costs; a month after the trial, he died.[95] Unlike John Slauson, who eventually remarried after his wife's murder and began a new family, this distraught husband did not have the strength to go on. His wife remained in the Hartford jail for another eighteen months, despite continuing pressure for her execution. "Some were very hot to be at her again," Bulkeley reported, but no ruling was handed down until May 1693.[96]

Another controversial prosecution that inflamed the colony while Brown was in prison likely influenced the final disposition of her case. In May 1692 a witch-hunt began in southern Connecticut, instigated by a "possessed" young girl who had accused several local women as her spectral tormenters. Mercy Disborough, a Fairfield resident who had once worked as a servant in the Bulkeley household, was convicted of witchcraft. As in Brown's case, Bulkeley raised questions about the composition of the jury that reached this verdict, but in this instance he objected not to the jurors' place of residency but to an illegal jury substitution. This procedural irregularity was cited by a group of the alleged witch's supporters in a petition requesting that the court overturn her conviction. In response, she was granted a stay of execution and a committee of magistrates was formed to investigate the charge.[97] Ruling that the jury substitution had been improper and that the conviction should be overturned, these members of the colony's governing elite articulated a clear commitment to judicial due process. "Due form of law is that alone wherein the validity of verdicts and judgments in such cases stands," they observed, "and if a real and apparent murderer be condemned and executed out of due form of law it is indictable against them that do it." This ruling embraced a core element of Bulkeley's argument. If a defendant is denied due process, a guilty verdict cannot be sustained, particularly when a life is at stake. "Blood is a great thing," the magistrates pronounced, "and we cannot but open our mouths for the dumb in the cause of one appointed to die by such a verdict."[98]

The men who "opened [their] mouths" to invalidate this witchcraft conviction could not have failed to observe the applicability of their judgment to Mercy Brown's murder case. Disborough's committee issued its report in May 1693, at the same session of the Court of Assistants that made a final determination in Brown's case. Both convictions had been challenged by charges of procedural irregularity and both were capital cases in which the life of the defendant was at stake. Furthermore, all three men on the committee had been members of the court that had heard Brown's murder case, and all three were still in office a year and a half later, when she was finally sentenced.[99] In the interim, witch-hunts not only in southern Connecticut but, more important, in Salem, Massachusetts, had generated a heightened concern for judicial due process. When the Court of Assistants met for its spring session, the judges decided to temper justice with mercy. Making no mention of any procedural irregularities, their decision focused only on the issue of *mens rea*. Having reviewed the evidence of incapacity presented at trial, they ruled that Mercy Brown "hath Generally been in a Crazed or distracted Condition as well Long before She Committed the Fact, as at that time." Given this finding of *non compos mentis*, they refused "to pass Sentence of death against her," ordering instead "that She Shall be kept in Custody" in her hometown of New Haven to prevent "her doeing the Like or other Mischief for the future."[100] Having provided for the people's safety, the court closed Brown's case.

Mercy Brown did not take a place beside her brother Benjamin on the Hartford gallows. As with brother David, however, madness stole her independence and forced her to rely upon others for her support. Having no record of dangerousness, he remained within the care of his family, who presumably allowed him to come and go as he pleased. Mercy, by contrast, was a public ward, whose movements were restrained to protect the community from further harm. No institutions existed for the confinement of criminal lunatics in colonial Connecticut. Where she was kept is uncertain, as is the duration of her incarceration. Although the custody order appears to allow for her release if her illness abated, no record exists that she was ever freed. Upon returning to New Haven where family and friends could contribute to her care, she may have shown some improvement, but in 1695 she was still apparently held in custody by the town magistrates.[101] Just forty-one years old when the crime was committed, she probably lived for many years imprisoned by both madness and iron shackles.

The Tuttle family had been afflicted by a severe trial. This hardy group of puritan pioneers who had left their Northamptonshire home to begin a new life in a new world was struck in its second generation by a chain of tragic losses. Benjamin Tuttle's murder of his sister Sarah stretched to its limits the explanatory framework within which the family ordinarily interpreted extraordinary events. It also stirred predestinarian fears. They inhabited a theological universe in which all sinners deserved damnation. God in his infinite mercy elected a few for heavenly bliss, while abandoning the vast majority of humankind to eternal torment. Struggling to comprehend these impenetrable mysteries, the Tuttles likely met each successive tragedy with increased religious devotion and self-scrutiny. But with one family member murdered and another hanged, these colonial Jobs also probably implored God to reveal the cause of their afflictions and were baffled by the apparent injustice of their continuing trials.

Burdened with these awful mysteries, David and his sister Mercy descended into madness. That Mercy's religious melancholy focused on the welfare of her children was not surprising, given that a woman's sphere in colonial New England comprised only the roles of wife and mother. The sudden cessation of childbirth was an early sign that something was amiss. Why bring new life into the world, she may have thought, when it was doomed for destruction? Then in a tragic repetition of her brother's primal crime, she murdered her eldest son, hoping to rescue him from a terrible fate. The destructive force that was unleashed when Benjamin first swung the axe was, however, not yet spent. Throughout this protracted period of family crisis, Elizabeth Tuttle was living with her husband, Richard Edwards, and their children in Hartford. This struggling household, fragile from its rocky beginning, was Benjamin Tuttle's final victim.

A MESSY DIVORCE

In October 1691, the Connecticut General Assembly agreed to free Richard Edwards "from his conjugall tye to his wife Elizabeth." Unlike the majority of divorces granted in the Connecticut colony in the seventeenth century, this decision had been difficult to reach. Twice denied by the Court of Assistants, Edwards's plea eventually received a more sympathetic hearing in the Assembly, which also rejected it twice before ultimately ruling in his favor. To mute any criticism, the legislators noted that they had "considered the case with seriousnesse and taken the best advice they could com at by the word of God and learned and worthy divines."[1] Only when cloaked in religious authority did they feel free to overrule the Assistants, who had primary jurisdiction in such cases. This bill of divorce, therefore, represented the culmination of a protracted legal campaign that Edwards had waged over two years and in two separate jurisdictions. As we have seen, however, our story of family failure had a much earlier beginning.

The puritans who settled New England enacted in the Massachusetts and Connecticut colonies the most permissive divorce laws in the Anglo-American empire.[2] In seventeenth-century England, because regulation of marriage was part of canon law, its termination fell under the jurisdiction of ecclesiastical courts. No divorces permitting either party to remarry (divorce *a vinculo matrimonii*) were granted—only annulments if there was proof of a pre-existing impediment, such as incest, impotence, or bigamy, and legal separations (divorce *a mensa et thoro*) on grounds of either adultery or extreme cruelty. In the 1690s, Parliament began passing private acts of divorce with the right to remarry for wealthy members of the aristocracy whose wives had committed adultery. Such legislative divorces were rare and costly, however, intended primarily to protect the orderly transmission of property to legitimate heirs. Although reformers, following the lead of continental Protestants, had been agitating for liberalization of English divorce law since the reign of Henry VIII, no significant change occurred until the passage of the Divorce and Matrimonial Causes Act in 1857.[3]

New England puritans implemented the radical revision of matrimonial law that had long eluded English reformers. Rejecting the sacramental view of marriage upheld by both Catholics and Anglicans, they redefined the marital relation as a civil contract between husband and wife whose terms were regulated by secular courts. Bed and board separations, the only alternative for most English couples in troubled marriages, were condemned as a "popish invention, with no basis in the Gospels."[4] Therefore, when a violation of the marital covenant occurred, the innocent party could escape the "chains of matrimony" by suing for a full divorce with right to remarry. Divorce *a vinculo matrimonii* was, in this view, integral to the maintenance of an orderly family structure, the best legal remedy for men whose wives had strayed and women whose husbands had disappeared or deserted them. Dissolving such dysfunctional unions allowed for the formation of new, stable marriages and reduced the incidence of bigamy caused by informal self-divorce, which was common in England.[5]

Although a dramatic departure from English practice, divorce in colonial New England had limits. Not every source of domestic discord was sufficient grounds for divorce by either law or custom. Massachusetts Bay's first statute, passed in 1660, did not specify permissible grounds, but in practice petitions were most commonly granted for desertion and adultery.[6] Connecticut subsequently adopted a statute that empowered the Court of Assistants to award bills of divorce for only four causes. "[N]oe bill of divorce," the General Assembly ordered, "shall be granted to any man or woman lawfully marryed but in case of adultery, fraudulent contract, or willfull desertion for three years with totall neglect of duty, or seven years' providentiall absence being not heard of after due enquiry made and certifyed."[7] Although these grounds differed little from those employed in other New England colonies, Connecticut was more generous than its neighbors. By 1800 its courts had terminated almost 1,000 marriages, making its "divorce policy the most liberal in New England, and, indeed, in the English-speaking world." Most of these cases, because they clearly met the terms of the statute, were routine and easily dispatched by the magistrates. But on rare occasions an unhappily married man or woman tested the limits of the law by requesting a divorce in uncommon or controversial situations.[8] Richard Edwards was one such petitioner.

When Richard Edwards first petitioned for divorce, he and his wife, Elizabeth, were a middle-aged couple who had been married for more than twenty-two years. They were raising five children: The eldest was a boy of twenty-one, while the four younger girls ranged from nineteen to four years of age.[9] According to Edwards, however, this household had been troubled by serious conflict for some time. He noted that after their marriage he and Elizabeth had lived together "in som measure of Comfort" for "About Eight or Nine years," at which time the disorder began.[10] The few available clues to the nature of their domestic partnership confirm Edwards's claim, suggesting that their marriage functioned adequately for about a decade—despite its rocky start.

When we last encountered our protagonists, Richard had made a seemingly advantageous match with the daughter of a prominent New Haven householder who was apparently already pregnant with his child. Only months after the wedding, however, the young couple became entangled in the first crisis of their marriage. Elizabeth gave birth to an early baby, a not uncommon or particularly scandalous event in colonial New England. Her humiliated husband's accusation that another man had fathered the child transformed this common sin into an irreparable betrayal. The legal system provided no relief for these poisonous emotions or means to resolve this family conflict.[11] The court judgment that Edwards was the "reputed" father of the child resolved nothing, for he persisted in denying his paternity. Likewise, no satisfaction came from his father's lawsuit against the suspected other lover, which was dismissed for lack of evidence. By repudiating the child and forcing his wife to surrender her care to her family in New Haven, Edwards established his patriarchal authority as head of his new household, but this "bastard" daughter provided a constant reminder of his wounded manhood. The festering of this unhealed wound likely crippled their marriage from the outset.

Finding no solution to this crisis, the unhappy couple had little choice but to get on with their lives. Working together to run a household was one way to escape the messy beginning of their domestic partnership. Seventeenth-century puritans understood marriage to be a covenant of reciprocal obligation. As the English moralist William Whately observed, "[M]an and wife are bound to each other, in a mutuall bond of dutie." A successful marriage was not dependent upon the "momentary" and "fickle" affection of romantic love.[12] Puritans elevated the companionate end of marriage over its traditional procreative end, but the love that created this companionate union was itself the expression of duty. Enjoined by scripture commands, it was considered "a common mutuall dutie belonging to husband and wife." Spouses cultivated this love by fulfilling the responsibilities defined by their places in the domestic hierarchy. A well-governed household, wherein "all duties will readily and cheerefully be performed," was, therefore, a loving household.[13] For struggling couples like Richard and Elizabeth Edwards, this mutual duty was perhaps a welcome refuge. It provided a way forward, a means of regaining the love that had been lost in the first months of their marriage. Of course, we cannot peer inside their small dwelling on Hartford's north side to glimpse the interiority of their daily lives or gauge the quality of their affection.[14] Judging by the orderliness of their household, however, their marriage was not in its early years absent love.

As family head, Richard Edwards had the duty to govern his dependents and provide for their spiritual and material needs.[15] "Ordinary Anglo-Americans in early New England measured manhood by a man's ability to produce and provide for a wife and children."[16] Trained to make barrels by his father, Richard depended not only on his cooper's craft but also on his business skills to achieve the economic competency desired by all colonial men. Having married young and having been raised in a disorderly household in which his father's financial mismanagement regularly undermined the family economy, Edwards likely struggled in his duty to provide. No evidence suggests, however, that he perpetuated his family's intergenerational record of financial failure. Less than a year after the wedding he signaled his entrance into the community of adult men by making his first appearance in Hartford County Court to prosecute an action for breach of contract.[17] Adult male householders occupied the public sphere of the marketplace, in which each man's credit was dependent on his reputation as an honest and trustworthy trader. Although all craftsmen were at times forced to enter an action to preserve their credit with other traders, Edwards only rarely resorted to formal litigation to collect a debt, and on these occasions he apparently came to court with a solid case, for he commonly won the suit. This record of judicious litigation suggests that, unlike his father, skillful financial management ensured that he met his duty to provide.

Economic competency was not, however, an individual achievement. Without a dutiful wife, a man could not establish a public identity as an able provider for his family. She was his "helper" and "deputy" in governing the family, who supplied "the female labor needed for successful housekeeping."[18] As Richard Edwards's "helpmeet," Elizabeth Tuttle was responsible for the traditional "housewife's domain," centered primarily in the interior spaces of the home, especially the kitchen, but also encompassing such essential components of the household economy as the kitchen garden, henhouse, and cow barn, located outside on the family house lot.[19] This craftsman's wife also likely helped from time to time with the family business. Because her husband's shop occupied one of the outbuildings on their property, no clear boundary separated his male workplace from her female living space.[20] A common presence in the shop while her husband was coopering, she probably acted as his "deputy" in his absence, selling a cask on occasion or dealing with creditors.[21] Without her labor inside the home and her assistance without, the family economy would have faltered.

Women's financial activity, conducted in a largely informal and private manner, left few traces in public records. Elizabeth's participation in her household economy became visible on only one occasion, when she and Richard violated the colony's laws prohibiting unlicensed alcohol sale. Puritans recognized that beer, cider, and distilled alcohol, particularly rum, were staples of every colonist's daily diet, regularly consumed at meals and virtually all social occasions.[22] That the Edwardses produced their own homebrew was, therefore, not unusual, especially given Richard's calling as a cooper, a trade with historic ties to the brewing industry. But when in 1671 they sold a small quantity of alcohol to some local Indians, who were then "fownd In drink," they violated longstanding Connecticut statutes.[23] Richard's £10 fine was cut in half when he confessed his sin and pledged to reform; Elizabeth was likewise fined £5.[24] Three years later, Edwards confessed to a second, more serious, alcohol offense, but in this instance his wife was not involved.[25] These misdemeanor convictions are the only suggestions of disorder in the Edwardses' household in the early years of their marriage.

But economic competency alone did not make Edwards a man. In Anglo-American society the "traditional marker of manhood" was not marriage so much as fatherhood.[26] A complete household typically comprised three classes of dependents—wife, children, and servants—ordered hierarchically with the husband at the head. Without children, then, a man's household was incomplete and his authority was insecurely established. These dependents were the objects of his care and the consumers of the goods he produced; they were also the subjects of his judicious government. He guided all the weak and subordinate members of his household with a firm hand, ensuring that each received proper nurture and that each performed his or her particular duties. In return, they provided a valuable asset. Child labor was integral to the family economy, with boys assisting their father in his calling and girls helping their mother with the housework. Like an obedient wife, a brood of productive and pious children, whose parents had "nurture[d]" them "with good discipline" and "instruct[ed]" them "in the ways of God," promoted patriarchal success.[27]

During the first decade of their marriage, Elizabeth gave Richard Edwards the children he needed to establish his manhood. Less than a year after their wedding and probably only a few months after the contested daughter was born, she was again pregnant. In May 1669 she gave birth to a son named Timothy, and over the next nine years she safely delivered three more children, daughters named Abigail, Elizabeth, and Anne.[28] Any newly established householder would have celebrated this succession of successful births, but for Edwards, who believed his wife had cuckolded him even before their marriage, it likely had heightened significance. Perhaps the most fundamental expression of a man's authority was his control over the marriage bed. The "ideal husband" was "physically potent and virile, capable of meeting his wife's needs and of impregnating her."[29] Regular childbirth was, therefore, a sign of a properly ordered household, an expression of manly dominance and control. By quickly impregnating his wife, Edwards established his place of authority in his household and displayed his ability to govern his wife and keep her in her place. Although the alleged discovery of another lover had at the outset of the marriage placed his authority in question, the appearance of a son and heir restored his wounded manhood and completed the small domestic society that was subject to his government. This child demonstrated to the larger community his status as mature household head, capable of ruling his "little commonwealth" and therefore qualified for public office.[30]

On becoming husband, father, and household head, Edwards acquired new political status. Independent male householders ran the local town meetings and elected the colony's officers. Edwards was admitted into this political community with little delay. Less than two years after his marriage, when only twenty-two, he became a Hartford freeman, a position his father had not achieved until he was almost twice that age. Conferring full political rights, freemanship qualified Edwards to vote in colonywide elections, hold elective office, and serve in other civic capacities.[31] Over the next decade, he was appointed to small town offices, such as chimney viewer and surveyor, and served on county court juries with some regularity.[32] These positions of authority reflected public acknowledgment of his capacity to govern, an ability first developed in the family before it was exercised in the larger community. His father, an inept financial manager, was awarded such responsibilities only late in life. That his son began early to acquire the status markers that defined manhood in colonial New England suggests that he had, at least for a time, escaped his family's history of patriarchal failure.

Despite their tumultuous start, therefore, the Edwardses appeared to have made a success of their marriage in its early years. On this foundation, Richard began moving up in the world. He established an identity as an orderly householder, equitable in his trading and worthy of public trust, and he was rewarded with positions of responsibility in his community. Further social advancement, however, required the ongoing cooperation of his wife. In colonial New England, manhood was a relational virtue, obtained through the assistance of a loving spouse and easily threatened by her rebellion. For about a decade Elizabeth appears to have willingly subordinated both her body and her labor to the joint interest of her family. But such harmonious cohabitation did not last. When the next crisis struck this fragile family, their domestic partnership began once again to break down.

Our principal sources for reconstructing the internal factors that led to the disintegration of this marriage are, in addition to the supplementary papers preserved in the court records, Edwards's two divorce petitions. The deficiency of these sources frustrates any approach to the truth. On the most basic level, these texts are incomplete. Documents recording important evidence may have been lost; some of the extant manuscripts are damaged and only partially legible, and oral testimony of witnesses in court was unrecorded.[33] Most problematic is the absence of Elizabeth Tuttle's voice. In this, as in all troubled marriages, there must have been two stories—the husband's and the wife's.[34] As their union broke down, Edwards was surely not alone in constructing a narrative tracing the etiology of this failure. Elizabeth's version of the story, however, was either not recorded or not preserved, and in its absence her husband's angry accusations have loudly filled the void. Unchallenged by a competing explanation, he has controlled the tale.

Of course, this controlling narrative is itself incomplete. Although Edwards entitled his first petition "A *True* Abreviate of the Case of Richard Edwards Respecting Elizabeth his Late wife," it records only *his* truth, which is at best only a partial truth.[35] As the historian Joanne Bailey notes, "reality" in legal records "is difficult to pin down, for the 'truths' they contain are diverse, contradictory and dependent on the teller."[36] Unlike many court documents, Edwards's petitions were not mediated by an attorney paid to cast a litigant's story into proper legal prose. An educated man who by the

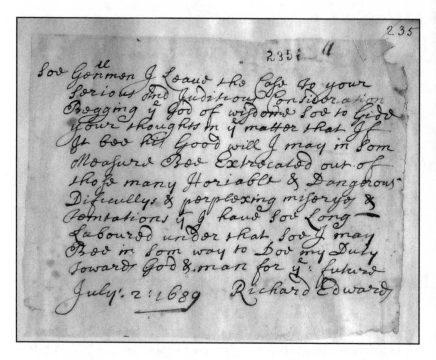

Concluding paragraph of "A True Abreviate of the Case of Richard Edwards Respecting Elizabeth his Late wife." Connecticut Archives, Crimes and Misdemeanors, 1st Ser., 235i. Courtesy of the Connecticut State Library. Photo by Bill Keegan.

date of the divorce had begun fashioning for himself a second career as an attorney, Edwards composed his own petitions.[37] His voice is, therefore, heard clearly in these texts, and, like all litigants, he speaks to persuade. He constructs his narrative to achieve a desired end, the termination of his marriage. This end, in turn, shaped the evidence presented to secure it. His self-serving story of family failure did not need to contain outright lies, but it omitted and obscured contradictory evidence that would have hindered the prosecution of his case. These texts, therefore, must be read with suspicion, but we cannot wholly escape them. Because they provide our only window into the lived experience of this marriage, we must peer through it, ever mindful that the image it discloses of our unhappy couple is a fragmentary reflection of the husband's frustrations and desires.

One omission is the larger, external context that likely precipitated this family failure. Edwards's only explanation for why, after eight or nine years, his marriage began to falter is the willful rebellion of his wife. She, in his telling, is the sole and sufficient cause of all the trouble. He neglected to mention, however, that his chronology dated the beginning of the breakdown to the murder. Benjamin Tuttle struck down his sister Sarah with an axe on 17 November 1676, two days before his sister Elizabeth's ninth wedding anniversary. This sudden act of violence had many victims. It left the large and flourishing Tuttle clan in disarray, stunned by a terrible act of God's providential judgment. Brother David's fragile mental state rapidly declined, leaving him disabled and dependent on his elder siblings' care. Sister Mercy's mind also apparently became increasingly unbalanced. What effect this crisis had on Elizabeth and her husband, Richard, can never fully be known. But its likely last casualty was their marriage.

Living in Hartford, the Edwards family was separated geographically from the crime's central locus of disorder in New Haven, where the majority of the Tuttles resided. They were, however, uniquely positioned to experience their own kind of hell. Upon his arrest, Benjamin was transported by the authorities to the colony's capital and imprisoned in the town jail to await trial. This confinement stretched out over seven long months before climaxing in his conviction and execution. This was surely a difficult time for the Edwardses, especially Elizabeth, who likely held a particular affection for both the murderer and his victim. In a large family like the Tuttles', siblings separated by many years may be joined by weaker emotional bonds. But only three years separated Elizabeth both from her younger brother Benjamin and from her sister Sarah, her next-older sibling. These three children, along with brother Simon, who was born between Elizabeth and Benjamin, surely spent much time together when young, playing games, learning lessons, and watching out for one another's welfare. When Benjamin killed Sarah, the attachments formed in these early years were violently broken. Elizabeth, perhaps more than her other siblings, was left to deal with the mess.

Like many towns in colonial New England, Hartford built its jailhouse on the town green to reinforce the assertion that compliance with the law was central to the social order. The first "house of Correction" was erected in 1640 in the northeast corner of the green, across from the meetinghouse, where it remained throughout the seventeenth century.[38] While all Hartford residents had easy access to the jail, the Edwardses had a particular familiarity with its precincts. As a boy, Richard grew up in homes neighboring the jail. His father's home lot abutted the eastern boundary of the prisonhouse yard.[39] Living next door, William Edwards on occasion did odd jobs around the jail. In the winter of 1680, for example, he was paid ten shillings to remove and bury the body of a convicted murderer who had died in the jail's dungeon, first "[c]utting off his legs to save his Irons."[40] Richard's grandmother likewise lived nearby, on a small lot just south of the prison, which she had purchased after her husband's death.[41] Given the nearness of the family relations and their proximity to the place of his confinement, providing for Benjamin's care during his imprisonment naturally would have fallen to his sister and her kin.

In colonial New England, prisoners were liable for the costs of their incarceration.[42] Richard Edwards later acknowledged that his family had shouldered much of their relation's financial burden. "Brother-in-Law Benjiamin Deseased Lying long In prison Last winter," he complained, "we were forsed to Be at sum Considerable Disbursements And Truble towards his Comfortable Subsistanse."[43] Much of the comfort was probably provided by Elizabeth. When walking to the jail and climbing down into its dungeon to visit her brother, pray with him, and bring him a blanket or a simple meal, she must have experienced a confusion of emotions. Rage likely competed with grief over the sudden loss of her sister. The impending death of a second sibling surely stirred further sadness, conflicted with a desire for vengeance. During this difficult ordeal, however, her love for her brother apparently remained strong. Of all the members of his extended family, Benjamin rewarded only his sister Elizabeth for her "great love and pains" during the "long teyme of my affliction."[44]

As was expected of all puritans looking death in the face, Benjamin Tuttle in the fifth month of his imprisonment put his financial affairs in order. Having no direct heirs, he gave "all my estate both parsonall and reall" to "my welbeloved sister Elizabeth Edwards." In part, this gift was compensation for his care, and when the estate was probated Richard Edwards received payment for a debt of about £6.5. But when all outstanding obligations had been discharged, a small legacy remained, which Benjamin bequeathed to his sister. He gave his estate to her, he wrote, as a testament to "our near [r]elation," and in "remembrance of that love that was allwaies between us."[45] Elizabeth was, however, apparently unwilling to profit from her brother's crime. Although her husband pressed the court to disburse this almost £15 estate, at probate he agreed to give the legacy to his aged mother-in-law, who, widowed and suffering from financial loss, was mourning the deaths of two of her children.[46]

No causal connection can be clearly established between the trauma of the murder and the breakdown of the Edwardses' marriage. The timing is, however, suggestive. It corresponds not only to Edwards's own telling of the story

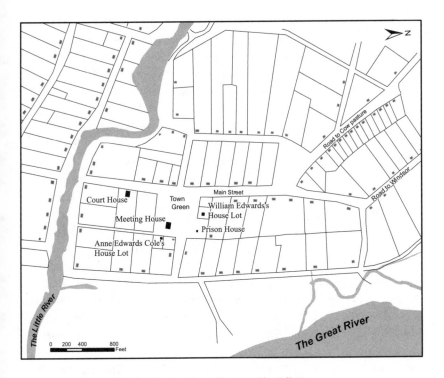

Hartford in the 1670s. Illustrated by Bill Keegan.

but also to the downward spirals two other Tuttles experienced in the years after the murder. Unlike her siblings, Elizabeth was daily by her brother's side as he awaited execution. Having shared his anxious preparations for death, she may have had particular difficulty getting past this crisis. Richard himself probably provided little comfort. He likely harbored little fraternal feeling for this brutal killer, only shame at his association with such a heinous crime. To have a murderer in the family was a setback for a man whose fortunes had just begun to rise, and for the second time since his marriage he may have regretted the hasty alliance he had contracted as a young man. Elizabeth also likely felt shame, but her love for her brother would have complicated this emotion with a volatile mixture of grief over his death, rage at his crime, and fear for his eternal fate. This external stressor would have strained even the strongest relation, but for the Edwardses' fragile domestic partnership it was a staggering blow.

Again, birthrate may provide an index of disorder. Prior to the murder Elizabeth had given birth at a steady pace, delivering, after the couple's contested first child, three more children in seven years. She had another daughter the year following the execution, but for the seven years between 1678 and 1685, when a fourth and final daughter was born, there was apparently no issue.[47] Elizabeth's younger sister Mercy followed a parallel pattern of births. As noted in the previous chapter, she produced children at regular intervals until 1679, when a six-year hiatus began, ending also in 1685 with the birth of a son. Of course, such apparently fallow times, which occurred when both women were young and fertile, could have a number of explanations, including illness, miscarriage, stillbirth, and incomplete vital records. Why Mercy apparently ceased for a time to bear children is unknown; Elizabeth's hiatus, however, was either the cause—or the effect—of the breakdown of her marriage.

Edwards's primary allegation against his wife was sexual incontinency. That conflict about sex was the principal symptom of this family's failure is not surprising, given that the marriage began in a sexual crisis. Unlike most men petitioning for divorce on these grounds, however, Edwards did not build his case on an adultery charge. If he could have substantiated such a charge, his petition would have been uncontroversial, for adultery was one of the four statutory grounds for divorce established by Connecticut law. Edwards's principal complaint was that his wife had violated their marriage covenant not by an act of infidelity but by a refusal of sexual services. "I Aledge," he wrote in his first petition, that she "Broake the Mariage Covinant in Her obstinately Refusing Conjugal Comunion with mee Her Husband." She "desert[ed] my bed," he complained, "not only In Som fitt but in a Generall way for Many years." Sexual and marital disorder were matters of public concern in colonial New England, regularly policed by the informal public of neighbors, relatives, and friends.[48] When word of the Edwardses' domestic difficulties spread, their neighbors tried to intervene. Through "the persuasions of som neighbours," Edwards reported, his wife "(for a short time) behaved herself with som more moderation." This interval of restored order likely occurred around 1685, for in this year Elizabeth again delivered a child, but according to Edwards, she quickly fell back "into Her old fitts of obstinacy and perverseness." By his estimation, then, Edwards had endured a protracted period of marital abstinence, lasting "about seven or Eight years together."[49]

"The truth is," notes the historian Richard Godbeer, "Puritans celebrated sexual passion"; they "sought not to repress their sexual instincts but to keep them within ordained borders."[50] Sex outside of marriage was condemned as a violation of both divine law and colonial statute, but within marriage sex was extolled not simply as a means of procreation but, more important, as an expression of what the English theologian William Perkins called that "solitarie and secret societie, that is betweene man and wife alone."[51] Husbands and wives should, counseled another divine, "mutually delight each in other" and yield "that *due benevolence* one to another which is warranted & sanctified by God's word." The scriptural term "due benevolence" captured for puritan moralists the complexity of the conjugal relation. Marital sex "is said to be *due*," William Gouge explained, "because it is a debt which the wife oweth to her husband, and he to her," and "it is called *benevolence* because it must be performed with good will and delight, willingly, readily, and cheerefully."[52] As an obligation, sex was a key term of the contract agreed upon by husband and wife at marriage, but the debt was to be paid with love. Through sexual communion, married persons "cherished" and "solaced" each other "in a mutuall declaration of the signes and tokens of love and kindness."[53]

Although spouses were bound by a duty of mutual "delight," this shared bond did not establish equality of persons. The marriage bed was a microcosm of the hierarchical yet companionate union that ideally joined husband and wife.[54] A well-ordered household was built upon the wife's willing submission to the superior authority of her husband. This inequality "authorized a man to think of his wife as property, as a package of rights he could lay claim to."[55] Part of this package was sex. Marriage conferred upon the husband a property right in his wife's body, to own and control at will. He "possess[ed] his wife's body through regular sex and her mind through authoritative control of her behavior."[56] A common early modern metaphor clearly expresses this unequal relationship. "He is her head," wrote Gouge, and "[s]he is his bodie." This figure of the "body domestic" represented both the "neere equality" of husband and wife and her complete subjection to him. A wife was subordinate to her husband "because she is set under him, as his bodie under his head."[57] She was his body in the household, subject to his superior wisdom and authority, and she was his body in the marriage bed. By giving her body to him she surrendered her will to his in all matters of family government.

Given the centrality of sexual submission to domestic order, the charge Edwards made against his wife represented a serious breach of contract. The charge also likely expressed the central cause of this family's failure. Because Connecticut law made no provision for divorce on grounds of sexual refusal, a suit alleging this violation would be by definition weak. It was also unprecedented. In its forty-six-year history, the Connecticut Court of Assistants heard no other divorce case based on similar allegations.[58] Edwards was clearly aware of the weakness of his suit, and to bolster his argument he appended to his petition an unconventional exegesis of several scripture passages used by reformers to justify legalizing divorce. Contrary to common interpretation, for example, he argued, when Jesus says, in Mt. 19:9, that fornication is the only lawful cause for divorce, he intended "fornication" to include "Any Escencyall Breech of the marage Bond." He also cited the case of Galeacius, the "Great Itallian Convert," who obtained a bill of divorce from a council of Protestant ministers when his Catholic wife, who had refused to move with him to Calvin's Geneva, also "Refused his bed Sosiety."[59]

The veracity of Edwards's primary charge is, therefore, supported by what New Testament scholars call the "criterion of discontinuity," which judges original or unprecedented sayings of Jesus more likely to be historical. It also fits the "criterion of embarrassment."[60] Just as Edwards would have pled his case on more standard legal grounds if such had been available, he also would probably have chosen a less humiliating cause of action. Edwards believed he had begun marriage cuckolded by his wife. To lose control of her sexuality after a decade of apparently successful government would have reopened this early wound, allowing the festering shame again to surface. This fresh humiliation also began at a particularly vulnerable time, when Edwards was on the cusp of full manhood, the "pinnacle" of a man's life cycle.[61] For early modern men, manliness was not a quality of youth but an achievement of middle age. When the crisis erupted, Edwards was in his early thirties, just entering the age when his mastery of the art of family government should have been firmly established. Sexual potency was, likewise, believed to peak in middle age. For him to lose sexual control of his wife when entering this crucial time diminished his manhood and placed in question his authority as household head. Even more humiliating, such an inability to govern would inevitably have been linked to his insufficiency in bed.[62]

Edwards was on a trajectory to full manhood when his marriage began to break down. His father's headship had been undermined by a lack of financial mastery. While Richard had apparently learned to control his money, he had failed in his duty to control his wife. As household head, he was responsible for Elizabeth's body. Her breach of contract was ultimately his patriarchal failure. Woman "was ordained as a *Helper*, and not a hinderer," observed the English puritan Robert Cleaver. "And if they bee otherwise, it is for the most parte, through the fault, and want of discretion, and lacke of good government in the husband."[63] The law, however, required Edwards to prove fault to obtain a bill of divorce. The colonial divorce mechanism was an adversarial process, demanding a clear showing of one party's violation of the marriage covenant. To succeed, therefore, he not only had to show that his plea fit the statutory grounds for divorce established by Connecticut law, but he also had to deflect blame from himself. To achieve these ends, he constructed a story of the breakdown of his marriage in which good and evil, praise and blame, were neatly apportioned between the two parties.

Divorce is a contest of competing narratives. When a private family dispute becomes a pubic legal contest, each party has the opportunity to construct what the historian Laura Gowing has called a "litigation narrative." In their narratives husbands and wives retell the stories of their unhappy marriages, employing the stock characters of victim and villain to demonstrate praise and blame. While not pure fabrications, these accounts are fashioned to prove innocence and guilt. Heated words are selected and recorded, contested events remembered and retold, as each party tries to construct a story having sufficient narrative coherence to sway the court.[64] The two themes that dominated divorce petitions in colonial New England were abandonment and betrayal. Edwards appropriated these themes to retell the messy story of his marriage as a familiar tale of family failure.

The theme of betrayal framed his first petition. In this text, Edwards constructed from the detritus of his marriage a narrative depicting himself as the innocent victim of his wife's sexual rebellion. Litigation required this process of self-fashioning to be oppositional. His innocence had to be established in contrast to her guilt. To show her guilt, he presented to the court a figure of Elizabeth Tuttle that fit the common stereotype of the rebellious woman. In seventeenth-century Anglo-American culture, female deviance was primarily a quality of will. Unlike the goodwife, who was submissive to her husband and obedient to his command, a "badwife" was assertive, disobedient, and difficult for her husband to control. The most significant measure of a woman's willfulness was her sexuality. The chaste wife surrendered her sexuality to her husband's desires; the unchaste wife flaunted her rebellion by giving her body to other men. In his divorce narrative, Richard Edwards casts Elizabeth as the threatening figure of the unchaste woman. To construct this image required some creative storytelling. Sexual refusal had to be redescribed as uncontrolled sex. Absence of sexual desire had to be changed into voracious sexual appetite. To effect this transformation, Edwards reached back to the beginning of the marriage to retrieve his memory of the contested event that had damaged the unhappy couple's union at its outset.

In his version of the early-baby story, Edwards portrayed Elizabeth as a deceptive and untrustworthy woman who was unable to control her sexuality from the start. "About three months after I had maried Her," he recalled, "I found Her to Bee with C[hild by] An Other Man." In this statement Richard portrayed the pregnancy as a double betrayal. Surprised by his wife's condition, he was even more shocked by the infant's paternity. The uncertainty that permeates the records documenting the birth of this contested baby is absent from Edwards's account. He voiced no doubt that Elizabeth was pregnant with another man's child when they married. As evidence he cited his wife's alleged testimony when first charged with fornication. "Before two of the Honorable Magistrates," he asserted, she under oath "Accused by name" another man "to Bee the father of said Child she was then Bigg with." To support this assertion he named the two magistrates who had supposedly witnessed this confession, but because both men were dead neither was able to testify in support of Edwards's story. A consideration of the legal approach to analogous fornication cases, moreover, suggests that only portions of his account were likely accurate.[65]

Women suspected of fornication were first questioned privately by local authorities before appearing publicly in court.[66] Although no official record of her testimony has survived, Elizabeth may have confessed at this first examination to having had another lover, especially if she was questioned under oath. Judicial oaths were common in Hartford courtrooms, but New Haven magistrates did not adopt the practice until the union with Connecticut. During New Haven's colony period, defendants and witnesses were expected to testify truthfully without swearing to do so.[67] Raised with this strict rule, Elizabeth probably needed no reminder of the biblical injunction on oaths when directly questioned by the Hartford magistrates about her early baby. If she had hidden the other lover from her new husband, she may have felt compelled in this setting to break her silence, whether or not she testified under oath. And if the magistrates demanded a name, she may also have divulged under questioning the identity of this rival.

Contrary to Richard Edwards's assertion, however, nothing in the Hartford court records indicates that Elizabeth Tuttle believed that this man was the father of her child. If under questioning she had made a "constant" accusation, to use the language of the bastardy statute, against someone other than her husband, the court would have handled her case differently. A year before the court heard the Edwardses' fornication case, another paternity suit involving a recently married couple had appeared on its docket. Soon after she married William Buckland, Elizabeth Williams accused another man, John O'Neal, "of bringing [her] with child." Although English common law assumed that a child born to a married woman was her husband's issue, this presumption of paternity was apparently not absolute.[68] Investigating Elizabeth Williams's accusation, the magistrates found "that the said Oneal hath by his expressions rendred himself deeply suspitious that he is guilty of the fact," and ordered him to pay £8 maintenance to her father, who presumably had agreed to take custody of the child.[69] The disposition of this analogous case suggests that had Elizabeth Tuttle accused another man, the court would have considered her claim, and had her accusation been credible, he would have had to pay. According to court records, however, the only question considered at the Edwardses' fornication trial was that of Richard's paternity. The judges' ruling that he was the child's reputed father should have settled this question, but Edwards persisted in his denial. Some two decades later, he recalled this story to establish his wife's identity as a woman by nature prone to sexual sin.

The story of the early baby also establishes Richard Edwards's identity as an innocent victim who had patiently suffered his rebellious wife's train of abuse for years. He claimed the contested pregnancy provided grounds to terminate the marriage, but his "Compassionate and pitiful Disposition" prevented him from taking legal action and allowed him to be "Drawn in by her many faire promises of her future Good Demenior." More likely he hesitated because in the seventeenth century Connecticut did not grant annulments or divorces to men whose wives had given birth to another man's child after marriage.[70] Moreover, as he admitted, "It was then suspected by som that I was guilty of beeing the father of that first Child." This suspicion was, however, just another injustice, for, he complained, "I was Altogether Inocent in that matter."[71] To buttress this claim of innocence, he omitted mention of either his conviction for fornication before marriage or the legal judgment naming him as the responsible party. These inconvenient facts clouded with moral ambiguity a story designed to neatly distribute praise and blame.

Edwards also insisted that he sustained this posture of the long-suffering husband throughout his marriage. To emphasize his forbearance, he refused even "to Speak" of the "Intricate, Hart-breaking miseryes, the most pinching pressures of spiritt, that Have been my meat Day and Night." Following the common storyline developed in colonial divorce petitions, he adopted the role of the rational household head who responds with manly self-control to his wife's "Intolerable and unsupportable Afflictions."[72] We hear only distant echoes of the heated words and vicious recriminations that must have disrupted their home with some regularity. Edwards included accounts of only a few verbal jousts to buttress his claim that marriage had chained him to a sharp-tongued scold. Benjamin Tuttle had killed his sister to teach her not "to scold." Although Edwards refrained from using this term of abuse, his anger likewise took as its object this common early modern stereotype of the rebellious woman.

Edwards depicted Elizabeth Tuttle as a disorderly woman who used her tongue to belittle her husband and undermine his manhood. He complained that "shee Hath more than once said to my face" that another man "was worth A thousand of my selfe." Authors of domestic conduct manuals regularly counseled married couples not "to twit one another in the teeth with the husbands and wives of other persons."[73] Given his fragile manhood, Elizabeth's "twits" must have hit Richard especially hard. But Edwards could also turn his wife's loose tongue to his advantage, for the scold's taunting words were symptomatic of a more profound failure of self-control. A woman with a sharp tongue was likely also an unchaste wife. As the historian Lynda Boose observes, "the two crimes—being a scold and being a so-called whore— were frequently conflated."[74] A second undoubtedly heated exchange, which Edwards presented as a "quasi-legal" interrogation, allowed him to transform his wife's taunting hints about other men into a full confession to adultery. When "I asked her som Questions," Edwards reported, she answered, "Shee had Committed folly, or, as I Remember, Her own words were that she had Lyen with sutch a man." To substantiate this admission, Edwards noted that she named the alleged lover and identified the "Time and place" of their liaison. The veracity of the confession is, however, undermined by Edwards's curious failure to provide either the man's identity or any further corroboration of this serious allegation, saying only that "the person's name I omit for som Reasons."[75]

This hearsay evidence completes Richard Edwards's construction of Elizabeth Tuttle as a sexually deviant woman. Framed by the early baby and the alleged adultery confession, her lack of "due benevolence" becomes part of a pattern, identifying her as a rebellious woman habitually prone to disorderly sex acts. She first displayed her turbulent nature when young, and this early sin gave the uncorroborated confession more weight. "[A]n old fornicator will be a new adulterer" observed two English divines in an exposition on the seventh commandment, for premarital fornication "is a secret poyson that lurketh within; and if it be not stayed, it will break out to adulterie."[76] As an "old fornicator," Elizabeth was prone to adultery. Her apparent unwillingness to engage in licit marital sex also suggested, according to early modern gender images, that she was likely to seek illicit sexual pleasure elsewhere. In seventeenth-century Anglo-American society, women were believed to have strong sexual appetites that could be controlled only by subjection to manly rule. Insubordination, therefore, naturally led to infidelity.[77] Playing on this correlation, Edwards casts his wife in the familiar role of the defiant shrew who through her repeated rebellions and betrayals had kept his household in a state of permanent disorder. Such a threatening figure makes for compelling narrative and has a weight that is difficult to escape. By presenting this powerful image of female deviance to the Court of Assistants, Edwards hoped to sway the reluctant magistrates to his cause.

Like most unhappy couples in colonial Connecticut, Richard and Elizabeth Edwards endured many years of marital misery before he decided to take legal action. A crisis of rising expectations may have sparked the suit. In the winter of 1685 things were looking up in the Edwards household. After several years of turbulence following the execution of Benjamin Tuttle, order had begun to appear amidst the chaos. Richard's business was flourishing, and to facilitate his expansion into trade the Hartford proprietors had granted him a small "pees of land" at the town docks on the Connecticut River "too set a warhous upon."[78] Elizabeth had given birth to another child, a daughter fashionably named Mabel. Edwards likely was a bit disappointed that the new baby was another girl, for male children were proof of the father's virile constitution, but he was surely pleased his wife had returned to their marriage bed.[79] The following year, his only son, Timothy, enrolled at Harvard College with the class of 1690 to begin preparing for the ministry, a distinction his father had probably anticipated for many years.[80] The first Richard Edwards had been a university-trained minister, occupying the genteel post of master at a London boys' school. His son, William, was likewise an educated man, but his prospects for social advancement had been cut short by the schoolmaster's untimely death. Enrolling Timothy at Harvard therefore represented a restoration of that status the Edwards family had lost and had been striving to regain for two generations since immigrating to the colonies.

This semblance of order did not last. Elizabeth soon returned, in her husband's words, to "Her old fitts of obstinacy and perverseness." Perhaps the period of temporary abstinence colonial couples may have observed following the birth of a child became once again permanent habit.[81] This relapse, according to Edwards's story of the disintegration of his marriage, broke his patience. "I thought It time," he declared, "to Renounce that woman from Beeing my wife that had first soe many waies Deserted me and broken Her

Covinant with mee." He evidently began making preparations to petition for divorce as early as March 1688, for in that month Timothy and his younger sister Abigail gave a deposition attesting that "our Mother" has "been absent from" our Father's "Bedd and Society for about five or six years."[82] Timothy had returned to Hartford around this time after some unspecified disciplinary infraction committed in the first quarter of the 1688 school year resulted in his apparent dismissal from college.[83] Although this new disgrace may have been unrelated to the Edwardses' dysfunctional family, it surely increased Richard's conviction that things were falling apart.

Edwards composed his first divorce petition in the summer of 1689, but he waited until the following spring to enter his plea, at which time the Court of Assistants deferred ruling on the case. Having heard Edwards's case and considered the testimonies submitted in its support, the Assistants did "not find themselves in a Capacity to Answer his desires at present." Instead, they appointed a committee to investigate the charges and "referr[ed] the Issue of this Case to the next meeting of this Court." In October, however, the Assistants denied Edwards's petition, noting only that they "do not find sufficient ground and reason to grant him a Divorce." He immediately appealed to the General Assembly, which was also convened for its fall session. As in England, the Connecticut legislature was more liberal than the lower courts in its divorce rulings. "Spouses whose marital grievance was without remedy under statute law," observes the historian Cornelia Dayton, "could petition the General Assembly in its capacity as a court of equity."[84] But the Assembly provided Edwards no relief. It affirmed the Assistants' judgment, likewise declaring only that "they doe not find reason to grant his petition."[85]

Why were the Connecticut courts, which implemented the most generous divorce policy in colonial America, reluctant to grant Edwards judicial relief for his miserable marriage? This, of course, is one of the central mysteries in our story. That the plea failed to comply with the terms of the colony's divorce statute made it a difficult case. But this difficulty was not impossible to overcome, for the General Assembly employed an expansive reading of the statute. On the rare occasion when a divorce petition was denied, the ruling likely reflected a lack of community support, for a successful "divorce petitioner had to muster community validation of the broken marriage *before* resorting to the legal process."[86] The failure of Edwards's plea accordingly suggests that the informal public was not on his side. Colonial towns were rumor mills, kept constantly turning by settlers eager to share the titillating details of their neighbors' lives. Unhappy marriages were particularly hard to hide. What did Edwards's neighbors know about his marriage that is hidden from us today? They knew that his story was not the whole story. But what else did they know? Combing the records for clues to his omissions and obfuscations, we can identify at least two bits of common knowledge that surely complicated his simple tale of an abused husband driven beyond his endurance by the insufferable behavior of a rebellious wife.

First, the neighbors undoubtedly knew that Richard Edwards was not as innocent as he tried to appear. On 5 June 1688, a single woman named Mary Talcott was presented in Hartford County Court for the crime of fornication. Twenty-seven years old, Mary Talcott was the daughter of one of Connecticut's first families. Her grandfather had served repeatedly in such prestigious posts as Deputy in the General Court, Assistant, Treasurer, and Commissioner of the United Colonies. Continuing the family tradition of public service, her father likewise held multiple public posts and served as an officer in the Connecticut militia, leading the Connecticut forces as commander-in-chief during King Philip's War.[87] For a daughter of one of the colony's ruling families to be charged with such a common crime was scandalous, and to avoid pubic humiliation Mary refrained from appearing in court. In her absence, the magistrates imposed a fine of 50 shillings and ordered that "Richard Edwards be sumened to the next sesions to answer to what shall be layd against him."[88]

Although Edwards's alleged offense is not specified, this order suggests Mary Talcott had identified him as her partner in crime. Women accused of fornication were expected to confess and name their lovers.[89] In 1685, for example, Mary Williams appeared in Hartford County Court and "accused James Benitt of committing Folly with her." As with most single women in this difficult situation, her guilt was clearly displayed by the birth of a child; the alleged father, however, was bound by a £40 recognizance to ensure he later appeared "to Answer the complaint" made against him. Like James Bennett's, no record remains of Richard Edwards's subsequent appearance in court, and both men probably settled their suits privately.[90] Edwards's case was simpler than Bennett's, because his lover was apparently not pregnant, but as a married man he had committed a transgression that was more grave. Mary Talcott's conviction put this established householder's apparent violation of his marriage vows on public display.

This conviction was likely the precipitating factor leading Edwards to begin proceedings to terminate his marriage.[91] He omitted from his divorce petition any explicit reference to his own moral failings. But by publicly airing the story of his wife's breach of duty, he deflected blame away from himself. To protect his innocence, he shifted the guilt onto his wife. He strayed

from their marriage bed only because she had abandoned it first. One purpose of marriage, universally cited in domestic conduct manuals, was to
safeguard against fornication. God ordained marriage, counseled an English divine, "that the wife might bee a lawfull remedie to avoid whoredome,
fornication, and all filthie uncleane lusts."[92] Not having a regular outlet in
marriage, Edwards confessed, his "own naughty Hart" had run rampant. He
begged the Court that "I may in som Measure Bee Extrecated out of those
many Horiable and Dangerous Dificul[t]ys, and perplexing miseryes and
temtations, that I have soo Long Laboured under." A divorce was, he urged, a
matter of "nesesaty."[93] The magistrates entertaining his case, of course, knew
the necessity he labored under. His cry to be delivered from temptation was
not simply a general admission of the universal depravity of human nature
but an oblique reference to what everyone in town understood quite well. He
had already succumbed to a temptation all too common among men with
difficult wives: the allure of a younger, sexually compliant woman.

This affair compromised Edwards's legal case. Colonial courts rarely
rewarded adulterous spouses with permission to divorce and remarry a new
mate. Elizabeth's own faults did not mitigate his. A successful suit required
the identification of a single guilty party. "[E]qual fault," as the historian
Linda Kerber observes, "seemed to justify continued misery."[94] Richard's
breach of duty does, however, make Elizabeth's apparent silence even more
perplexing. Although a countersuit may also have proved unsuccessful, his
involvement with another woman surely provided grounds for her to contest
his case. Colonial divorce narratives commonly tell detailed stories of such
spousal battles.[95] In 1676, for example, James Wakeley sued for divorce, citing his wife's refusal to move with him to Rhode Island. In her countersuit,
Alice Wakeley argued that he had deserted her.[96] Likewise, in 1702, when
Elizabeth Reynolds was convicted of adultery, she charged that her husband
was "notoriously known to the neighbors" for "many Intollerable wrongs and
Abuses" of her.[97] Elizabeth Tuttle surely could have used her husband's failure of manly self-control to contest his charge of sexual incontinence. At the
very least, she would have gained from a countersuit the personal satisfaction of publicly exposing his hypocritical plea. Her silence, however, suggests
that she submitted without objection to this protracted character assault. A
strangely passive posture for a defiant shrew! Her curious response points to
the second thing the neighbors likely knew, that Richard Edwards's wife was
not as guilty as he wanted them to believe.

In cataloging his wife's alleged crimes, Edwards stressed the volitional
nature of her rebellion. In value-laden words, he repeatedly condemned

her "obstinate" and "willful" breach of duty. She "obstinately refus[ed] Conjugall Communion with mee," he complained. "All sutch women" who "Obstinately and willfully Refuse Due Benevolence," he argued, "are not Acounted wives." He likewise deployed the term "perversion" to emphasize the unnatural character of her willfulness. He observed that she "Began her perversions" at a particular time; he hoped "Shee might Relent and Turn from Her perverseness," and he exasperatedly noted that she returned to "her old fitts of obstinancy and Perversness" following a brief period of submission.[98] By using these descriptors Edwards confirms his wife's guilt. As Mercy Brown's murder case clearly illustrates, a guilty mind, or *mens rea*, was a necessary element of criminal liability. To be ruled the guilty party, Elizabeth Tuttle had to be a domestic rebel who knowingly and willfully rejected her marital duty. Edwards accordingly presented to the court an image of a woman with a guilty mind, but once again local knowledge apparently placed his construction of the case in question.

Hartford magistrates were reluctant to accept Edwards's careful construction of his wife as a willfully rebellious woman. Again, we ask, what did they know that is hidden to us today? Evidence suggests that they knew that illness compromised the volitional quality of her acts. Illness in colonial New England was a matter of community concern. If Elizabeth suffered from a physical incapacity, surely the community of women who had attended her in childbirth and were wise in the secrets of nature would have known of the condition. Given the frequency of difficult childbirths, pelvic damage was probably commonplace among colonial women. Connecticut courts did, at times, terminate marriages on proof of sexual incapacity. In 1693, for example, Sarah Dorman was granted a divorce, arguing that her husband, John, had since their marriage been "wholly disabled to perform Conjugall duties to her, or granting her due benevolence." But impotence or incapacity that developed later in marriage was not as clearly actionable.[99] Men whose impotence preceded marriage could be charged with fraudulent contract, but a subsequent disability was a trial the couple had to bear. A husband whose wife suffered a long illness had no remedy but "praier made for the gift of continency," as did a wife whose husband contracted a "contagious disease that cannot be cured."[100] Spouses were bound to bear each other's burdens and care for each other in times of affliction. The affliction, however, that burdened the Edwardses' marriage was not a physical but a mental disability that placed in question Elizabeth's capacity for criminal intent.

The Edwards family had suffered a paralyzing blow when Benjamin struck down his sister Sarah. In the years following the murder their fragile domestic partnership began to break down. Unable to withstand this trial, Elizabeth appears to have withdrawn both emotionally and physically from her husband. The union had been wounded from the start, and neither she nor the marriage had the strength to recover from this second crisis. Within a decade, neighbors and kin evidently judged her—like both her brother David in New Haven and her sister Mercy in Wallingford—to have a distracted mind. One possible indication of her incompetency occurred when Edwards first entered his plea. After hearing his complaint, the magistrates did not order her to appear in court and answer the charges, as was common procedure. Instead, they appointed the investigative committee that visited the Edwardses' home to "inform the Said Edwards his wife of her husbands desires" and report to the court her response. They also ordered that notice of the charges be given to her brothers and sisters, her nearest relations, "that they (if they se cause) may appear and Object what they have to Say in the Case."[101] These deviations from ordinary procedure suggest that the court questioned Elizabeth Tuttle's ability to speak for herself. The clearest evidence of her incapacity, however, is displayed in Edwards's second divorce petition.

When Edwards renewed his plea for divorce at the spring 1691 session of the General Assembly, he was a frustrated and angry man. The prior winter he had irately accosted William Pitkin, a long-serving member of the Court of Assistants, shouting repeatedly "that he had wrong, that he was sure he had wrong in the case, and al with much vehemency." Believing the judge was biased against his suit, he rashly accused him with "falsely informing the Court about it." For this slanderous accusation, Edwards was cautioned that his heated words had been "Injurious and dishonorable to the Court," but this loss of manly self-control was evidently not a serious setback for his case.[102] Although in May the Assembly again deferred judgment, the language of its ruling expressed a new-found sympathy for his plea. The magistrates were not yet ready "to alter their apprehensions from what they were formerly," but they assured Edwards that they "are willing to doe what they can for his reliefe."[103] Judicial sentiment was coalescing in his favor.

A year had passed since Edwards had begun his suit, and evidently during this time the informal public had rallied to his support. Reflecting this shift, the members of the Assembly gradually reached consensus that their fellow householder must be provided an escape from his troubled marriage. Courts in seventeenth-century Connecticut employed an "informal case-by-case approach" to divorce that "drew on local knowledge to fashion ad hoc remedies."[104] Edwards's repeated petitions allow us to witness this ad hoc procedure at work, as the authorities searched for a rationale that would justify granting his bill of divorce. Persistent domestic instability had kept his household in disarray for more than a decade, leaving its members dangerously exposed to sin. Edwards's inability to form a sexually satisfying relationship had apparently become a particular source of alarm for the community of adult men that governed the colony. Expressing particular sympathy for "the deplorable estate of the petitioner, and the many intolerable temptations he lyes open too," they began fashioning a remedy.[105]

Edwards likewise attempted to strengthen his case by addressing some of the court's specific concerns. His first failed narrative had emphasized the theme of sexual betrayal, a crime of which he was likely more guilty than she. When this plea was rejected, he reframed his wife's breach of duty as an act of desertion. "I Claime the Benifitt of that Law Title 'Divorces,'" he asserted in his second divorce petition, "which Gives Liberty for A separation for three years Disertion only." Desertion was the most common ground for divorce in seventeenth-century Connecticut, and also the most successful.[106] An action that fit the statutory definition of desertion was, therefore, virtually guaranteed success. Because his wife had never physically left home, Edwards's new argument rested, once again, on a tenuous statutory foundation, but it had some merit. Although divorce actions entered by deserted husbands and wives were both commonly granted, Connecticut magistrates defined a woman's desertion more by the statute's "total neglect of duty" clause than by her physical absence. "Thus, while a husband's desertion consisted of non-support and an unexplained withdrawal of his presence as household head for three years, the signs of a wife's desertion were her withholding those special 'Offices' she provided in her husband's bed and at his board."[107] No evidence suggests that Elizabeth had neglected any of her household duties, such as food preparation or child care, but she had abandoned the marital bed. "I Conceive," Edwards asserted, "I Have prooved As Clearly as Is possible to Bee Done," that such a protracted withdrawal of sexual services fulfilled the statutory definition of desertion.[108]

To make this argument required a showing of *mens rea*. If Elizabeth had not willfully deserted her husband, Richard could not claim intentional breach of duty. Without intent, her guilt could not be established and the suit could not succeed.[109] Edwards framed his second action specifically to address this objection, which the magistrates had apparently raised in response to his first plea. "I here [ac]cept," he conceded, "that the woman Hath Been Distracted for many years, &c." To convince the court that an apparently incompetent woman should be held liable for her actions, he constructed a novel legal argument without clear precedent in Connecticut law.[110] He claimed that her desertion preceded her distraction and so began as a willful act. "Let it bee Considered," he proposed, "that when shee went of[f] from me In her Afections and Behaviour, it was when shee was in A Composed and not a Distracted frame." Following this initial act of willful desertion, she subsequently became distracted, but, he urged, because her "Desertions and obstanesy Is prooved to bee Before that as well as After," she should be held responsible.[111]

No clue remains to the character of Elizabeth Tuttle's affliction. Richard Edwards describes no symptom of her illness beyond her refusal to have sex with him. Is this a sign of insanity? Seventeenth-century physicians at times identified insubordination as evidence of mental unbalance.[112] In a world of fixed hierarchical structures, a woman who refused to be ruled by her husband was likely to be thought insane. But Elizabeth was probably not an "uppity" woman judged mad by men jealously guarding their patriarchal perquisites. More likely she, like her brother David, suffered from an episodic mental illness. Edwards's argument does bear some analogy to the common-law approach to periodic lunacy, for if she had an intermittent disability then during "lucid intervals" she would legally be considered *compos mentis* and so responsible for her actions. But unlike the murder of a child or the signing of a contract, desertion was not a momentary act but an ongoing condition that had to have persisted for a minimum of three years to meet the statutory requirement. Even if her rebellion predated her illness, her intent to rebel did not apparently persist for the statutory minimum. Edwards's legal invention did not, therefore, clearly establish his wife's competency as a deserting spouse. It could, however, provide a kind of legal cover as Hartford's ruling elite became increasingly sympathetic to their fellow householder's cause.

Questions about mental competency had also, on first hearing, undermined another central element of Edwards's case: Elizabeth's alleged confession to adultery. Although such hearsay evidence was likely insufficient for a criminal conviction for adultery, it was admissible in colonial divorce proceedings, which allowed "almost any kind of evidence, including hearsay evidence [and] out-of-court admissions."[113] If, however, this confession had been made while she was in a *non compos mentis* condition, its veracity as well as its admissibility would have been compromised. To overcome this objection, Edwards swore under "oath in court that his wife did confess to him that she had Commited adultery and that she was not distracted when she made this confession."[114] This oath provided the Assembly some firm ground on which to stand and reinforced the image of Elizabeth Tuttle as a sexually deviant woman. Further support came from the judgment of a council of ministers that the court had appointed at Edwards's request. Colonial judiciaries commonly employed such ministerial councils in difficult cases, to judge whether the scripture rule fit the legal facts. In Edwards's case, however, the council offered the magistrates little more than an ecclesiastical fig leaf for the desired outcome. Several divines had championed Edwards's plea from the outset, testifying as early as December 1689 that "it doth not seem to be within the Compass of any humane power to deny him the Liberty of putting away his former and marrying another wife."[115] That one of these original supporters, the Hartford pastor Timothy Woodbridge, was subsequently appointed to the ministerial council likely ensured its ruling would be in Edwards's favor.[116]

As the judicial stars began auspiciously to align for our unhappy householder, an unforeseen event occurred that sealed the Assembly's judgment. About a month after Edwards had resubmitted his plea, Elizabeth Tuttle's sister Mercy Brown murdered her son Samuel in his bed while he slept. Once again the Hartford jail harbored in its dungeon a member of the Tuttle family charged with a heinous act of intimate violence. This time, however, the accused murderer was not an angry young man who had killed in a moment of uncontrolled rage but a deranged goodwife who had struck down her child in a fit of criminal lunacy. If the first axe murder delivered to the Edwardses' marriage a life-threatening wound, the second axe murder proved to be the fatal blow. The link between Mercy and Elizabeth was too strong to ignore. The two women were sisters, separated in age by only five years, and both were suffering from distraction. Edwards reinforced this association by an additional accusation that he included only in his second petition. "Alsoe I am reddy to Confirm with my oath," he declared, that she has "often Threaten[ed] my Life to Cut my Throat when I was Asleep," and he voiced "Great fear of my Life by Reson of her soe threatening."[117] Mercy's shocking murder of her son gave urgency to Edwards's professed fear that his wife's uncontrolled passions would drive her to kill. This alleged threat also played on the link between adultery and murder common in early modern popular print, which "conflate[d] unregulated sexuality with murderousness" and represented murder as the "last danger that adulterous women posed for their husbands."[118] By transforming Elizabeth into the "domestic danger" her sister so starkly represented, Richard tied his divorce suit to her murder trial, thereby joining both sisters' judicial fates.[119]

Mercy Brown was put on trial for her life at the October 1691 session of the Court of Assistants. After the guilty verdict was delivered, the judges deferred sentencing to weigh additional testimony concerning her competency. The following week the members of this court convened as the upper house of the General Assembly, which in its capacity as a court of equity entertained for the third and final time Edwards's divorce action. In both cases, the question before the magistrates was the same. Was she mad or was she bad? Mercy's very life depended on the answer to this question, and with great reluctance the court had postponed its judgment. Elizabeth's destiny also hung in the balance, but the stakes were not so high. If distraction was the cause of her domestic "perversions" then she, like her sister, could not be held responsible for her actions. But the authorities were not twice to be denied by madness the satisfaction of a conviction. Already predisposed in Edwards's favor, they rejected the pathetic image of a goodwife unhinged by an intolerable grief and embraced the threatening image of a defiant shrew whose uncontrolled sexuality was a dangerous, if not lethal, source of community disorder. Edwards's protracted campaign, waged over two years and in two separate courts, was finally over. We "doe see reason," the Assembly ruled, "and doe release him the sayd Richard Edwards from his conjugall tye to sayd Elizabeth his late wife."[120]

Richard Edwards and Elizabeth Tuttle were an unhappily married couple. He placed all the blame for this unhappiness on his wife. Our reconstruction of the other side of this story suggests, however, that there was plenty of blame to share. The circumstances that contributed to the marriage's collapse began with two very different migrations. While the Tuttles were pulled by the hope of New World opportunity, the Edwardses were pushed by the shame of financial ruin. The contested early baby crippled the union of this mismatched pair from the outset. Although the seeds of family failure were sown in these early days, their germination was not inevitable. A brutal murder dealt a life-threatening blow to the flourishing Tuttle family. This sudden death was too much for some to bear. David and Mercy developed debilitating mental illnesses. Elizabeth withdrew from her marriage, apparently unwilling to bring more children into the world. The festering sexual crisis that had afflicted this union from the outset reemerged with renewed force. The old feelings of mistrust, anger, and betrayal returned. Unhappy at home, Richard began looking for greener pastures abroad. Having superior inner strength, financial resources, and legal knowledge, he eventually began divorce proceedings, intending to form a new union with a more attractive mate patiently waiting in the wings.

This story of marital breakdown is framed by titillating tales of murder and madness, but it ends with a sexually dissatisfied husband unhappily yoked to a mentally unstable wife. Connecticut law did not recognize such an unremarkable explanation for conjugal misery as an actionable cause for divorce. This judicial remedy was necessary to preserve domestic stability, but it was not intended to make people happy. In colonial New England, unhappiness was the "shakiest of grounds for divorce."[121] Nevertheless, when this bill of divorce was finally granted, it certainly made one man happy. In less than six months Richard Edwards had married Mary Talcott, his own illicit lover, and had begun fashioning for himself a new, more comfortable life.

Elizabeth Tuttle's future is unknown. After the divorce she simply disappears; no record even notes the date of her death. Like her sister Mercy, she probably lived out her days alone and impoverished, sustained by the small maintenance her husband had agreed "out of mere Compassion and pity of Her Condition" to provide.[122] The first part of our likely tale must, then, end here. But even though we don't know the final chapter of Elizabeth's story, we can write its sequel. The divorce was both a conclusion to one story and the beginning of a second. While the first has explored the limits of historical retrieval, the second will trace the wanderings of historical memory. In the years following the divorce, both Richard Edwards and his son Timothy struggled painstakingly to forget Elizabeth Tuttle, and within several generations she had been erased from the family's memory. But the legacy of her illustrious grandson, Jonathan Edwards, would in the nineteenth century revive the threatening image of the defiant shrew, made even more menacing by the discovery of the science of genetics.

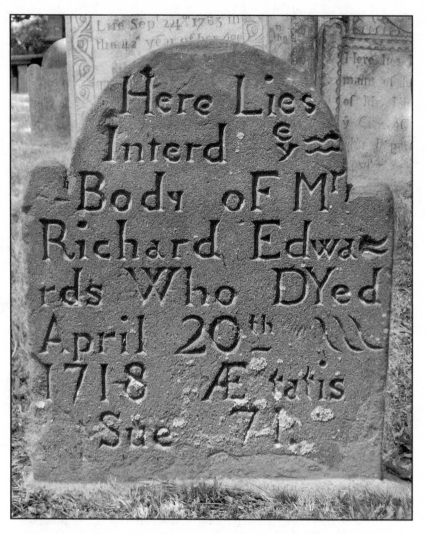

Gravestone of Richard Edwards, Ancient Burying Ground, Hartford.

[6]

THE INHERITANCE

In the spring of 1718 Richard Edwards knew he was dying. "I have been of the mind all along that This sickness will be my Death," he told his son Timothy, who kept a meticulous record of his father's every word and action in the last days of his life. Timothy had traveled to Hartford from his East Windsor parish to join the family and friends who surrounded the seventy-one-year-old man's deathbed during this difficult time. Four of Richard's younger children still lived at home, and his married daughters were all settled nearby. His young son Daniel also probably returned home from neighboring Wethersfield accompanied by his fourteen-year-old nephew, Jonathan, who was his roommate at the recently formed Yale College.[1] All these children and grandchildren had gathered at the patriarch's bedside to comfort him in the "Great and sore sickness that was upon him," and weep "Over him under preapprehensions of his Final departure from them, and the Great Loss they were like shortly to sustain thereby."[2] But this large puritan family knew in these last days that they also had a more serious responsibility: to help their aged father prepare for his death.

Puritans believed that God called them to live life in preparation for death, and to take each sickness as an occasion for renewed devotion. "Preparation for death was the culminating exercise of the entire devotional system," for beyond death lay eternity and the hope of union with Christ.[3] Popular devotional manuals regularly exhorted believers to anticipate death and included aids, such as prayers and meditations, to assist in preparation. "Put not farre off the day of death," warned *The Practice of Piety*; "thou knowest not, for all this, how near it is at hand; and (being so fairly warned) be wiser."[4] The approaching certainty of death put this lifetime of preparation to its final test, and according to his son, Edwards was not caught unawares. "[T]his time I have expected," he assured his children, "this time I have Look'd for, and now it is Come." Adopting the proper posture of faith, he resigned himself to the "violent distemper that was upon him," asking God to "enable him, patiently to bear his afflicting hand, and quietly submit to his will, even to the end." He died on a Sunday morning, eagerly anticipating to "keep Sabbath with saints, and Angels in Heaven."[5]

By the standards of puritan devotional practice, Richard Edwards "Died Well, he made a Comfortable and Good End." This good death was not quick and free from suffering. Christians desire, Timothy Edwards observed, to die "not by some Casualty or Accident as by a fall, Drowning or the Like," for accidental death allowed no opportunity for preparation by repentance, submission, and prayer. The length of the senior Edwards's sickness, lasting a "little above Eight dayes and a half," was also a mercy, and during this time he quickly applied "himself with all possible seriousness unto the Great and solemn work and business that was before him." Part of this business was the patient endurance of suffering, the final trial of the dying man's faith. It tested the truth of his humble submission to God's will and allowed him to face death "well satisfied concerning the state and Condition of his soul."[6]

During this time of intensive devotion, Edwards also followed the standard advice to "set thy house in order."[7] He had acquired a considerable estate during the latter years of his life—valued at more than £1,100 at probate—and two days after the onset of his illness he dictated his last will and testament. Having in the customary pious preamble "Commend[ed] [his] sole into the bosom of my most mercifull God and father," he left the family home to his second son, John, who assumed the responsibility of caring for his aging mother and distributed the remainder of the estate to the other eight living children. Three days after the will was signed and witnessed, however, Edwards added a curious codicil to this conventional document. He bequeathed that "Mary, the Eldest Child of my first wife, shall have two shillings out of my Estate," and directed John, the estate's executor, "to pay unto the above said Mary two shillings upon her demand."[8]

Richard Edwards had spent much of his adult life trying to forget the recipient of this small bequest. This conflicted past is clearly displayed in the awkward description used to identify Mary in the codicil. For fifty years Edwards had maintained that she was not his daughter, but "the Eldest Child of my first wife." In his final hours she was a lingering reminder of her troublesome mother, Elizabeth Tuttle, whom he had many years before fought tenaciously to divorce. As he prepared to "make an happy departure out of this world," he did not restore Mary to his family. This codicil suggests that on his deathbed he recalled her, and indirectly her mother, to once again renounce them.[9]

Puritan devotional manuals recommended reconciliation with one's neighbors as an integral part of preparation for death. Lewis Bayly, the author of *The Practice of Piety,* exhorted the "sick party that is like to die" to "heartily forgive all wrongs and offenses done or offered unto thee by any manner of person whatsoever."[10] In his final days Edwards apparently tried to follow this advice. He "manifested a Good Christian spirit towards One That he thought himself to have been Greatly Injured, and abused by," and forgave a neighbor who had "offended or grieved him."[11] He did not, however, extend this spirit of reconciliation to Elizabeth Tuttle or to her daughter Mary. Her two-shilling bequest was designed to protect his estate by preventing his "reputed" daughter from making a more substantive claim. It effectively disinherited Mary by leaving her a token amount. The English jurist William Blackstone noted that according to Roman law a will risked challenge if it "disinherited or totally passed by . . . any of the children of the testator." But passed-over, or "pretermitted," heirs could not bring suit if they were left "any legacy, though ever so small." Although common law did not acknowledge the principle of "pretermission," the "one-shilling rule" was part of Anglo-American folk tradition. This rule, which Blackstone called a "groundless vulgar error," required "leaving the heir a shilling or some other express legacy, in order to disinherit him effectually."[12] As attorney for the Hartford County Probate Court, Richard Edwards was undoubtedly aware that Connecticut law did not formally recognize this rule. Protecting his estate against this nonexistent threat, the codicil declared that the distance he had fought to maintain from this child during his life would be kept after his death. With two shillings he both acknowledged and annulled Mary's status as a marginal member of his family.

When John Edwards informed his not-quite half-sister of this preemptive bequest, it likely reminded her of the train of rejections that had marked her early years. Mary's "reputed" father had disowned her at birth and separated her from her mother, leaving her with an ambiguous identity, legitimately neither Tuttle nor Edwards. The divorce action had likewise left her mother in a liminal space, neither married nor free to marry, her reputation compromised. Separated from her home and children, the youngest of whom was only six years old, Elizabeth may have returned to New Haven to live near her first daughter's household, but even the restoration of this relationship would not have been full compensation for the years of loss. If Mary accepted this small legacy, then, she surely took it with bitterness. And like the man who granted it, she probably could not quite forget the failed family signified by these two silver coins.

The ease with which Richard Edwards rebuilt his life following the divorce undoubtedly helped him to forget. He remarried less than six months after the divorce was granted, and in less than a year his new wife delivered their first child. The haste with which he reconstituted a family was common for men in his situation. In colonial New England, a "man alone was an oddity, a thing to be remedied."[13] Although most men found themselves wifeless through death, not divorce, once single, Edwards behaved no differently from his peers: he quickly remarried.[14] Men married for love and companionship, but, more important, from necessity. Forty-four years old and responsible for several small children, Edwards needed a wife for his household to flourish.

Marriage also legitimized the adulterous relationship he had begun several years before the divorce was granted. Mary Talcott was quite a good match for a divorced, middle-aged man. Although ambition had gradually propelled him to a place of some prominence in Hartford, Edwards's social status did not equal that of his new wife's family, who were leading members of the colonial Connecticut oligarchy. This marriage also gave him the loving and harmonious domestic partnership that Elizabeth Tuttle had failed to provide, at least in the latter years of their marriage. Sixteen years younger than her predecessor, Mary Talcott was apparently the model colonial goodwife, submissive and obedient to her husband. For a man who had long struggled to maintain his authority in the marriage bed, her sexual compliance must have been particularly gratifying. Having six children in ten years, she produced a second family for her husband, and, unlike his first, this new family was predominantly male. Whereas all but one of Elizabeth's six children were girls, Mary had five boys and one girl.[15] Edwards likely perceived this preponderance of sons as additional affirmation of his manly virtue.[16]

This orderly household established a foundation for further achievement. Three years after his second marriage Edwards acquired a new spiritual and social status when he and his wife joined Hartford's First Church in full membership.[17] His rapid economic rise was even more striking. Mary Talcott's father had left a substantial estate of almost £2,300, which included two African and two Indian slaves, a rare mark of status in seventeenth-century New England.[18] Although no record of her portion remains, Mary surely brought a respectable settlement to her marriage, likely having received after her father's death a legacy of almost £180.[19] But she also brought a less tangible, and ultimately more lucrative, form of capital to her marriage. Through her well-connected family, she provided her husband access to the powerful social network of Connecticut's governing class. These family connections quickly enhanced his business prospects and allowed him to develop a second, more prestigious career.

Richard Edwards practiced his barrel-making trade, which he had learned as a boy from his father, throughout his life. The inventory of his estate indicates that at the time of his death his shop contained a "parcell off Coopers Tools off all Sorts," "Twenty three Barrils new but not quite finisht," "Two Churns not finisht," and "A new pale."[20] He also continued his father's interest in litigation, appearing occasionally in court to administer an estate through probate or to litigate an action for a third party.[21] Such routine court appearances during his first marriage cannot foretell how rapidly his work as an attorney grew in the decade following his divorce and remarriage. Edwards's new alliance with one of Connecticut's ruling families likely contributed to this sizeable increase in caseload. For example, only a few months after remarrying, he represented Edward Randolph, an agent of the Crown widely despised throughout the colonies, in a controversial case concerning a violation of the Navigation Acts.[22] Nothing in Edwards's past prepared him for such a high-profile case. However, the Talcott family, while not militant royalists, had maintained cordial relations with the English government and its colonial representatives during the Dominion period.[23] Edwards's marriage into this family may have recommended him to Randolph, who was the first of a number of out-of-town clients for Edwards, especially merchants and tradesmen from Boston. By 1700 he regularly appeared and argued cases on all three levels of the Connecticut judicial system.[24]

Another controversial client surely reflected Edwards's checkered past. For a man looking to extricate himself from some marital trouble, a divorced attorney probably appeared to be a good advocate. Nathaniel Finch, however, was not petitioning for a divorce; he was struggling to prevent the annulment of his illicit second marriage. This union was truly scandalous because his new wife was the "own Naturall Sister of the Said Finch his first wife." Rooted in scripture, the prohibition against a man's marrying his dead wife's sister was an ancient principle of common law, which defined the degrees of affinity and consanguinity that were impediments to marriage.[25] In Finch's defense, Edwards directly challenged not only this longstanding legal principle but also the ruling of a council of ministers that had issued an opinion supporting the prosecution. He argued that Leviticus prohibits a man from marrying his sister-in-law only while his wife is living. It is not "unlawfull," he asserted, "for A widdower to marry His Late wife's sister," for he has "becom a single man Againe and is freed from all those former Conjugall obligations." The Court of Assistants was not, however, impressed by this novel argument. Judging his plea to be "insufficient, and also of an Offensive nature," they ruled that the marriage was "Incestuous and Unlawfull."[26]

Despite this public reprimand, Edwards's legal career continued to advance. In 1699 he first appeared in the General Assembly with Daniel Clark "as attorneys for the country" to prosecute a land dispute. Clark had been presenting capital cases for the government on an irregular basis since 1694. But in 1705, after passage of a statute creating a position "to prosecute and implead in the lawe all criminall offenders," Edwards was named the colony's first Queen's attorney, a post that he held for thirteen years, until his death.[27] Three years later he was also appointed attorney for the Hartford County Probate Court and was the first man admitted to the newly formed Connecticut bar.[28] Edwards's rising fortunes paralleled those of his "Good friend" Joseph Talcott. He became Hartford's prosecuting attorney in the same year that his brother-in-law took his seat among Connecticut's ruling elites as Justice of the Peace for Hartford County. This post was the first of many civil and military honors, culminating in Talcott's long service as the colony's governor.[29]

As Queen's attorney Edwards prosecuted another high-profile case that also must have dredged up his well-buried past. In 1706 a Farmington woman named Abigail Thompson was indicted for capital murder, having thrown a "Pair of Taylors Shears" at her husband that pierced his "Skull into his Brains." No colonist had been tried for murder in Connecticut since Mercy Brown's controversial case, and Edwards presented for the Crown a strong body of evidence. With the informal public clearly favoring conviction, a parade of witnesses testified that Abigail had a long history of abusing and threatening her husband. These shocking accounts ensured that Edwards easily obtained a conviction, but following sentencing the case became embroiled in controversy.[30] Gershom Bulkeley, who had worked to overturn Mercy Brown's capital conviction, once again intervened, arguing that Abigail Thompson had been charged with the wrong crime. "I find that the woman's act was in the nature of a chance medley, done in a quarrell upon a sudden provocation," he wrote to the governor, who recommended that her charge be reduced to manslaughter. Although the General Assembly apparently considered this recommendation, the "bloody woman" ultimately went to the gallows.[31]

Edwards's flourishing legal career suggests that his new family connections paid off well, but more impersonal forces were also at work. His reinvention as an attorney coincided with a transitional period in American legal history, during which the underlying conditions necessary for the emergence of the modern legal profession first took shape. Throughout most of the seventeenth century, the colonial courtroom was a "chaotic and extremely informal place, where adversaries talked at the same time and audience members shouted out their opinions." Litigants unable to attend a particular court session "would execute a power of attorney to a friend, neighbor, or relative to appear in their stead and act for them," but these "attorneys-in-fact" were the only attorneys present in the court. Given the informality of the pleading, most defendants were capable of representing themselves. By the end of the century, however, the layperson's courtroom was giving way to the more formal and orderly world of professional lawyers and technical pleadings that marked the English common-law courts. Courtroom contests focused less on matters of fact and more on legal procedure as litigants learned to employ technical pleadings to advance their interests. The increasing complexity of the legal system created a demand for a new class of professional "attorneys-at-law," persons skilled in the intricacies of common-law procedure, who were paid a fee to accompany their clients to court and present their cases. [32]

In this rapidly changing legal climate, Edwards was well positioned to take advantage of a new opportunity for professional advancement. His lack of formal legal training was not a liability, because all early colonial lawyers were self-taught. Using his "quick Ready wit," he learned pleadings and rules of evidence by studying the substantial collection of law books he acquired for his library.[33] Lying on his deathbed, he had every reason to feel proud of his earthly accomplishments. Although his first marriage had ended in failure, once freed from that heavy yoke he had flourished. Married to a woman whom "he highly Esteemed, and Tenderly Loved," he became a "Man Considerable in the Town where he dwelt."[34] His oldest son, Timothy, had taken his place among the colony's ministerial elite, effectively surpassing—as had Richard Edwards—his father's own social position. His daughters from his unfortunate first alliance had married well and had started families of their own. And his younger son Daniel and his grandson Jonathan were readying themselves for prestigious public careers. This proud patriarch had come a long way from the struggling cooper's son who, facing a fornication charge, had married young and with uncertain prospects.

Had he lived out his life married to Elizabeth Tuttle, Richard Edwards likely would have traveled some of this distance. The times created opportunities for an ambitious man like Edwards to improve himself. The divorce, however, did not harm his prospects; acquiring a new young wife from an

Timothy Edwards doodled this musing about his father in the margin of a
sermon on Eccles. 12:1. Gratz Sermons Collection, box 322, vol. 18.
Courtesy of the Historical Society of Pennsylvania.

elite family was, in fact, a benefit. But the decisive benefit was the very ability to remarry. Unable to form a new family and start anew, Elizabeth was
left after the divorce with nothing but her unhappy and tragic past. Richard
could make a better future for himself. Being a man, of course, helped him
move forward. He could start new business ventures and develop new career
paths, avenues for self-advancement closed to Elizabeth, whose only sanctioned social role lay within the family. The right to remarry, however, was
contingent not upon gender but upon guilt. Guilty men, who forfeited only a
third of the marital property, fared better than guilty women, who lost everything.[35] But when a man was declared the injured party, his future was bright.
Financially secure and with custody of the children, Edwards could forget his
past failure by fashioning for himself a new identity. And the makeover continued after his death. Burdened by memories of the past, Timothy Edwards
formed an image of his flawed father that recalled only the happy second half
of his bifurcated life.

Timothy Edwards was a child of divorce. His parents' marriage began to
break down when he was a boy of only six or seven years old, and for many
years he had lived in a household that was torn by unhappiness and conflict.
Because colonial houses were small structures affording little personal privacy, the Edwards children knew the intimate details of their parents' marital
strife, especially Timothy, the oldest child and only son. Like many children

caught in the crossfire between warring parents, he took sides. Providing crucial support for his father's divorce case, he testified that "our Mother for many Years hath demeaned an[d] behaved her selfe with very great obstinacy and averseness against our Father."[36] The bond forged during this moment of crisis became increasingly close as the two men aged. "My Father was to me in this Life-time," the son lamented, "so Great and dear a Christian friend." Had he lived, "how often should he and I have taken sweet Counsel together in the Night season" or conversed about religion "as we were Going to, or coming from Boston together."[37] These words echo the reverence for patriarchal authority common in puritan families; for Timothy Edwards, however, such idealization was complicated by his father's divorce.

The ambiguity of this intimate relationship is clearly expressed in the encomium on the life of his father that Timothy Edwards composed after his death. Biography was a popular genre for second- and third-generation colonists lamenting the declension of their commonwealth from its pious foundations, and biographies of both actual and metaphorical fathers were widely admired. "All the World allows a Son, to Erect a Monument for, & Preserve a Memorial of, his Departed Father," Cotton Mather wrote in the opening line of *Parentator*, his account of the life of his father, the renowned puritan theologian Increase Mather.[38] Timothy Edwards, however, could not appropriate a literary genre designed to praise figures of unquestioned and widely recognized virtue without erasing the messy particulars of his father's first marriage. He accordingly adjusted the biographical form to accommodate a life as much to be forgotten as remembered.

Unlike the great majority of hagiographies written by New England puritans during this period, Edwards's narrative does not recount his father's ancestry, birth, and education, nor does he include the story of his conversion and calling. A chronological account of Richard Edwards's early years would not have revealed the pious foundation for a life of heroic virtue, the common narrative frame employed by puritan biographers. Unable to tell his father's story from his birth, Edwards gave his life a new beginning. After an oblique reference to a time of "very Great and sore tryal" suffered by his father, Edwards stated that "In what follows I shall principally and almost wholly have Respect to the Time that hath passed since what I have but now hinted at." This period "took up or Contained the Last seven and Twenty years of his Life," which locates his father's new beginning in 1691, the year of the divorce. Edwards, however, conflates this humiliating event with a more admirable moment actually occurring some four years later, when his father

"Join[ed] in full Communion with the Church." This important religious milestone is thereby transformed into the true beginning of the "best part of his Life."[39] Edwards takes this "best part" for the whole, to reconstruct his father in the image of a godly puritan man.

Edwards began by recounting his father's "Natural and moral Qualifications." This description conforms in every particular to the puritan ideal of manliness, which, in the son's estimation, his father exemplified "in a More than Ordinary manner." He was a "Comely person," with a "Healthy constitution" and a "Lively vigorous stirring spirit," Timothy observed, whose rationality allowed him "to Command and Govern his spirit, as became a wise man and a Christian." Equally important was his ability to govern his relations with others. "He was a very kind, careful, Tender, Loving Husband to his wife," the son recalled, "and I think One of the best Fathers to his Children." He was also a "Good master," who was "Just and kind, to his Servants" and even "kind and mercifull to his very beasts." Outside the domestic sphere, moreover, he was a "sincere, plainhearted, honest man," who in the conduct of his business was satisfied with a "midling moderate advance up on what he sold" and would not "go high in his prices." With both the dependent members of his household and his fellow men in the community, then, Richard Edwards was an admirable man. "The Truth is," his son concluded, "he had many Amiable things in his Natural Temper and was a very manly and Ingenuous Spirited man."[40]

This account of Richard Edwards's manliness obscures all memory of his failed first marriage and leaves one important question unspoken. Timothy reports his father had felt a "very Tender affection and Dear Love" for his wife. But which wife? Even if this question is not asked, its answer is clear. Richard had once used very different words to describe his wife. "Her Cariage," he had noted with exasperation, "was so Exceeding Intolerable and unsupportable that I Could noe Longer Indure what I mett with from her."[41] Thirty years had passed since these words had been written, and much had been forgotten. Elizabeth Tuttle had been replaced by a new, more lovable, woman. But even if his father had moved on, Timothy could not wholly escape troubling thoughts of his lost mother. Her absence complicated his remembrance of his father and led him to doubt the truth of the divorced man's religious faith.

Faith was the most basic manly virtue. "A man's calling," notes the historian Lisa Wilson, "was to a Christian life as well as to a profession that would glorify God."[42] Biographies of New England patriarchs were, accordingly, spiritual narratives tracing the direction of God's providence in the conversion, calling, ministry, and death of great exemplars of the puritan faith. Attempting to follow this design in his own biography, Timothy Edwards depicted in detail his father's "qualifications as a Christian." He had an "awfull sense of the Infinite Greatness and Majesty, and absolute Sovereignty of God," Timothy related. He acknowledged his "Utter Unworthiness" of God's mercy and "seemed heartily to Close with the way of salvation by Christ." His father's "Inward spiritual sense and understanding of [the] excellency" of Jesus Christ also produced "Tender Religious affections," the pastor observes with approbation. He "prayed twice a day with his family," spent time alone in "his Chamber" on the "Morning before the administration of the sacrament," and took "Delight" in studying "Excellent Books [of] Divinity." Edwards embellished this account by including an extract from his father's will and a detailed description of his deathbed scene, both common seventeenth-century biographical conventions.[43] In every detail, therefore, his representation of Richard Edwards's faith conforms to the puritan ideal. "Though I have been in the Ministry for Now very Near four and Twenty years," Edwards reports, "I don't Remember that I have met with Any that seemed to be more in Living such a Life then My Dear Father was."[44]

Undermining this extravagant conclusion, which is not inconsistent with the puritan biographical form, is another type of authorial intrusion. Edwards repeatedly inserted his own voice into the text to make assessments of the truth of his father's spiritual state. "I have reason to hope," Edwards frequently concluded, "that he understood and Believed what he Read"; that his affections were "from the Gracious Influence and Operation of the spirit of God upon his heart"; "that God had savingly brought him home to himself."[45] These first-person judgments transformed this biography into a search for signs of grace. The uncertainty inherent in the doctrine of predestination made discerning signs of grace a characteristic of puritan piety. This penchant for self-examination produced several autobiographical forms, including the diary and the conversion narrative, which traced the dialectic of faith and doubt that marked a genuine quest for assurance of salvation. But the doubt common in puritan autobiography is foreign to biography. The biographical subject was represented as an exemplar of faith, whose authenticity was beyond question. Because Edwards conflated the first- and third-person positions, doubt permeated his biography; it tormented, however, only the son. By making his father's religious beliefs and practices the object of his anxious examination, Edwards drew attention away from his subject and directed it back toward himself. This redirection created a hybrid text, as much about the son as his father.[46] As puritans struggled to turn doubt into assurance by daily recording their religious experiences, Edwards wrote to conquer his own doubts about his father's spiritual state.

Edwards declared this self-reflexive purpose in the opening paragraphs of the text. "The following things are written," he stated, "because I hope from what I have already experienced, the Reading of them over hereafter may be for my Soul's profit and Comfort." But lasting comfort was always just beyond his grasp. This anxiety manifested itself with increasing intensity in Edwards's relentless analysis of the last days of his father's life. He dissected each moment of his father's final agony with microscopic precision, scrutinizing every word and action for evidence that he died in a state of grace. After watching his father suffer through the night, Edwards stated with satisfaction that "he seemed then to be very patient, submissive, and much Resign'd under the afflicting hand of God, and to his holy sovereignty." Submission, especially in times of trial, was a most distinguishing sign of grace, and the "manner of his speaking it was," Edwards observes, "very Refreshing and Comfortable to me." He similarly took comfort that his father spoke "with an air of much Inward satisfaction Concerning his Interest in God's favor." Nevertheless, he repeatedly questioned his father about the strength of his assurance. During his final night, "when he was Labouring under very Great pain and manifestly Dying," Edwards "asked him whether his hopes of salvation still held." And "but a few hours before he died," he again pressed him. His father reassured him "by squeesing my hand," but this final gesture provided no lasting assurance.[47]

Timothy Edwards, like all good puritans, knew not to strive for complete assurance. Certainty was a mark of hypocrisy, suggesting insufficient self-examination and incomplete awareness of sin. As a result, "the surest earthly sign of a saint was his uncertainty; and the surest sign of a damned soul was security." Edwards's anxiety, however, was evidence not of "faith in its proper imperfection" but of his own inability fully to control the memory of his father.[48] He tried to construct an image of Richard Edwards which ensured that he and "my fellow Mourners of the same family with myself" would remember his father as an ideal Christian man.[49] He expunged from this image the messy divorce and the difficult years of his father's first marriage, but a residue of anxiety remained, permeating the biography and preventing him from comfortably resting in the hope of his father's salvation.

Edwards's intricate exegesis of his father's signs of grace clearly communicates this lack of resolution. Following the chronological account of his final days, he summarizes his father's last words in a thirty-five-point list. This lengthy catalogue is then followed by a ten-point list of his father's responses to various questions, a twenty-point summary of his manner of death, a seven-point analysis of the ways he "glorified God at his Death" (which is reprised in a more liturgical format), and a seventeen-point list of the mercies that accompanied his death. This obsessive analysis of his father's internal state is accompanied by extensive extracts from the writings of English puritans that demonstrate, Edwards concluded in a fleeting moment of clarity, that his father died with an "Infallible Evidence" of grace. Anticipating, however, a lifelong battle with doubt, he recorded his tortuous quest for signs of his father's salvation. By rereading this account "from time to time even as Long as I Live," he could repeatedly renew the fading memory of assurance. This "Treasure" and "precious Remembrance" of a father who was not quite holy was a devotional guide for a son who could never feel sure enough.[50]

Predestinarian anxiety was one sign that the memory of Elizabeth Tuttle stubbornly endured, despite her son's painstaking efforts to forget this unpleasant reminder of the past. Other signs surfaced in surprising ways in Timothy Edwards's own domestic relations. Compounding his family's rapid rise in social status in the years after the divorce, he married in 1694 the daughter of Solomon Stoddard, the influential pastor of one of the most prestigious pulpits in the Connecticut River valley. The same year he belatedly received his degree from Harvard and accepted a ministerial post in the new village of East Windsor, conveniently located just north of his hometown of Hartford.[51] Over the course of his lengthy pastorate, Timothy and his wife, Esther, raised eleven children—one boy, Jonathan, and ten girls.[52] Haunted by the specter of a disobedient and distracted mother, Edwards could have acquired a deep-seated fear of female power. Defying these expectations, he governed his female-dominated household with a light hand.

Although women in colonial New England were commonly not as well educated as men, all of Timothy Edwards's children received equal attention in their father's schoolroom. Putting the girls through the same college preparatory course as their brother, he taught them Latin, mathematics, theology, and logic and sent them to finishing schools in Boston to perfect their learning. This elite education was empowering. Edwards's daughters became "women of highly cultivated intelligence, characteristically headstrong and assertive, who espoused views on gender and marriage roles" well ahead of their time. Praising the "Single Life" as preferable for women who "can make Religion and knowledge their chief end," they deferred marriage, forming families of their own five or six years on average later than their peers. The

Edwards girls were also notoriously choosy in their marriage partners. Perhaps because he knew all too well the troubling consequences of unhappy unions, Timothy refrained from controlling the courtship of his daughters and allowed them to choose mates based more on romantic love than on the traditional colonial pragmatism. Taking full advantage of her freedom, the eighth daughter, Hannah, left a trail of broken hearts and broken marriage contracts in her wake before settling down and marrying at age thirty-two.[53]

Such patriarchal permissiveness did not extend to Edwards's ecclesiastical family. Adopting the high definition of church office common among colonial ministers of his generation, he governed his flock with a heavy hand.[54] This autocratic leadership style created frequent conflicts with his congregation, which preferred a more democratic model of church governance. One common locus of conflict was marriage formation. When Edwards's niece Abigail Stoughton secretly married a man of "veri bad Carracter" named John Moore, her irate father petitioned the East Windsor church to intervene, but the congregation was unwilling to support an annulment. Edwards then took the case to the local ministerial association, which ruled that the couple had "Acted very sinfully" and "ought to make publick satisfaction." Moore, however, appealed to the Superior Court, the only legal body empowered to void the marriage, which overturned the ministers' ruling and judged the marriage valid.[55] Some years later when another young parishioner married without her parents' consent, Edwards again took an uncompromising position. He refused to baptize the couple's first child until its father had made a public confession of his "Scandalous Offence." This conflict dragged on for three years, during which time Edwards suspended communion, arguing that "the church in its divided state could not celebrate the love feast."[56]

These clandestine unions were opportunities for Edwards to defend not only his ministerial prerogatives but also a traditional concept of marriage in which filial desire was subordinate to parental will. For unhappily married couples, however, he had greater sympathy. During his pastorate an "epidemic" of divorces spread throughout the region of East Windsor. Most were uncontroversial cases of desertion and adultery, but Edwards became embroiled in a few protracted and ugly contests. After Hannah Thrall left her home, alleging spousal abuse, her husband countered with charges of desertion and adultery and appealed to his church to mediate the dispute. When the case was referred to a ministerial council, Edwards and his colleagues rejected the adultery charge as unproven and argued that the blame for Hannah's desertion lay with her spouse. Citing the English divine William Ames, they reasoned that "if a man by hard usage and cruel treatment drive his wife away from him . . . he is to be esteemed the Desertor."[57] Although cruelty was not a statutory ground for divorce in Connecticut, this expansion of the definition of desertion had precedent. Twenty years earlier, when Hannah Merriman had left her husband and returned to her parents' Windsor home, a supporter similarly cited Ames to argue that "if one party drives away the other with great fierceness and Cruelty . . . that very person plays the Deserter." Edwards and his ministerial colleagues likewise took this position, asserting in their ruling on the Merriman case that "if the deserted be the Cause of the desertion" then "he is to be accounted the deserter."[58] This interpretation may also have led Edwards to veto his niece Abigail's conviction on a "scandalous violation" of several of the Ten Commandments, when after more than a decade of marriage she separated from her husband, who had been confined in the house of correction as a "Dissolute and Idle Person."[59]

In these cases Edwards's reasoning paralleled that employed by his father during his long divorce contest. Although Richard Edwards had not explicitly petitioned for divorce on cruelty grounds, he had depicted his wife as an abusive spouse. He had even admitted having once left home to escape her mistreatment. Because "I could noe Longer Indure what I mett with from her," he confessed, "I tra[v]illed Abroad for Som Time Hopeing by my Absence that Shee might Relent and Turn from her perverseness." He had likewise argued that the desertion clause in the Connecticut divorce statute should encompass his wife's sexual refusal, thereby expanding the range of actionable behavior beyond physical absence from the home. By "Deserting my bed" she "Deserted mee," he had reasoned. Timothy Edwards and his ministerial colleagues applied a similar logic in both the Merriman and Thrall cases. Although in his father's divorce action the wife, not the husband, was the alleged deserter, this reversal of gender roles did not alter the reasoning. Husbands and wives could abandon their partners by, to use Richard Edwards's language, "Any Esencyall breach of the marage Bond."[60]

This debate over the meaning of desertion engaged a question central to the evolution of modern divorce law, the amount of spousal cruelty tolerable in a marriage. John Merriman's attorney argued that separation was justified only when the husband's abuses would cause a "reasonable woman" to be "afraid [for] her life."[61] Richard Edwards had tried this tactic, claiming that Elizabeth had threatened to kill him in his bed, and her sister's filicide gave his claim weight. Colonial authorities, however, had greater difficulty with nonlethal levels of abuse. The Superior Court rejected Hannah Merriman's claim that her husband's "frantick and raveing" actions caused her to fear for her life and was apparently unwilling to apply a lesser standard. The ecclesiastical council likewise identified her as the deserter, asserting that the "husband be not so to blame as may Justify a separation." This decision placed a heavy burden on future petitioners suing for divorce on cruelty grounds, and over the next eighty years the justices granted only one plea, brought by a woman whose husband had committed a triple homicide.[62]

Despite this chilling precedent, the pastors considering the Thrall separation appeared willing to lower the bar. They ruled that William's violence cleared Hannah of a "Scandalous Offense," even though it was not severe enough to threaten her life. In this case Timothy Edwards testified separately in support of Hannah's innocence.[63] Puritan divines since the beginning of the English Reformation had championed liberalizing divorce laws, but Edwards's support for this cause likely had a more personal motivation, rooted in a childhood spent in a troubled home. In his flourishing East Windsor household, however, the disorder that had fractured Edwards family life for almost a century had finally been left behind. By the third generation, memories had faded of the breakdown of Richard Edwards's marriage to Elizabeth Tuttle. Only a few small traces of this troubling legacy can be found in Jonathan Edwards's illustrious pastoral career.

On the occasions when Jonathan Edwards considered his ancestry, his grandfather's successful legal career and his father's lengthy pastorate likely obscured the family's humble colonial beginnings. Even more deeply buried were the messy facts of the divorce that had in so many ways secured the Edwardses' social ascendancy. When, therefore, he campaigned to regulate sex and marriage formation in his Northampton parish, his efforts were shaped more by the challenges of the present than the embarrassments of the past. In the mid–eighteenth century new gender constructs were forming that would, by the beginning of the next century, revolutionize domestic roles for both men and women. Of particular concern to Edwards was the emergence of a double standard regarding moral and sexual behavior. He defended the traditional single standard of virtue, which required chastity outside of marriage, public confession of sin, and equal punishment of offenders of both sexes.[64] This stance created frequent conflicts with his parishioners, who were increasingly adopting a more permissive attitude toward male sexual indiscretion. In policing the boundary separating licit from illicit sex, Edwards refused to let the boys in his congregation "just be boys."

One conflict clearly reveals the distance his family had traveled from the hasty union that had first set Richard Edwards and Elizabeth Tuttle on their collision course. When a young unmarried woman named Martha Root gave birth to twins in Edwards's parish, she was convicted of fornication and required to pay the customary fine. Elisha Hawley, the "reputed" father, did not appear in court; his family simply tidied up the mess by privately negotiating a financial settlement. Dissatisfied with this arrangement, Edwards tried to use the powers of his office to force the couple to marry. Citing the scripture rule requiring a man to wed a virgin whom he had "humbled," the church excommunicated Hawley for his persistent refusal to confess his sin and marry his illicit lover, the godly choice of responsible Christian men.[65] Eighty years earlier, Richard Edwards had, like most of his peers who found themselves in this compromising position, apparently made this godly choice. His grandson now looked back to that time as a golden age of virtuous manhood, having apparently forgotten—if he had ever known—the tragic consequences of that ill-conceived union.

A second marital dispute suggests that Edwards combined this campaign against male irresponsibility with a more liberal reading of colonial divorce law. When a woman named Eleanor Gray became entangled in a protracted divorce case, his family apparently championed her cause. Eleanor had fled her home and petitioned for divorce, charging her husband with both cruelty and adultery, and taken refuge in the Edwards household working as a servant.[66] This case occurred a decade after similar circumstances had forced Hannah Thrall to leave her husband, and Edwards was evidently familiar with the reasoning his father had used to justify that unhappy woman's desertion. In an entry in the *Blank Bible*, he defended the traditional grounds for divorce but expanded the definition of desertion to include other violations besides physical absence. When a husband makes it "utterly intolerable for [his wife] to live with him," he asserted in a brief commentary on Mt. 5:32, "as when she cannot live with him without apparent hazard of life, etc., she is at liberty." In this situation, as William Ames had reasoned, "Her husband departs from her."[67] The Gray case, however, focused not only on the meaning of desertion but also on a guilty husband's irresponsible behavior. After the Massachusetts governor and his Council had granted the couple a bed and board separation, Samuel Gray had refused to provide his wife the financial support that had been mandated by the magistrates. With the Edwards family's assistance, she petitioned them to enforce the maintenance order.[68]

Throughout his pastoral career, Jonathan Edwards combated changing gender roles that left women like Eleanor Gray to bear the consequences of male misbehavior. He struggled to uphold the image of the godly Christian man that had defined the puritan ideal of manliness. If he was aware of the patriarchal failures that had crippled his family in its early generations, little evidence remained of that legacy. Burdened by his past, Timothy Edwards was afflicted with anxious doubts about his father's eternal fate. Had Jonathan Edwards looked back, he likely would have seen an irresponsible young man reflected in his grandfather's image. Although he had married his pregnant lover, Richard Edwards had refused to take responsibility for his "reputed" child. Having strayed from his marriage bed, he divorced his difficult and emotionally troubled wife to marry a younger and more compliant mate. In his domestic life, Richard Edwards resembled more the new nineteenth-century man who used the rhetoric of liberty to justify his sexual freedom, than the traditional puritan patriarch. His grandson, however, was likely ignorant of much of this story. Two generations of refashioning and forgetting had lifted from him the burden of this conflicted past.

Casting this retrospective gaze upon Elizabeth Tuttle, Jonathan Edwards also would not have seen in his grandmother the exemplar of female piety that he so effectively promoted in his writings. His accounts of the heroic religious experiences of women like Abigail Hutchinson, who had met her premature and agonizing death "in a kind of beatific vision of God," foreshadowed the emerging "cult of true womanhood" that depicted women as naturally more virtuous than men.[69] According to this new gender role, women were called to be pious, pure, domestic, and submissive to their more licentious and worldly mates. Whether from perverse willfulness or mental illness, Elizabeth Tuttle had failed to embody these "cardinal virtues" of true womanhood.[70] No evidence suggests that she mismanaged her household or flouted the Christian faith, but she was disobedient to her husband, and this lack of submission made for a disorderly home.

The way Elizabeth Tuttle expressed her rebellion, however, did not comfortably fit this gender construct. Nineteenth-century images of femininity equated submission with chastity and represented female "passionlessness" as a virtue. "The belief that women lacked carnal motivation was the cornerstone of the argument for women's moral superiority," notes the historian Nancy Cott.[71] As the inversion of virtue, the rebellious woman had to be unchaste, driven by unnatural sexual desires to compromise her purity. The cult of true womanhood had no place for a wife who was both rebellious and passionless, as Elizabeth evidently became in the latter years of her marriage.

When, therefore, after generations of repression, memories of the Edwardses' messy divorce reemerged in the latter nineteenth century, her passionlessness had been erased. Freed of this awkward fact, the representation of Elizabeth Tuttle as an uncontrolled and promiscuous woman acquired an irresistible weight. The simple story of family failure, which Richard Edwards had only with difficulty convinced the Connecticut courts to accept, gained new life as leaders of the growing eugenics movement looked to their colonial past for evidence that "blood will tell."

BLOOD WILL TELL

The first published biography of Jonathan Edwards appeared in 1765, seven years after the theologian's death. Samuel Hopkins, who had trained for the ministry under Edwards, observed that he wrote the volume not so much as an "act of friendship for the dead, as of kindness to the living." Nevertheless, in a brief account of his mentor's forebears he fashions a respectable past for the man he describes as "one of the greatest—best—and most useful of men, that have lived in this age." Emphasizing the aristocratic elements of the family tree, he notes that Edwards's English progenitor was a London minister, whose wife had made a "ruff for the Queen." He also comments that William Edwards, the New England migrant, had made a respectable match to a woman whose brothers were mayors of English towns. His son, the first American-born Edwards, had also married well. According to Hopkins, the facts of Richard Edwards's domestic life were both ordinary and admirable:

> His first wife was Mrs. Elizabeth Tuttle, daughter of Mr. William Tuttle of New Haven in Connecticut, and Mrs. Elizabeth Tuttle his wife, who came out of Northamptonshire in England. His second wife was Mrs. Talcot, sister to Governor Talcot: by his first wife he had seven children, the oldest of which was the Reverend Mr. Timothy Edwards of Windsor. . . . By his second wife, Mrs. Talcot, he had six children.[1]

Because death—not divorce—was the most common reason for remarriage in colonial America, a reader of this note would clearly assume what is not explicitly stated, that Elizabeth Tuttle died prior to Richard Edwards's second marriage. It suggests that she was an unremarkable goodwife, who like many women of her time died at an early age and that her husband recovered from this loss in the ordinary way, by marrying another woman and starting his family over again. Whether Hopkins failed through ignorance or design to mention the divorce cannot now be known, but his silence ensured that the nineteenth century would inherit an unblemished record of Jonathan Edwards's past.

Sereno Edwards Dwight brought to completion the multigenerational reinvention of his colonial ancestor Richard Edwards. His monumental biography of Jonathan Edwards, published in 1829, includes an edition of Timothy Edwards's encomium on the life of his father that figured Richard Edwards as a "bright example of [C]hristian resignation and triumphant faith." This text is not, however, a simple abridgement of the original manuscript, which Dwight noted he had "before me, while writing," but a new and revised edition. The most significant omission from the text was its anxiety. He removed the son's obsessive search for signs of grace, leaving, in Dwight's words, "an accurate moral picture of the man, who moulded the character of the father" of Jonathan Edwards. Writing more than a hundred years after Richard Edwards's death, Dwight could not have noticed the gap between this image and the actual life it represented. Nor was he aware of Jonathan Edwards's troublesome grandmother. Echoing Hopkins, he makes the expected inference from the information available to him. Richard Edwards, he notes, first "married Elizabeth Tuthill," and had "seven children, the eldest of whom was the Rev. Timothy Edwards. *After her decease*, he married a Miss Talcot, of Hartford," with whom "he had six children."[2]

By the year of the publication of this biography, the scandalous first marriage of Jonathan Edwards's paternal grandparents had been so effectively forgotten that Richard Edwards could be depicted as the pious and respected patriarch of a distinguished colonial family. This story of the virtuous grandfather had been constructed by preceding generations who chose what memories to include and exclude in their family story. One person who had been forgotten over the years was Elizabeth Tuttle. Dwight's representation of Richard Edwards's first wife was empty of content, with the exception of two details that ensured the ordinariness of this apparently unremarkable woman's life. That Elizabeth gave birth to a succession of children suggested she dutifully fulfilled the role of wife and mother expected of all colonial women; that she apparently died in middle age provided an uncomplicated explanation for her husband's second marriage. Taken together, these commonplace events figured Elizabeth Tuttle as a grandmother suitable for a great theologian.

One hundred years after Dwight's volume, a new biography of Jonathan Edwards appeared. In *Jonathan Edwards: The Fiery Puritan*, published in 1930, Elizabeth Tuttle dramatically returns as the "skeleton in the family cupboard." Richard Edwards, Henry Bamford Parkes notes gleefully,

> had been inveigled into marriage by a rich and attractive New Haven girl, Elizabeth Tuttle, who within a few months gave birth to a child whose paternity her husband disowned; after twenty years of marriage she seems to have become insane, for her husband secured a divorce; one of her sisters committed infanticide; and one of her brothers was hanged for murdering another sister; Timothy Edwards was her second child.[3]

Unlike Dwight's empty placeholder, Parkes's description of this eminently unsuitable grandmother is full of content. In the intervening century, Elizabeth Tuttle acquired all the attributes of a rebellious woman. She is "rich and attractive" and uses her sexual charms to "inveigle" an unsuspecting man into marriage. Her uncontrolled sexuality is confirmed by the birth of an early baby of questionable paternity. And the inconvenient appearance of this child is emphasized by the added detail that "Timothy Edwards was her second child," not the eldest as stated by Hopkins and Dwight. After marriage, her unseemly behavior degenerates into actual insanity, a condition seemingly confirmed by her siblings' two homicides. For Richard Edwards to divorce such a wild, and perhaps dangerous, woman was a rational response to a continuing train of female abuse.

What happened to transform Dwight's innocuous grandmother into Parkes's menacing grandmother? The story of the construction of this new image over the course of the nineteenth century forms the sequel to our reconstruction of the breakdown of the Edwardses' marriage. Just as the memory of Richard Edwards's failed first marriage was slowly erased by subsequent generations, the awakening of this memory in the years following the publication of Dwight's biography took time. The fashioning of the figure of the crazy grandmother is a surprising byproduct of Jonathan Edwards's iconic status in nineteenth-century American culture. A clue to her origin is found in the curious conclusion to Parkes's account of the Edwards genealogy:

One of Jonathan's sisters was distinctly queer, and two of his nieces became confirmed opium-eaters; his own youngest son [Pierpont] was a clever and erratic Don Juan; and one of his grandsons was Aaron Burr. The cross between Puritan solidity and the morbid brilliance of the Tuttles seems to have caused all the ability of the Edwardses, a family dear to enthusiastic eugenicists.[4]

The claim that the Tuttles contributed a streak of hereditary deviance to the Edwards family tree originally developed, as Parkes suggests, during the eugenics movement. Eugenicists, who maintained that procreation control was the key to social betterment, regularly cited the Edwards family to support their claim that "blood will tell." This complex bloodline, however, contained not only an array of brilliant and accomplished men but also several disreputable descendants, including the notorious libertines Pierpont Edwards and Aaron Burr, Jonathan Edwards's "queer" sister, and her allegedly drug-addicted daughters.[5] A figure of Elizabeth Tuttle emphasizing uncontrolled sexuality and hereditary deviance was constructed to explain this conjunction of contradictory traits. This crazy grandmother became a standard feature of the modern Edwards myth.

The new image of Elizabeth Tuttle could not appear until the proper material foundation was in place. Colonial Connecticut legal records document the conflicted and tragic lives of our protagonists, but in the early nineteenth century these manuscripts were largely inaccessible to the public. New England colonists had no method of organizing and preserving the records they produced at such a prolific rate. Without centralized record repositories, birth notices, probate records, land titles, and legal papers were scattered throughout the region in private homes, courthouses, and churches. Records were lost, neglected, and destroyed by fire and ransacking British troops.[6] Following the Revolution, however, these piles of old papers were gradually transformed into valuable artifacts of the nation's origins and history. Reflecting this new relation to the past was a growing concern for the collection and preservation of colonial documents.

As early as 1744, the Connecticut General Assembly had directed its secretary "to sort, date and file in proper order, all the ancient papers that now lye in disorder and unfiled in his office." In 1770 the legislature acted to acquire all public documents remaining in private hands, noting that they "properly belong to the Colony, in whose custody soever the same may be found."[7] Despite this directive, Connecticut took many years to organize and publish its records. A turning point in our story occurred in 1841, when the Assembly appointed the Northampton antiquarian Sylvester Judd to organize its archives. Once completed, the Connecticut Archives comprised more than 40,000 documents dating from 1635 to 1820, bound and indexed in large folio volumes.[8] This collection made accessible for the first time a wealth of information about colonial Connecticut. By the mid–nineteenth century, interested antiquarians and genealogists could peruse these volumes looking for curious details of their ancestors' daily lives. With some effort, a diligent researcher might even discover the long-ago forgotten fact that in 1691 Richard Edwards had been granted a divorce from his first wife, Elizabeth. Rescuing these records from historical oblivion provided the material foundation for the recovery of this memory.

Another turning point occurred in 1851, when the Connecticut Assembly created a State Library Committee, which appointed a librarian "whose duty it shall be to take charge of the State Library, to arrange, catalogue and index the same." The early occupants of this post, James Hammond Trumbull and Charles J. Hoadly, presided over the preservation and development of the state's manuscript collection. Their most significant accomplishment was the publication of the *Public Records of the Colony of Connecticut*, a fifteen-volume collection that made available to the interested public the minutes of the state's colonial legislature.[9] Volume four, covering the years 1689 to 1706, contained the record of Richard Edwards's final divorce decree. After 1868, the date of the publication of this volume, a quick look through its index would easily have revealed this forgotten fact, but someone had to care enough to look. Without a cultural context that encouraged interest in the colonial past, no memories of Elizabeth Tuttle would return.

The collection and preservation of colonial-era manuscripts was one part of a larger nineteenth-century narrative tracing the development of a distinctive New England regional identity. Following the Revolution, as the historian Joseph Conforti has observed, the "old Puritan notion of a 'peculiar people'" was transformed into "an ethnic identity." This sense of "New Englandness" was based on a conviction that the region had a "common history and ancestry, which distinguished [it] from other parts of the Union."[10] Documents and other curious objects, like buildings and furniture, were the scaffolding upon which this common history was erected. Relics of a lost golden age, these artifacts connected Yankees with the heroic men and women who populated the imagined landscape of puritan New England.

Joseph Badger, *The Rev. Jonathan Edwards*, c. 1750, Yale University Gallery, Bequest of Eugene Edwards, 1938. Courtesy of Jonathan Edwards College.

Jonathan Edwards was one of the most useful and adaptable of these iconic colonial figures. The nineteenth-century appropriation of Edwards occurred in several phases, as successive generations of New Englanders deployed him "to serve new cultural needs." One familiar image, which animated seminary classrooms and doctrinal debates, emphasized the theologian's powerful intellect and relentless defense of orthodox doctrine. A second image stressing his personal piety and fiery preaching style gave religious leaders from diverse Protestant denominations a "useable past" for the emerging American evangelical tradition. More important, however, for our story of the recovery of Elizabeth Tuttle's memory was the "reinvention" of Edwards as "a de-Calvinized cultural icon" during the colonial revival period of the latter nineteenth century, when New England styles and themes predominated in art, architecture, and literature.[11] He became an "object of nostalgia and veneration," Conforti observes, representative of the traditional values that modern American society was rapidly losing through the forces of immigration and industrialization.[12] In contrast to the ethnic immigrants rapidly filling the squalid tenements of urban slums, Edwards embodied the manly, morally earnest, strenuous life that Victorians imagined their puritan ancestors had pursued in their orderly villages. "He represents the concentrated vitality and aggressiveness of the occidental peoples," judged A. V. G. Allen in his 1889 biography of Edwards, and "of the Anglo-Saxon race in particular, of which he was a consummate flower blossoming in the new world." As the last and greatest of the puritans, this figure of Edwards inspired the ancestor-worship of several generations of genealogically obsessed Yankees.[13]

Genealogy was the principal way many New Englanders made contact with their colonial pasts. Newly formed state library collections provided the information that descendants required to prove their aristocratic ancestry.[14] Dwight had little genealogical data beyond that provided by Hopkins. With the publication in 1856 of the first substantive genealogy of the Edwards family, some facts became newly available. Nathaniel Goodwin lists in his *Genealogical Notes* all of Elizabeth Tuttle's children, including her first (Mary), and the birth dates for each. But he perpetuates the erroneous claim that Elizabeth Tuttle's death freed her husband to marry a second time, as do several subsequent nineteenth-century family genealogies that appeared after information about the divorce decree became readily available in the Connecticut Archives and *Public Records*.[15] The 1883 Tuttle family genealogy, for example, fails to mention either the divorce or the murders and promotes a counter-image of Elizabeth Tuttle, emphasizing that she possessed the "nervous, sensitive and excitable temperament of genius." And the bicentennial genealogy of the Edwards family, issued in 1903, once again directly asserted that Richard Edwards remarried following his first wife's death.[16]

Dwight constructed in ignorance the myth of Jonathan Edwards's pious puritan ancestors, but its repetition was surely a conscious calculation. Some memories are, it appears, more difficult to recover than others. As the historian Michael Kammen observes, "[M]yths and traditions have their own resilience, not completely controllable."[17] The Edwards myth was perpetuated at national family gatherings, a popular Victorian pastime. The first Edwards family reunion, held in Stockbridge in 1870, established Jonathan Edwards's former mission post as a shrine to the "foremost pure intellect of his time."[18] Nearly 200 descendants visited the family home and saw the "room, and the very spot in it, where the great man sat when he penned" his famous treatises. Also on display was a collection of Edwards relics, including his wife's wedding dress and a "silver porringer" from which he ate "his simple meal of bread and milk."[19] In 1900, when Northampton organized a similar tribute to the colonial pastor's legacy, visiting pilgrims were able to stand upon the granite doorstep that had graced his parsonage; bask in the shade of a massive elm tree that, according to legend, had been planted by the divine himself; and view the unveiling of a large bronze bas relief of the town's most distinguished colonial resident. These commemorative activities were but a prelude to the more widespread celebrations that occurred throughout New England in 1903 on the bicentennial of the great theologian's birth. "Everywhere," Conforti concludes, "Edwards was hailed as a sacred Anglo-Puritan, and thus American, cultural icon."[20]

The men and women who flocked to these events admired the passion of their ancestor's revival rhetoric and the intellectual force of his doctrinal writings, but they preferred to dwell nostalgically on the curious details of his domestic life and pastoral labors. This tendency to idealize the daily lives of the puritans worked against the revelation of uncomfortable facts. "[S]urely," urged the bestselling author Alice Morse Earle, "they have no traits to shame us, to keep us from thrilling with pride at the drop of their blood which runs in our backsliding veins."[21] This filiopietistic approach was, however, challenged by the increasing accessibility of early manuscripts. Driven by an indiscriminate passion for collecting past facts, nineteenth-century antiquarians and local historians combed records for quaint habits and odd features of colonial life. Under such scrutiny, the crazy-grandmother story eventually emerged with the force of a long-repressed memory.

This image of our protagonist first appears in a local history of Timothy Edwards's East Windsor parish, published in 1883. In *Windsor Farmes: A Glimpse of an Old Parish,* the antiquarian's "unchecked license to retail facts" is on full display.[22] Its author, John A. Stoughton, aimed to fill "what may be called a gap in the history of the Edwards family." He had discovered a "large heap of papers" steadily deteriorating on the "garret floor" of a house "belonging to the Edwards estate." Astonished that Dwight had "overlooked so valuable a mass of material," Stoughton made extensive use of this treasure trove, boasting that "most of my quotations are from what are in the pure sense 'original records.'" And to display his devotion to recorded facts, he strung together with little apparent method or organization large extracts from letters, sermons, account books, the newly published *Connecticut Public Records,* and other relevant materials housed in the Connecticut State library.[23]

Through his research Stoughton discovered the divorce as well as several other incongruous features of Jonathan Edwards's family tree. To explain these anomalies he adopted a new image of Elizabeth Tuttle that combined uncontrolled sexuality with hereditary madness. "There can be no question," Stoughton asserted, "that this branch of the Tuttle family, from which Jonathan Edwards' grandmother came, was erratic to the degree of insanity." He cited as evidence of this hereditary taint not only the murders committed by the two Tuttle siblings but also the alleged opium addiction of Edwards's two nieces. That Elizabeth also inherited the "peculiarities of the Tuttle blood" was displayed, claimed Stoughton, by her uncontrolled sexuality. He noted her early baby but insisted, following the divorce petition, that her husband was "ignorant of her condition when he married her." Omitting her marital abstinence, he implied that she regularly strayed from the marriage bed. This alleged promiscuity reappeared in Jonathan Edwards's son Pierpont and in his grandson Aaron Burr, causing their "curious outbreaks of depravity." But it bypassed Elizabeth's more illustrious descendants, thereby preserving the purity of the Edwards family's male line. Timothy Edwards, Stoughton insisted, "seems to have inherited none of his mother's propensities." From his untainted bloodline, Jonathan Edwards acquired his genius; it was a "hereditary strength, bearing the paternal impress of an original, richly endowed, godly character."[24]

In this provocative account Stoughton displayed his passion for the facts, but he interpreted these facts through a cultural lens. As the historian David D. Hall observes, the "nineteenth-century effort to re-imagine a lost world gave us the Puritans not as they *really* were, but as a mixture of invention and fact interlaced with nineteenth-century values."[25] One value added to the reawakening memory of Elizabeth Tuttle was heredity. Stoughton's emphasis upon the transmission of the "peculiarities" of the Tuttle blood reflects the pervasive influence of hereditary explanations for disease, insanity, and moral degeneracy in nineteenth-century America. The eugenics movement transformed this interest in the lineages of individual persons and families into a powerful social reform program.[26] When, therefore, *Families of Ancient New Haven* appeared in 1922, its Tuttle genealogy included for the first time records of the divorce, the two murders, and several *non compos mentis* judgments. Like Stoughton, the author of this monumental genealogy, Donald Lines Jacobus, was motivated by a passion not only for the facts but also for heredity.[27]

Jacobus, who has been called the "founder" of the "modern American school of critical genealogists," advised family historians not to "worry about the deviations from rectitude of our remote ancestors." A "conscientious" genealogist, he chided, "will not even consider falsifying the facts as the records disclose them." But as a fellow traveler in the eugenics movement, he also encouraged the preparation of a "eugenicized type of genealogy" that included the "kind of data concerning physical and mental traits that the science of eugenics requires."[28] Eugenicists used genealogies to investigate inheritance patterns displayed by families of eminent men and to compile pedigree charts tracing the incidence of social pathology across multiple generations. Through this work hereditary deviance became a national obsession, and the figure of Elizabeth Tuttle became an American cultural icon.

Eugenics represents a generally unrecognized episode in the cultural appropriation of Jonathan Edwards. Eugenics had its origin in the work of Francis Galton, an amateur British naturalist, who coined the term and organized the movement in England.[29] Galton had, like biologists throughout the nineteenth century, only a rudimentary understanding of the laws of human heredity. Nevertheless, in his foundational work *Hereditary Genius*, published in 1869, he argued that "man's natural abilities are derived by inheritance, under exactly the same limitations as are the form and physical features of the whole organic world." Noting that animals had for centuries been bred for particular traits, he reasoned that human inheritance patterns must follow similar lines. To demonstrate this claim he collected hundreds of genealogies of judges, politicians, authors, musicians, scientists, clergymen, and, turning his attention from "brain" to "muscle," oarsmen and wrestlers. Analysis of this data led him to the two-part position that would define the eugenics movement throughout its history. From the observation that human ability "clings to certain families," he concluded that intellect, talent, and even moral character were hereditary traits. This theoretical claim had an important practical application. "[I]t would be quite practicable," he asserted, "to produce a highly-gifted race of men by judicious marriages during several consecutive generations." Just as horses could be bred to win races, the results of human reproduction were "largely, though indirectly, under our control."[30]

Galton's theories arrived in America during the colonial revival period and attracted many of the same constituents. Promoters of eugenics were "largely middle to upper middle class, white, Anglo-Saxon, predominantly Protestant, and educated."[31] Although the movement was active in all regions of the country, its strongest base of support was concentrated in Long Island, Connecticut, and New York City, among New Englanders who proudly displayed their puritan ancestry through membership in hereditary organizations.[32] Even the university geneticists and Progressive reformers who adopted a eugenic approach to social change were overwhelmingly "old stock" Americans.[33] The American eugenics movement easily, therefore, appropriated the cultural reverence for Jonathan Edwards and other iconic colonial figures, whose descendants seemed to demonstrate the value of cultivating superior or "aristogenic" traits. Accompanying this emphasis on "positive" eugenics, however, was a negative program whose aim was to prevent propagation by "cacogenic" or "unfit" families.[34]

Sensational studies of extended families of "hereditary degenerates" dominated the American eugenics movement from its outset. Robert L. Dugdale, a social reformer and member of the New York Prison Association, conducted the earliest and most influential of these studies. In 1874 he began investigating the kinship relations of prisoners in Ulster County jails, eventually compiling a genealogy involving seven generations and 540 individuals, all descended from five Revolutionary-era sisters. *The Jukes: A Study in Crime, Pauperism, Disease, and Heredity* detailed the high rate of criminality and poverty among the male members of this family, and the even higher rate of "harlotry" and "illegitimacy" in its female members.[35] To explain this clustering of dysfunctional behaviors, Dugdale cited both environmental and hereditary factors. Nevertheless, in subsequent years his study was repeatedly used to confirm the eugenic belief that "social deviance and hereditary biological degeneracy were inextricably linked together."[36] When Arthur H. Estabrook, a eugenics field worker, returned some forty years later to conduct a follow-up study of the "Jukes," his analysis of the data was more rigidly hereditarian, attributing, for example, such traits as "licentiousness" and "feeble-mindedness" to "defective germ plasm."[37]

The first of numerous similar studies of rural families, *The Jukes* was the prototype for the most influential body of literature of the American eugenics movement. These family studies, with such provocative titles as *The Tribe of Ishmael, The Smoky Pilgrims, The Zeros*, and *The Happy Hickories*, were filled with titillating narratives of sin, sex, and redemption, enacted by figures given such demeaning pseudonyms as "Margaret, the Mother of Criminals," the "Old Horror," and "Sam Sixty," sixty being the subject's I.Q. score.[38] These studies also made effective use of visual aids. Some included photographs that illustrated the "unmistakable look of the feeble-minded."[39] And most summarized their intricately detailed results in simple pedigree charts that mapped the relationships between "feeble-minded girls," their "licentious" and "syphilitic" partners, and their numerous offspring. These charts depicted in a visually striking format one of the movement's central claims: that a high incidence of a given trait across multiple generations proves that the trait is hereditary. Such graphic representations of the "feeble-minded menace" attracted many followers who had neither the time nor the training to read scientific literature, and they generated support for eugenics legislation mandating compulsory institutionalization or sterilization of those deemed unfit.

The Jukes, considered the "most influential American work on heredity during the nineteenth century," also provided the occasion for the movement's preeminent study of "hereditary ability."[40] In *Jukes-Edwards*, Albert E. Winship, a prominent author, editor, and educator, matched Dugdale's compelling argument for negative eugenics with an equally striking example of positive eugenics. Since the appearance of *The Jukes*, Winship noted, there has been a "call for a companion picture. Every preacher, orator, and editor who presented the story of the Jukes, with its abhorrent features, wanted the facts for a cheery, comforting, convincing contrast." According to Winship, who was himself a descendant of early colonial settlers, only the Edwards family had the reputation, intellect, and character such a companion portrait required.[41] Jonathan Edwards's iconic status in American culture made him a natural foil for the Jukes. In 1900, the year *Jukes-Edwards* appeared, the figure of Jonathan Edwards had reached the height of its cultural influence. He was memorialized in Northampton as the "only American intellect that deserves a place in the ranks of the world's great thinkers," and he was inducted into the American Hall of Fame, newly established at New York University "to stimulate patriotism and high endeavor." Three years later, the country celebrated not only the bicentennial of Edwards's birth but also the glorious birthright he had passed on to his numerous descendants.[42]

"Whatever the Jukes stand for, the Edwards family does not," Winship proclaimed. "Whatever weakness the Jukes represent finds its antidote in the Edwards family." After more than twenty years of notoriety, the Jukes image was well established in American culture. Prone to "idleness, ignorance, and vulgarity," this family had produced 1,200 descendants who tended "to disease and disgrace, to pauperism and crime." The image of Jonathan Edwards was equally well established. As the Jukes had passed to their posterity a legacy of degenerate habits, Edwards had bequeathed to his an "intellectual capacity and vigor, moral character, and devotion to training which have projected themselves through eight generations." To demonstrate this claim, Winship gathered data from a variety of genealogies, biographical dictionaries, and other reference works. From this data he complied detailed descriptions of the numerous accomplishments of a "family of more than 1,400 of the world's noblemen."[43]

Jukes-Edwards is filled with lists of the many college professors, ministers, lawyers, government officials, military officers, authors, and captains of industry who swelled the ranks of Jonathan Edwards's descendants. Various versions of this Edwards honor roll are ubiquitous in eugenics literature. One of the most frequently reproduced variants first appeared in Henry M. Boies's *The Science of Penology*, published the year following Winship's study. Among Jonathan Edwards's 1,400 descendants, Boies noted,

> 295 were college graduates; 13 presidents of our greatest colleges; 65 professors in colleges . . . ; 60 physicians, many of whom were eminent; 100 and more clergymen, missionaries, or theological professors; 75 were officers in the army and navy; 60 prominent authors and writers . . . ; 100 and more were lawyers, of whom 1 was our most eminent professor of law; 30 were judges; 80 had held public office, of whom 1 was vice-president of the United States; 3 were United States senators; Several were governors, members of Congress, framers of State constitutions, mayors of cities, and

ministers to foreign courts; . . . It is not known that any one of them was ever convicted of crime.⁴⁴

Statistics like these had weight. With the spread of numeracy in the nineteenth century, the systematic collection of quantifiable data was commonly recognized as a source of objective truth. "Counting was presumed to advance knowledge," the historian Patricia Cline Cohen asserts, "because knowledge was composed of facts and counting led to the most reliable and objective form of fact there was, the hard number." Such hard facts were also an effective agent of social change. Social reformers calculated the economic effects of slavery, the number of prostitutes in a given city, or the average yearly consumption of alcohol not simply to advance knowledge but to express concern. Armed with statistics, they rallied other distressed citizens to their cause.⁴⁵

Eugenicists, who saw themselves as implementing a scientific program of social reform, understood the power of numbers both to reveal truth and to effect change. Paired with equally impressive tabulations of the immoralities and crimes of the Jukes and other cacogenic families, lists enumerating the Edwards family accomplishments were among the movement's most effective forms of propaganda. Reduced to a parade of statistics, these twin pedigree studies acquired a force only numbers could provide. And although the studies of cacogenic families multiplied, the Edwardses almost single-handedly carried the movement's positive message. Other distinguished American bloodlines, like the Adamses' and the Lees', were at times cited, but the Edwards family was consistently deployed as the paradigmatic example of eugenic mating. Their achievements, noted one biologist, "show unmistakably that 'blood counts' in human inheritance"; another concluded that "no other family has contributed more to the national welfare than has this."⁴⁶ Grounded in hard fact and figures, the conclusion that the Edwards family embodied a hereditary elite appeared inescapable.

As the eugenics movement grew in the early decades of the twentieth century, the contrast between the Jukes and the Edwardses permeated American culture. Winship regularly delivered a "highly appreciated" lecture, entitled "Rascals and Saints," summarizing the argument of *Jukes-Edwards*, and published the entire text in serial form in the *Journal of Education*.⁴⁷ Educators eagerly promoted his findings, which became a common topic of study in American classrooms. Of forty-one high school biology texts published between 1914 and 1948, almost 55 percent cited the Edwards family to demonstrate that "good inheritance" is an "important factor in the production of a stronger race."[48] Students in college and university eugenics courses also learned from their texts of the accomplishments of that "old Puritan strain which is one of the familiar examples of eugenics."[49] The Edwards honor roll likewise appeared in such periodicals as *Scientific American, Popular Science Monthly,* and *The World's Work.* Even the eleventh edition of the *Encyclopaedia Britannica* included in a footnote to its entry on Jonathan Edwards an abbreviated list of the "great, brilliant and versatile men" descended from the puritan theologian.[50]

The record of the Edwards family accomplishments also reached a more popular audience. Albert E. Wiggam, who spread the eugenics gospel in frequent appearances on the Chautauqua lecture circuit, used as the frontispiece for his best selling book *Fruit of the Family Tree* a pedigree chart listing a "few of the best known" of the Edwards descendants and cataloged in its opening chapter the family's achievements to illustrate the maxim "Good blood is more precious than rubies."[51] An article appearing in *Good Housekeeping* in 1922 cited this record to convince its readers that "our first duty is to provide future generations with respectable, healthy, normal, and industrious parents."[52] In the same year, the notorious racist Lothrop Stoddard used these statistics to promote the creation of an "ever-perfecting super race."[53] And the minister who placed first in the 1926 eugenics sermon contest quoted the same statistics in his prize-winning sermon to persuade his congregants that "germ plasm" is, paraphrasing Rev. 22:1, a "River of Life from out the Throne of God." When families competed in the "fitter families" contests that the American Eugenics Society promoted at Midwestern state fairs, the Edwards family was well established as the standard example of positive eugenics.[54]

Elizabeth Tuttle originally had no place in the Edwards honor roll. In his brief account of Jonathan Edwards's forebears, Winship described the theologian's paternal grandparents as "ideal American Christian educated persons," despite readily available evidence to the contrary.[55] The figure of Elizabeth Tuttle was first introduced to eugenics enthusiasts by Charles Benedict Davenport, the Harvard-trained biologist who transformed Galton's theory into an American crusade. Davenport was born into an old Connecticut family of aristocratic puritan lineage. His father had compiled two extensive Davenport family genealogies that traced the family's American roots back

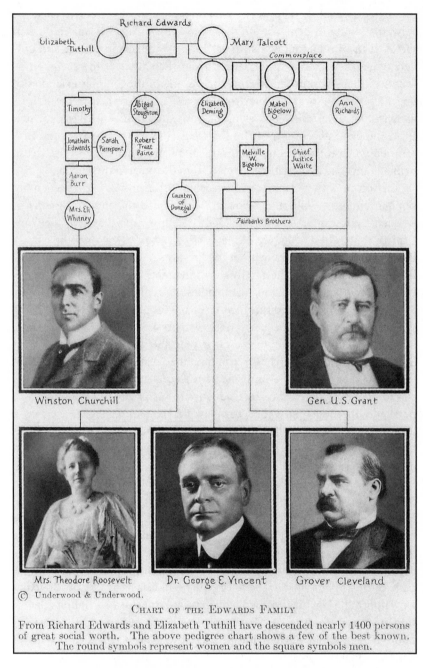

Richard Edwards

Elizabeth Tuthill · Mary Talcott

Commonplace

Timothy · Abigail Stoughton · Elizabeth Deming · Mabel Bigelow · Ann Richards

Jonathan Edwards · Sarah Pierrepont · Robert Treat Paine

Melville W. Bigelow · Chief Justice Waite

Aaron Burr

Countess of Donegal

Mrs. Eli Whitney

Fairbanks Brothers

Winston Churchill

Gen. U.S. Grant

Mrs. Theodore Roosevelt

Dr. George E. Vincent

Grover Cleveland

© Underwood & Underwood.

CHART OF THE EDWARDS FAMILY

From Richard Edwards and Elizabeth Tuthill have descended nearly 1400 persons of great social worth. The above pedigree chart shows a few of the best known. The round symbols represent women and the square symbols men.

Frontispiece to *Fruit of the Family Tree*, by Albert E. Wiggam (Bobbs-Merrill, 1924).

to the Reverend John Davenport, the pastor of the New Haven church in which Elizabeth Tuttle had worshiped as a child.[56] Charles Davenport inherited his father's passion for the family's colonial ancestors and imported into his scientific research the conviction that the roots of New England's regional superiority lay in its puritan past. Eugenics transformed this nostalgic appropriation of the past into a scientific program of social reform, grounded in the work of such pioneering biologists as Charles Darwin and Gregor Mendel. It provided a genetic foundation for the ancestor-worship common during the colonial revival and a scientific rationale for the general obsession with genealogy.

Davenport opened the Eugenics Record Office in 1910 in Cold Spring Harbor on Long Island. This office rapidly grew into the organizational center of the American eugenics movement. Believing that the "study of genealogy, under the stimulus of our modern insight into heredity, is destined to become the most important handmaid of eugenics," Davenport viewed the pedigree study as the movement's chief investigative tool. He and his colleagues trained many eugenics field workers, who combed backwoods areas to compile pedigrees of "feeble-minded" families.[57] They also distributed to thousands of individuals instructions for making a "Eugenical Family Study," a genealogical chart on which was "record[ed] as complete a picture as possible of the physical, mental, and temperamental constitution of as many as possible of the individuals charted."[58] Once coded and cross-listed according to an intricate cataloging system, these family studies became the foundation for Davenport's most influential publication, *Heredity in Relation to Eugenics*, which appeared in 1911.

In the pages of *Heredity in Relation to Eugenics,* considered the period's most important text on human genetics, thousands of Americans encountered a detailed construction of the figure of Elizabeth Tuttle.[59] Her appearance was a direct result of Davenport's methodology. He claimed that through extensive genealogical research the genesis of a particular trait could be traced not only to a specific region of the country but also to a specific individual who had migrated to that region at a particular time. He identified, for example, a couple who had lived in Milford, New Hampshire, as the progenitors of a family showing a high incidence of musical ability, and some early settlers of Windsor, Connecticut, as the source of their descendants' talent for the mechanical arts.[60] Davenport applied this same method to the Edwards family, noted for its extraordinary collection of eminent men. Searching for a source of this genius, he constructed the movement's most elaborate figure of Elizabeth Tuttle.

Davenport's Elizabeth illustrated the complexity of human heredity. First, she explained the Edwards family's aristogenic traits. Beginning with her physical appearance, he asserted that she was a "woman of great beauty, of tall and commanding appearance, striking carriage." Her husband was likewise "very tall and as they both walked the Hartford streets their appearance invited the eyes and admiration of all."[61] He arrived at this groundless description by employing the primitive hereditarian assumption that like begets like. Jonathan Edwards's more than six-foot frame was considerably above the height of the average eighteenth-century man, and the height and beauty of his ten sisters was legendary.[62] Employing the *post hoc, ergo propter hoc* reasoning common among eugenicists, Davenport constructed a matching description of their grandmother's physical appearance.

The "germ plasm of this wonderful woman" was also, claimed Davenport, the source of her descendants' intellectual accomplishments. The Edwards honor roll illustrated for him the multigenerational transmission of a trait predisposing its bearer to eminent accomplishment in multiple fields. Searching for the source of this trait in Jonathan Edwards's ancestors, he identified Elizabeth Tuttle as its earliest-known progenitor. She was a woman "of strong will, extreme intellectual vigor, of mental grasp akin to rapacity," Davenport noted. She transmitted to her grandson these "remarkable qualities," and from her germ plasm "have arisen statesmen, college presidents, men of science, great philanthropists from New England to California in extraordinary numbers." Further evidence of this "eminence" trait appeared in the descendants of Elizabeth Tuttle's daughters, for their lines also contained an abundance of accomplished men, including a signer of the Declaration of Independence, a chief justice of the United States, two presidents, and a vice president. "[H]ad Elizabeth Tuttle not been," Davenport extravagantly concluded, "this nation would not occupy the position in culture and learning that it now does."[63]

Complicating this positive portrait, Davenport's Elizabeth further explained the Edwards family's cacogenic behaviors. She carried an "evil trait" in her blood, Davenport judged, that predisposed its bearer to impulsive and violent acts. Because of this trait Elizabeth "evinced an extraordinary deficiency of moral sense." She was an "extraordinarily talented but erotic woman" whose "adultery and other immoralities" destroyed her family. This alleged moral deficiency explained how the puritan icon Jonathan

Edwards could have produced two such notorious libertines as Pierpont Edwards and Aaron Burr. Both these men had inherited from their fore-mother a "lack of control of the sex-impulse," in combination "with imagination and other talents." At least two of her siblings also carried this evil trait, "for one of her sisters murdered her own son and a brother murdered his own sister."[64] Several of Davenport's disciples searched for reappearances of this violent tendency in Elizabeth's descendants. Jacobus, for example, found the story of a nineteenth-century Tuttle named Thirza "specially remarkable," for she murdered her husband with an axe after a quarrel.[65] Evidently, poor Thirza inherited not only her ancestors' homicidal genes but also their choice of weapon.

According to Davenport, both "the good and the evil of Elizabeth Tuttle's blood" reappeared in subsequent generations of her descendants.[66] This complex heredity was, however, insufficient to identify her as the source of the Edwards honor roll. Elizabeth's real explanatory power lay in her position as a member of what Davenport called a "half-fraternity" or "double mating." In a double mating, two lines of descent trace their ancestry back to one man, who had produced two sets of offspring with two different sexual partners. The resulting bifurcated lineage appeared to eugenicists to function as a "controlled experiment." Because "economic and other environmental conditions are as similar as possible," Davenport reasoned, the "difference in the progeny is therefore the more readily ascribed to the difference in blood."[67]

The most influential of these duplex family studies was *The Kallikak Family*, whose fictitious name was a compound of the Greek words for "good" and "bad."[68] Martin Kallikak, the family progenitor, began this half-fraternity when he "step[ped] aside from the paths of rectitude" with a "nameless feeble-minded girl" whom he had met at a tavern while serving in the colonial militia. In this "unguarded moment" was born, the study's author, Henry Goddard, asserts, a "line of mental defectives that is truly appalling." Martin Kallikak's second mating, however, demonstrated that the "bad blood" was transmitted through the mother and not the father. When he married a "respectable girl of good family," the union produced offspring of a "radically different character." This line of descent is "our norm, our standard, our demonstration of what the Kallikak blood is when kept pure," Goddard observed. It proved that the first line's hereditary taint came from the "defective mentality" of the "feeble-minded girl."[69]

Jukes-Edwards did not trace a bifurcated lineage. In this study, as the author of *The Kallikak Family* noted, the "two families were utterly independent, of different ancestral stock, reared in different communities, even in different States, and under utterly different environment." This genetically unrelated comparison, therefore, presents "no sound basis for argument." Tuttle-Edwards, however, constituted just such a double mating praised by Goddard as a "natural experiment" in heredity.[70] In this pairing, Richard Edwards was the constant and his two wives, Elizabeth Tuttle and Mary Talcott, were the variables. Davenport constructed these two women with starkly contrasting characters. Unlike Elizabeth's "tall and commanding appearance," Mary was a "mediocre woman, average in talent and character and ordinary in appearance." In a striking departure from the gender roles common in Victorian America, he praised for her beauty and intellect the woman whose impulsive sexuality apparently destroyed her family and condemned as dull and plain the woman who dutifully fulfilled her role as a wife and mother. But what really condemned Mary Talcott was her offspring. "None of [her] progeny rose above mediocrity," Davenport reported, "and their descendants gained no lasting reputation."[71] As the control group in this duplex family study, her line of descent revealed the ordinariness of Richard Edwards's blood when unmixed with the germ plasm of genius.

Charles Davenport transformed Elizabeth Tuttle into a mother of genius. He elevated this obscure puritan woman, whose life had for many years been forgotten by her descendants, to the exalted position of matriarch of America's first family of genetic aristocrats. But, paradoxically, this noble figure was also tainted by a deficient moral sense that cropped up erratically in her relations and offspring. Few of Davenport's followers could hold together this construction of seemingly contradictory traits. For example, Albert Wiggam, one of the most important popularizers of the eugenics gospel, portrayed Elizabeth as a morally pure woman having no negative traits. In *Fruit of the Family Tree*, he declared that she was a "marvelous girl," whose descendants have "all left their mark upon American blood." He catalogued the accomplishments of these descendants and reported that many proudly wore a "gold badge known as 'The Tuthill Emblem'" in recognition of the "Blood of Greatness" that coursed through their veins. He ignored, however, the "evil trait" that Davenport believed tainted the Tuttle blood and implied, as had earlier Edwards biographers, that death, not divorce, occasioned Richard Edwards's remarriage to an "ordinary, every-day, commonplace woman" named Mary Talcott. Tales of murder, adultery, and divorce unnecessarily complicated the simple claim Wiggam aimed to communicate to his readers, that "from dogs to kings, from rats to college presidents, blood always tells."[72]

Wiggam, like most members of the eugenics movement, was an active promoter of the cult of true womanhood. In eugenics literature the virtuous woman was consistently depicted as the pious and pure guardian of the domestic sphere, but in addition to her duties as wife and mother she also had new eugenic responsibilities. One of these responsibilities was sex. A genetically superior woman who postponed or eschewed marriage by going to college and pursuing a career was an agent of "race suicide."[73] By choosing domesticity and reproduction, she fulfilled her "God-given" role as an agent of race betterment and "usher[ed] in a new era" by producing with her eugenically fit mate numerous genetically superior children.[74] Wiggam's Elizabeth was a woman of true eugenic virtue. She was a model mother who through judicious mating passed on her superior traits to a noble line of descendants. The moral deficiency identified by Davenport complicated this simple construction. By stripping Elizabeth of her negative traits, Wiggam assured her status as a member of the hereditary elite and clearly distinguished her from the threatening figure of the unchaste woman.

The unchaste woman was the eugenics movement's chief villain. Her uncontrolled sexuality not only corrupted the moral sanctuary of the home; it was the chief "dysgenic threat" facing the nation. To identify this threat, eugenicists employed the I.Q. test, which had been developed by a French psychologist in the early 1900s. Women with scores of "high-grade moron" were considered especially dangerous, for their good looks and charm allowed them to pass as "normal" and to attract mates unaware of their inferior intellects. An equally important and more common means of identifying this menace was sexual history. A female high-grade moron, eugenicists claimed, clearly displayed her hidden genetic deficiency by her "uncontrolled sexual instincts."[75] Because the "moron" category "linked mental deficiency with moral deficiency," every woman who engaged in sex outside of marriage was at risk of being classified as feeble-minded. Even a woman who tested normally could be labeled a moron and identified as a candidate for segregation or sterilization if she had given birth outside of marriage. "Moral deficiency alone—popularly and professionally accepted as proof of mental deficiency—was evidence enough of the need to institutionalize."[76]

Davenport's Elizabeth had all the traits of the female high-grade moron. Although he cast her as the heroine of the Edwards family romance, she more closely resembled the villain of the cacogenic family tragedies. Allegations of fornication, adultery, and homewrecking compromised her representation as a eugenically fit mother. The clustering of violent criminal offenses among her siblings further suggested a pattern of genetic depravity not unlike that found among the children of Ada Jukes or Martin Kallikak's nameless feeble-minded girl. Recognizing this apparent inconsistency, Wiggam omitted the incidents that compromised the reputation of his "marvelous girl." Critics of the eugenics movement delighted in revealing Wiggam's omission and seized upon the ambiguity of Davenport's Elizabeth to expose weaknesses in the movement's legislative agenda. Constructed as a woman whose penchant for casual sex revealed her hereditary insanity, the critics' Elizabeth functioned as an effective tool of opposition. This menacing figure became the most durable image of Elizabeth Tuttle.

The eugenics movement's principal legislative accomplishment was the widespread implementation of state regulations restricting reproduction of the "unfit."[77] "By 1890 the policy of lifetime segregation of feeble-minded women was widely accepted by officials," and states were turning their attention to less expensive approaches, such as marriage restriction and compulsory-sterilization laws. Connecticut enacted in 1895 the first marriage restriction law, which stipulated that any "epileptic, imbecile or feeble-minded" person who got married was subject to three years' imprisonment. By 1913 twenty-four states had passed similar laws. Indiana enacted in 1907 a statute mandating the compulsory sterilization of "confirmed criminals, idiots, imbeciles and rapists" confined in state institutions, and in 1927 the U.S. Supreme Court affirmed the constitutionality of sterilization laws in *Buck v. Bell*. By 1941 more than 38,000 institutionalized persons had been sterilized, the majority of them women.[78]

Advances in genetics placed in question the theoretical structure supporting this legislative program. The distinction between genotype and phenotype, the discovery that most traits have a polygenetic foundation that develops through a complex interaction between heredity and environment, and the demonstration that feeble-mindedness itself was not a heritable trait determined by a single gene led many geneticists to criticize both the effectiveness and the legitimacy of eugenic legislation.[79] But these theoretical developments were alone insufficient to discredit the movement, which had always depended as much on effective propaganda as on sound science to promote its claims. To counter the salacious stories and weighty statistics imbedded in eugenic family studies, critics employed alternate narratives, which revealed through wit and satire the limits of the movement's basic assumption that like begets like. Given the prominence of the Edwards family pedigree in eugenics literature, no story was as effective as that of Jonathan Edwards's crazy grandmother. As a consequence, this image of Elizabeth Tuttle emerged as a "staple" of anti-eugenics rhetoric.[80]

Critics of eugenic legislation deployed Elizabeth Tuttle as a trickster figure, who disrupted conventional thinking by her unexpected and even comic interventions. When the president of the New York Prison Association wrote in November 1909 to the *New York Times* to promote the state legislature's passage of a sterilization statute, he cited the Jukes-Edwards statistics to support his position. Several days later a rebuttal appeared that recounted the crimes of the Tuttle family and the unsavory details of Richard Edwards's divorce. "Had the penologists and criminologists of our day been in power then," this critic noted, obviously relishing the irony, "Elizabeth Tuttle could not have escaped them, so as to become, as she did, the ancestress of more genius and virtue than any other woman in the history of this country."[81] In response to the passage of Connecticut's sterilization statute later the same year, this same critic also sent an extended record of the "family history of Elizabeth Tuttle," transcribed from "original manuscript documents now on file in the State Library," to the vice president of the Connecticut Board of Prisons, suggesting that he read it "[b]efore the cutting begins."[82]

The ironic deployment of the figure of Elizabeth Tuttle by this sterilization opponent is representative of her role in anti-eugenics literature. The critics' Elizabeth was a woman who, despite her moral and mental deficiencies, gave birth to a superior line of offspring. Only this construction could expose the movement's arbitrary judgment, and as criticism grew, her appearances became more frequent. In the conclusion of his widely distributed genetics textbook, the biologist Herbert E. Walter told the story of Elizabeth Tuttle to illustrate a principal difficulty of eugenic reform, that there is no one "who is qualified to sit in judgment and separate the fit from the unfit."[83] The British author John Langdon-Davies made a similar point in a more playful manner by constructing an imaginary dialogue between Elizabeth Tuttle and Albert Wiggam, who assumed the role of the "Grand Inquisitor" leading the "Eugenic Inquisition" in colonial Connecticut. Young Elizabeth appears before the Inquisition to obtain a marriage certificate granting her permission to marry Richard Edwards. After questioning her about the Tuttle family's crimes, the inquisitor judges it a "case of manifest hereditary taint and probably dominant in the Mendelian sense." Accordingly, he rules that "the marriage cannot be allowed," much to the delight of the devil, who has been observing the questioning. "Thank heaven for eugenics," Satan snickers. "That saves me from the awful spectacle of a family with 12 college presidents, 265 college graduates, 100 clergymen. . . ."[84]

Figured as the victim of an imagined eugenic inquisition, Elizabeth Tuttle exposed the abuse of power that resulted when scientific ignorance and class prejudice conspired to judge "whose children will be great and whose will be worthless." She personified the misguided aims and potentially tragic consequences of eugenic legislation. "[I]t would have been a great eugenic mistake to have deprived the world of Elizabeth Tuttle's germplasm," Walter concluded, suggesting that the movement's policies would have resulted in this grave error.[85] "So, if eugenists had been in control three hundred years ago," the author Harvey Wickham similarly observed, "Mary Talcott would have been allowed to marry. But Elizabeth Tuttle would have been refused a marriage license even had she escaped a worse fate." Wickham contrasted Mary Talcott with Elizabeth Tuttle to suggest the magnitude of this misjudgment, which would have "inadvertently prevented each and every one of [the Edwards] notables from coming into being."[86]

Critics regularly constructed possible worlds in which apparently unfit mothers were kept from reproducing to reveal flaws in the eugenic paradise imagined by their opponents. A British critic observed that sterilization laws would have stopped Queen Victoria from having children, for she was "heterozygous for hæmophilia." According to Langdon-Davies, "[H]istory is packed with examples where eugenic interference would have impoverished the world beyond repair." The biologist Raymond Pearl even quantified the potential calamity, estimating that "95 percent of the greatest philosophers, poets and scientific men that have actually appeared during the history of our race would never have been born" had eugenics policies been in force.[87] Of all the imagined worlds created by these absent geniuses, however, the one in which Elizabeth Tuttle is judged unfit for procreation represented the most palpable loss.

In his satirical essay "The Edwardses and the Jukeses," Clarence Darrow similarly deployed Elizabeth Tuttle like a rabbit pulled with great dramatic effect out of the Edwards family hat. Like other critics of the eugenics movement, he began by using Elizabeth Tuttle to discredit the image of the eugenically fit mother. Having "discovered that Jonathan Edwards had ancestors," Darrow made another discovery, that Edwards's grandmother had a heredity moral deficiency that should have disqualified her from motherhood. Given the chance, Darrow speculated, eugenicists would have "united in the opinion that the [Edwards] line should have ended before it began." However, Darrow moved beyond this standard critique to question whether the inheritors of Elizabeth Tuttle's "precious germ plasm" were truly illustrious. We should not assume, he cautioned, that "all the twigs on this family tree are free from worm-holes." Of the 40,000 people he estimated had descended from Elizabeth Tuttle, only "something over 600" appear eminent, a percentage too small to be significant. "Genius cannot be proven," Darrow quipped, "by lumping together 265 college graduates." To Darrow, even the star member of the Edwards honor roll is unworthy of his illustrious reputation. Jonathan Edwards was a "Fundamentalist, stern and unyielding," he judged. "Except for his weird and horrible theology, he would have filled no place in American life." By labeling Edwards a "Fundamentalist" in an essay that was published in the *American Mercury* only three months after the lawyer's dramatic appearance in the Scopes trial, Darrow linked this puritan icon to William Jennings Bryan, the anti-evolution crusader. Surely this association only increased his astonishment that "anybody of this generation or any other should *want* to be traced to Jonathan Edwards."[88]

Clarence Darrow represented one voice in a diverse coalition of critics of the eugenics movement that formed during the interwar years. Well before the Nazi program of racial purification had discredited the imagined utopia of eugenics enthusiasts, Roman Catholics had organized to oppose sterilization laws, conservative Protestants had condemned the secular perfectionism of modern science, and psychologists had challenged the reliability of intelligence testing. With Charles Davenport's retirement and the closing of the Eugenics Record Office, a new generation of "reform eugenicists" emerged who were not as rigidly hereditarian as their predecessors. The study of heredity also advanced. Geneticists continued to compile pedigree studies of rare traits, but they increasingly relied on breeding experiments that were subject to laboratory control.[89] The new scientific literature, which focused more on peas and fruit flies and less on the "feeble-minded menace" and the declining birthrate of "old stock" Americans, rarely had occasion to mention the Jukes, the Kallikaks, or Jonathan Edwards. The line of illustrious descendants that Elizabeth Tuttle had bequeathed to the nation lost its scientific significance.

The conflicting images of Elizabeth Tuttle that had formed during the eugenics movement did not, however, fade into obscurity when the context that had produced them disappeared. The mad and immoral Elizabeth reappeared in a new context, as modern biographers imported her into their studies of Jonathan Edwards. Dwight's biography of Edwards, published in 1829, had contained a sanitized account of the theologian's ancestry. A century later, Parkes dramatically deployed the crazy-grandmother story in the opening pages of *The Fiery Puritan*, because her alleged immoralities and unsavory family connections effectively advanced his anti-puritan agenda. During the intervening years, the Edwards genealogy had been refashioned as a pedigree study illustrating the heritability of a variety of traits, including genius, madness, and licentiousness, and a menacing figure of Elizabeth Tuttle had become a common feature of American popular culture. With Parkes, this crazy-grandmother story entered the modern literature on Edwards.

Ola Elizabeth Winslow's Pulitzer Prize–winning biography of the puritan theologian was published in 1940, a decade after *The Fiery Puritan*. The first Edwards biographer to employ the methods of a social historian, Winslow conducted extensive primary source research into Edwards's ancestry. She traced his line of descent back to his first identifiable English progenitor and documented the lives of the first generation of Edwards and Tuttle settlers using the extensive collection of colonial materials housed at the Connecticut State Library. She was also the first biographer to consult the original sources documenting Richard Edwards's divorce. Nevertheless, this research did not produce a substantially new figure of Elizabeth Tuttle. Winslow's Elizabeth was a woman both unfaithful and insane. Her early baby revealed that she was "not of sound mind" when she married Richard Edwards. Her "periodic repetitions of infidelity" and "perversity" demonstrated that her insanity persisted throughout their marriage. The homicidal acts of "other members of her immediate generation" confirmed that this insanity was hereditary. Through her children, the "taint of insanity entered the Edwards inheritance," and this "erratic strain persisted" for several generations, cropping up in such likely suspects as Pierpont Edwards, Aaron Burr, and the two "opium-eating" nieces.[90]

Winslow appears to have gleaned these details from primary source documents, but she found in the colonial records only the story of Jonathan Edwards's crazy grandmother constructed by John A. Stoughton and deployed so effectively by critics of the eugenics movement. The original divorce petitions indicate that Elizabeth had refused to have sex with her husband for many years, but Winslow's explanation for the breakdown of the marriage omits this fact, saying only that her "folly" caused her husband to petition for divorce.[91] Absence of desire is a much more complicated explanation than uncontrolled desire. While the latter compromised only Elizabeth's morality, the former suggested that Richard's own passions drove him to seek a divorce. Winslow likely knew of his entanglement with Mary Talcott, for the record of his second wife's fornication conviction, which implicated Edwards, had appeared in print five years prior to the publication of her biography.[92] With neither his first nor his second wife had Richard maintained the puritan ideal of chastity before marriage. Nevertheless, Winslow indicted only Elizabeth for her alleged uncontrolled sexuality. This unchaste Elizabeth was made even more menacing by Winslow's adoption of one of the eugenics movement's central claims, that a woman who engages in extramarital sex must suffer from mental deficiency or insanity. And she substantiated the view that Elizabeth's insanity was hereditary by citing the criminal acts of her siblings and the peculiar and illicit behaviors of her descendants. This image offered nothing but the old crazy grandmother story dressed in a new historical guise.

In the context of Winslow's biography, however, this familiar construct does have a new explanatory function. It not only supplied a convenient cause for the divorce that secured Richard Edwards's innocence, but it also enhanced his integrity by linking him to his famous grandson. Throughout this difficult domestic trial Richard Edwards displayed, Winslow asserted, "the same sense of inexorable justice, the same ability to detach himself from that which concerned him intimately, and the same unassailable dignity" that guided Jonathan Edwards through his own contentious "divorce"—that is, the theological dispute that forced him to resign from his Northampton pastorate. Instead of forgetting the messy termination of Richard Edwards's first marriage, Winslow found in its memory confirmation of Jonathan Edwards's reputation as a great man. "In many such ways, he seems more the son of Richard Edwards," she mused, "than of his own father."[93]

Although no subsequent biographer has attempted to duplicate Winslow's primary source documentation of the divorce, all have without exception appropriated her construction of Elizabeth Tuttle. Even though Perry Miller in his magisterial biography of Jonathan Edwards focused upon the "drama" of the theologian's ideas, he noted in the "external biography" which framed his intellectual analysis that Elizabeth Tuttle "proved, by the most charitable account, to be of unsound mind" and implied that Richard Edwards divorced her because she had a child by another man. Reflecting the evangelical appropriation of Jonathan Edwards in the late twentieth century, Iain Murray's biography portrays Elizabeth Tuttle's repeated infidelities, which were "combined with evidence of insanity," as a trial of faith that God sent to her husband to keep him "in a faithful, watchful, humble, and praying frame." And in George Marsden's recent work, which he describes as the only "full critical biography" of Edwards since Winslow's, the familiar image of Elizabeth Tuttle appears with little modification. According to Marsden, Jonathan Edwards's "grandmother was an incorrigible profligate" who was a "scandal and disgrace" to the family. She was "afflicted with a serious psychosis," whose symptoms included "repeated infidelities," "fits of perversity," "rages, and threats of violence." In contrast, Richard Edwards is depicted as the patient and long-suffering spouse who tolerated his wife's peculiarities until her behavior became "so erratic" that he was forced to sue for divorce. Although Marsden does not explicitly state that Elizabeth's "psychosis" was hereditary, he perpetuates this interpretation by linking her alleged sex crimes with her sister's filicide and her brother's homicide. He retains the central features of the eugenical construction—insanity and uncontrolled sexuality—while removing the hereditary frame.[94]

Winslow ensured Elizabeth Tuttle's place as a standard feature of the Jonathan Edwards myth. But the figure constructed by Winslow has itself a history. Memories of Elizabeth Tuttle first began to stir during the colonial revival, as antiquarians searched colonial records for curious features of early New England life. During the eugenics movement, a permanent link was forged between this memory and two negative attributes: hereditary insanity and promiscuity. Although eugenicists proposed both a simplified, uniformly flattering image and a complex image having both positive and negative traits, the representation of Elizabeth Tuttle as an unstable and promiscuous woman proved most durable. Conforming to a common image of female deviance, it provided modern biographers of Jonathan Edwards with a convenient explanation for the divorce. Taking as their subject a man often identified as the greatest colonial American theologian, historians from Winslow to Marsden have pushed to the far periphery such minor characters as the long-forgotten ex-wife of Edwards's paternal grandfather. Even in this remote location, however, she had an important role to play. Her deviance secured Richard Edwards's virtue and kept pure the family line that produced Jonathan Edwards.

Taking Elizabeth Tuttle as its protagonist, the story told in this book has tried, without complete success, to shift the focus of the narrative away from these commanding male figures. From this perspective a series of images of Elizabeth Tuttle is revealed, each constructed to serve the interests of its author. Richard Edwards's Elizabeth persuaded the Connecticut magistrates to grant him a divorce. Sereno Dwight's Elizabeth was an unexceptional puritan goodwife who died a tragically early death. Charles Davenport's Elizabeth displayed in her genetic makeup the challenging complexity of human heredity. Clarence Darrow's Elizabeth exposed a troubling social injustice. Ola Winslow's Elizabeth preserved the purity of the Edwards family tree, as did George Marsden's. None of these images, however, satisfactorily answers the question with which we began: Who was Elizabeth Tuttle?

My Elizabeth provides a new answer to this question. She was an ordinary puritan woman trapped in an unhappy marriage with a man who, because of his own troubled upbringing, was both insecure and ambitious. Her early sex life was unexceptional for a woman of her time. She did, however, experience one exceptional tragedy. A brutal act of intimate violence struck her family a mortal blow. This opaque crime was a providential act of divine judgment. But what did it mean? Her Calvinist faith provided only one answer to this question. Sin. Innate depravity. Human corruption. God must have inflicted this terrible providence upon her family to warn them of the certainty of their eternal damnation. This hard doctrine was a common cause of religious despair in colonial New England, and an occasional trigger of mental illness. In the years following Benjamin's murder, brother David became increasingly unable to manage his affairs and was placed in the care of a guardian. An obsessive concern about sin led sister Mercy to believe that death was the only way to rescue her son from a terrible fate. And Elizabeth's unstable mental state caused her to withdraw emotionally and physically from her husband. He, then, strayed from their marriage bed, obtained a divorce, and married a less troublesome mate.

This narrative undoubtedly differs in many ways from the story that Elizabeth Tuttle told the committee that visited her Hartford home to investigate the charges Richard Edwards had made in his divorce petition. What facts have I left out? What interpretations are flawed? Because Elizabeth's voice has been omitted from the historical record, we will never know the answers to these questions. But, for the first time, someone has listened to her silence and given her the opportunity to speak for herself. Several fascinating stories have emerged from this small space, permitting a cacophony of new voices to be heard. Does the real Elizabeth make even a fleeting appearance in these intertwining tales? I have to believe that she does. But as with many women of the past, history tells us little about who she was and much about what others have wanted her to be. As a small villain in a much larger story, she has been cast as Jonathan Edwards's crazy grandmother. The cruel taunts and mad threats of this notorious figure will always sound more loudly than Elizabeth's inarticulate story of the divorce.

By shifting my gaze from the macrocosm to the microcosm, I have attempted in this book to free Elizabeth Tuttle from the gender stereotypes that have informed her identity. For three centuries she has been represented as a disobedient wife who destroyed her marriage by stubbornly refusing to submit to her husband. When this image was viewed through a hereditary lens, the sign of her rebellion—uncontrolled sexuality—became the symptom of her insanity. On my reading, Elizabeth did fail to obey her husband, but this disobedience was not displayed by promiscuity. The conviction that women are by nature deceitful and sexually voracious creatures transformed her well-documented sexual restraint into a pathological failure of sexual control. This narrative has proved so durable because this image of female nature has such an ancient pedigree. For centuries the stereotype of the rebellious woman has been deployed to legitimate male dominance. In this long history, Elizabeth Tuttle is a representative woman whose story has been shared by others who have, from willful rebellion, mental illness, or personal empowerment, strayed from their divinely ordained place. Many women of the past who did not conform to a culturally sanctioned model of female virtue have been, like her, transformed into sexual suspects. Although gender roles have changed dramatically since the seventeenth century, this construction of female nature endures.

It gives weight to adultery allegations in contested divorce cases and raises questions about the veracity of a woman's word in rape trials. Some readers of this book will likely still wonder if Elizabeth Tuttle really did lie to her husband and cheat with other men. But if we listen for her voice, she will tell us to be suspicious of such convenient explanations. There was more to her story than this.

CONCLUSION

In December 1693 Hannah Tuttle, the widow of the fifth Tuttle brother, appeared in New Haven County Court and accused a man named Daniel Sperry of slandering her late husband, Joseph, who had died in September 1690. In the intervening three years another awful providence had been visited upon the large Tuttle clan.[1] Once again, a family member had been butchered in a baffling act of intimate violence; once again, a family member had been convicted of homicide. Unlike Benjamin, Mercy had not been executed for her crime. Judged incompetent by the court, she had been sentenced to confinement in New Haven and, after a two-year incarceration in Hartford, had returned to her hometown in the custody of the local magistrates. This scandalous crime surely got tongues wagging, but it was not the only newsworthy event that had afflicted the Tuttle family in recent years. As we have seen, David, having lost his precarious hold on reality, had been placed in the guardianship of his brother, and Elizabeth had lost her home and children after a long and ugly legal battle. Divorced and alone, she also likely found her mental state in decline.

This cluster of tragedies surely shocked the Tuttles' friends and neighbors. Some may have looked suspiciously upon the family; others likely feared having a criminal lunatic in their town. Hannah's slander suit, brought in the months following her infamous sister-in-law's return to New Haven, provides a small clue to community sentiment. She charged Sperry with spreading false reports about the circumstances of her husband's death. Rumors, as the historian Mary Beth Norton has observed, were part of the "small politics of the neighborhood." Gossiping about neighbors "played a vital role as community members reached their collective assessments of fellow colonists."[2] The rumor spreading in New Haven about Joseph Tuttle suggested that his family had acquired a reputation for murder and madness.

According to Hannah's testimony, Sperry "had slanderously Reported that he heard that Joseph Tuttle senior, the father, deceased, dyed out of his bed (on his chamber floor as if he died not a naturall Death)." This rumor "reflected scandall upon him, his family and Relations," she protested, for it alleged her husband was an "accessory to his owne death."[3] Given all the real scandals that the Tuttle family had endured over the years, this malicious rumor seems hardly worth the bother. However, suicide was in the seventeenth century both a heinous crime and a diabolical sin. Tempted by the devil into hopeless despair, the *felo de se*, or self-murderer, committed the ultimate offense against God. This most intimate form of family violence accordingly represented, as the historians Michael MacDonald and Terrence Murphy observe, "the quintessential 'bad death.'"[4] Although the harsh penalties attached to the families of self-murderers in England had been reduced in the colonies, the stigma remained, clearly displayed by the handling of the body, which was traditionally buried at a crossroads and covered with a pile of stones.[5] This profane burial signified that the corpse was a "polluted being," the shell of a soul suffering the eternal torments of the damned in hell.[6]

The rumor that Joseph Tuttle had killed himself was so damaging precisely because it was so believable. A *felo de se* fit the pattern of violent and insane acts that set the Tuttle family apart from their neighbors. What family was more likely to harbor such a scandalous secret? And who was more likely to commit such a despairing act than a Tuttle? Family conflict, bereavement, and shame were commonly identified as motives for suicide, as was madness itself.[7] That the Tuttle family was marked by an abundance of such troubling experiences gave this rumor weight. Sperry confessed he had spread it, and he named Jonathan Atwater as its author. Atwater said he had heard it from another source. Community feeling had not, however, turned decisively against the Tuttles. Hannah appeared in court accompanied by "sundry others of the Relations and next neighbors to the family of the said Deceased." This group of supporters, who had likely visited Joseph during his last illness, easily impeached the slander. Providing "a full and Cleare accompt of the matter," they testified that Joseph had "died quietly in his bed as other Christian men [are] used to doo." The judge accordingly ruled that the rumor was "false and groundless" and indignantly cautioned its propagators against further defaming the "Deceased, who was Known to be a man fearing God and a member of the Church."[8] Despite his notorious siblings, this Tuttle could rest easily in his grave, his reputation unsullied by either murder or madness.

This rumor reflected the common early modern belief that mental illness and other forms of disease ran in families. The basic hereditary assumption that like begets like was, however, explained in this period not by the transmission of discrete traits from one generation to the next but by the heritability of temperament or character.[9] According to the humoral medical model, the body operated according to an economy of four fluids: blood, yellow bile, black bile, and phlegm. Health was a state of balance among these fluids, while disease resulted from their imbalance. Each person was born with a particular temperament depending upon which fluid tended to excess, and these individual temperaments in turn identified tendencies to particular diseases. A constitutional proneness to an excess of black bile, for example, produced a melancholic temper, while a proneness to an excess of blood produced a sanguine temper. Because tempers were heritable, particular diseases tended to cluster in families. Even asymptomatic members inherited their family's constitutional weaknesses, which needed to be treated prophylactically by the appropriate regulation of diet and activity.[10]

Employing this medical model as a diagnostic lens, members of New Haven's informal public would likely have concluded that the Tuttles had a temper prone to impulsive violence and mental illness. No member of the first generation apparently suffered from these debilities; Richard, John, and William Tuttle were all successful householders, as were the majority of their children. The unusual incidence of murder and madness in the second generation was not, therefore, explained by a simple application of like begets like. But it revealed a shared family constitution, which made the rumor of Joseph's suicide easy to believe and easy to spread. Almost a half-century later, when a member of Jonathan Edwards's Northampton congregation named Joseph Hawley slit his throat in a moment of religious despair, the distraught pastor attributed the shocking deed to inherited temper. "He was a gentleman of more than common understanding, of strict morals, religious in his behavior, and an useful and honorable person in the town," Edwards observed, "but was of a family that are exceeding prone to the disease of melancholy, and his mother was killed with it." This natural humoral cause acted, however, within a larger supernatural framework controlled by both divine and diabolical forces. Satan took advantage of Hawley's melancholy temper and "drove him into despairing thoughts," Edwards noted, but the devil was loose in Northampton only because the "Spirit of God" had withdrawn from the town. Such a desperate sin could be committed only with God's permission.[11]

By the beginning of the nineteenth century, the diabolical crime of self-murder had been transformed into a tragic outcome of mental illness. Madness was no longer explained by a combination of religious, biological, and moral factors. Supernatural agents were excluded, allowing natural explanations to grow in explanatory power.[12] Accompanying the naturalization of madness was an increasing interest in heredity. Decades before the formal advent of the eugenics movement, the concept of hereditary disease was "virtually ubiquitous" in both medical literature and popular culture. The biology of hereditary transmission shifted from temperament to discrete traits, which were mapped in intergenerational pedigree studies of individual families. Parents scrutinized their children's potential marriage partners for inborn defects to ensure the health of future offspring.[13] The eugenics movement transformed this concern for judicious mating into a comprehensive social program. It built upon a pre-existing linkage between heredity and disease to argue that reproductive control was the best means of addressing such intractable problems as crime, poverty, and alcoholism.

The belief that insanity was a heritable disease was particularly widespread in the nineteenth century. Most who treated mental disease, notes the historian John Waller, "unhesitatingly ascribed madness to tainted blood if an asylum inmate mentioned having an insane relation."[14] The diligent genealogists and antiquarians who discovered the cluster of murder and mental illness in the second generation of Tuttles in America similarly concluded that the lineage had a hereditary taint. This interpretation became commonplace during the eugenics movement, repeatedly appearing in literature written by both supporters and critics. The claim may be true. Modern geneticists have demonstrated that a "vast number of psychological traits or disorders have low-to-modest heritability." In psychotic illnesses like schizophrenia and bipolar disorder, genetic factors have strong causality, while more common mental conditions like depression and anxiety are less heritable.[15] Despite these findings, the claim that the early Tuttle family had an inborn propensity for mental illness is methodologically flawed.

Eugenicists who worked at the advent of modern genetics research had only a limited understanding of the patterns of human inheritance. The identification of what Charles Davenport, the founder of the American eugenics movement, called an "evil trait" in the Tuttle blood reveals several shortcomings. First is the failure to distinguish between heritable and nonheritable traits. Davenport quaintly claimed, for example, that a family with a preponderance of naval officers had an inherited factor for "thalassophilia," or love of the sea. More problematically, he believed that moral traits, especially sexual behavior, were as heritable as eye or hair color.[16] Elizabeth Tuttle's alleged promiscuity was, therefore, linked with that of her descendants Pierpont Edwards and Aaron Burr as evidence of the Tuttle taint. Like the murders committed by her two siblings, it appeared to express a genetic propensity to mental illness in the Tuttle pedigree.

A second, related failure lies in the pedigree method itself. In addition to the Tuttle-Edwards genealogy, Davenport collected hundreds of pedigrees to map the continuity of genetic expression within families. Many traced behavioral traits, however, that like thalassophilia were more "associate[d] with family traditions and mimicry rather than innate factors."[17] And even those pedigrees that traced heritable traits did not recognize the multifactoral etiology of many diseases, particularly mental illnesses. Modern research indicates that most psychiatric disorders follow complex patterns of inheritance involving the interaction of multiple genes, as well as non-genetic—that is, behavioral and environmental—influences. Davenport's pedigree studies were, however, "based on anecdotal and biased reports that could not distinguish between familial aggregations of characteristics based on environmental factors [and] true genetic traits."[18] This shortcoming is clearly revealed in the elaborate lists of the diverse intellectual and professional accomplishments of the descendants of Jonathan Edwards, which were common in eugenics propaganda. But just as the Edwards honor roll cannot isolate genetic from environmental factors, neither can a Tuttle genealogy charting a high incidence of so-called negative traits. Although the pedigree method can show that mental illness clusters in a particular family, it cannot determine whether this "clustering is attributable to familial genetic factors or to shared, familial environmental factors."[19] Davenport's overreliance on this method, therefore, promoted a strong form of genetic determinism that minimized the effect of experience on the development of disease.

In my reconstruction of the factors that likely contributed to the breakdown of Elizabeth Tuttle's marriage to Richard Edwards, I chose to disregard the genetic question. My aim was neither to prove nor to disprove the claim that an inherited trait for mental illness contributed to this family's failure. Although the understanding of human heredity has advanced since Davenport's day, developing a genetic profile for a family that lived more than 300 years ago remains methodologically challenging. Heredity, therefore, is at best an incomplete explanation; more important, it is a historically unsatisfying one. Reducing a complex series of past events to the transmission of a genetic trait empties their explanation of content. Applied retrospectively, genetics is a causal placeholder that, although having the appearance of an explanation, actually explains very little. Historical narratives are constructed from family conflicts, social forces, cultural constraints—the stuff of human experience. Biology undoubtedly shapes this experience, but it has little explanatory power.

According to the narrative I tell in this book, all the Tuttle siblings had one common moment of crisis when Benjamin suddenly and inexplicably murdered their sister Sarah. This acute life event surely caused the entire family to be troubled for a time with grief, anxiety, and depression, the normal emotional responses to traumatic loss. David, Mercy, and Elizabeth, however, apparently had neither the inner strength nor the external support to recover fully from this tragedy. Speculating why they, unlike their siblings, became in subsequent years afflicted with mental illness moves the plot forward. David, an aging bachelor suffering from a mental disability, was psychologically more vulnerable than his siblings to the effects of trauma. The apparent psychosis that prompted Mercy to murder her son Samuel is more difficult to understand, because its progression is not documented in any colonial records. But abundant sources indicate that Elizabeth had been burdened for years by a difficult marriage, a chronic condition that likely left her with weaker emotional resources.

In this telling, the murder was the principal stressor transforming the Edwardses' difficult marriage into a failing marriage. In the aftermath of this traumatic event, Elizabeth and Richard's domestic partnership, which had functioned adequately for almost a decade, began to falter. But additional stressors made their union fragile from its outset. Husband and wife came from very different social locations. An early baby likely occasioned their wedding. But the snake in this already weedy garden was Richard's conviction that he was not the father of this child. Their domestic life, therefore, began in crisis, poisoned by feelings of betrayal and mistrust. When Benjamin's shocking crime precipitated a second crisis, Elizabeth could not absorb the blow. The grief and confusion caused by this awful providence became a lasting mental "distraction" that proved too heavy a weight for the marriage to bear. Elizabeth was more the victim of tragic circumstances beyond her control than a genetic villain.

Piecing together the interrelationship among these stressful and traumatic events creates a unique story of family life in colonial New England. The normative image of the puritan family emphasizes order, companionship, and duty. Although order was primary, these three domestic virtues were interdependent. Without mutual affection, subordination became servitude;

without the willing performance of duty, family government failed. Because household order required each member to play his or her expected part, every deviation threatened domestic stability. But, as the historian John Demos has observed, "[N]either court records nor personal documents contain much evidence of intra-family conflict" in colonial New England.[20] Scant evidence of conflict does not mean, however, that domestic harmony always prevailed. Husbands and wives, brothers and sisters, surely bickered and fought, but these squabbles were too trivial, or too common, to attract much public notice. As a consequence, these small, often women-centered dramas are hard for a historian to see or to explain. Only in rare moments, when a family failed, for example, or was shattered by an act of intimate violence, do the sources of domestic disorder come fleetingly into view.

Our search for a thicker description of the breakdown of one unhappy couple's marriage is, therefore, an opportunity to explore in a magnified form a phenomenon more difficult to document in its ordinary expression. It opens up a rich and embodied world in which anxious patriarchs struggled to govern their households, unruly women disobeyed their husbands, and mental illnesses tore marriages apart. Following Elizabeth into this messy reality reveals that families were frequent sites of gendered conflict and violence in colonial New England. Gender drives the action in her story. On repeated occasions her behavior, and that of the many men and women located in the dense web of dual relationships that formed her extended family, failed to conform to normative gender roles. This gap between the actual and the ideal caused movement, shame, disorder, and even death. It produced the tensions and anxieties that shaped her life's narrative.

Elizabeth was born into a household governed by a patriarch who, after two migrations, had achieved the patriarchal ideal of manhood. She married into a family that had been pushed out of England by an inability to achieve this manly ideal and that struggled ineffectually to escape patriarchal failure once settled in the colonies. Through skillful management of the family business, her husband overcame this intergenerational history of financial incompetence and began moving up the colonial social ladder. Conflicts about sex, however, disordered their marriage from the outset and threatened her husband's authority as household head. Richard's wounded manhood transformed Elizabeth into a deceitful and sexually treacherous woman, unwilling to submit her body to his government. Although functioning for a time as his dutiful helpmeet, she strayed from her place in the difficult years following her sister's murder. This shocking crime, which brought another household to a violent end, was committed in a moment of gendered rage. Benjamin's frustrated manhood transformed Sarah into a scolding woman eager to pick and snipe at her dependent brother. Having no legitimate authority of his own, he silenced his sister with violence. Mercy's motive for taking an axe to her son's head was likewise gendered, a deranged expression of a mother's love for her child. This second murder, which corresponded with Richard's protracted campaign for a divorce, helped convince the Connecticut magistrates that Elizabeth was a domestic danger who should be separated from her husband. Once the union was terminated, Richard married a more submissive mate and achieved in this second family the patriarchal success he had long been denied.

This is an old story, but many of its features sound familiar. Although the structure of domestic life has changed dramatically since colonial times, the factors that prevent a family from flourishing have remained remarkably stable. Financial failure, mental illness, intimate violence, and sexual jealousy create marital crises from which many families, in the twenty-first century as well as the seventeenth, do not emerge intact. Gender constraints continue to cause spouses to quarrel, and these struggles for mastery frequently cause domestic partnerships to fail. For despite the shift to a companionate model of marriage involving a partnership of equals, vestiges of the older patriarchal model built on a hierarchy of dominance and submission persist. This traditional model suggests, as the historian Frances Dolan has argued, that "marriage is an economy of scarcity in which there is only room for one full person." Because conjugal unity is achieved by the wife's submission to her husband, the "full person" in the marriage, division inevitably results if both assert their individuality. As Dolan observes, "the presence of two wills—private rather than conjoined—means war." Inequality reduces conflict, while equality fosters it.[21]

Whether through willful rebellion or mental illness, Elizabeth declared war on her marriage when she stopped sleeping with her husband. This expression of individual identity created conflict, but she was poorly equipped for the battle. Well supplied for a protracted campaign, Richard formed new alliances and eventually emerged victorious from the contest. Recovering quickly from this family failure, he remarried, regained his economic position, and started again. Newfound domestic success erased troubling memories of this morally ambiguous divorce war, and although Timothy Edwards continued his father's efforts to reconstruct the past, by the third generation little memory of this unhappy marriage remained. In fact, its termination likely created the very conditions that made the illustrious career of Jonathan Edwards possible.

Jonathan Edwards was raised in an educated household governed by a member of colonial Connecticut's religious elite. His two most formative theological influences were his father, who pastored the congregation in East Windsor, and his maternal grandfather, Solomon Stoddard, who commanded the Northampton pulpit that Edwards would subsequently occupy. Nevertheless, Timothy Edwards might never have obtained his ministerial post nor made an advantageous match with Stoddard's daughter had his father's divorce action failed. His theological training was derailed in the tumultuous years preceding the divorce when a disciplinary violation led to his dismissal from Harvard. Returning to Connecticut in disgrace, he resumed his education apparently under the private direction of the pastor in nearby Springfield. Three years after the divorce, he received his Harvard degree, married Esther Stoddard, and began preaching in East Windsor.[22] Without the divorce, would he have established a household suitable for the raising of a great theologian? We cannot know the answer to this counterfactual question. But the rapid ascendancy of the Edwards family in the eighteenth century suggests that if Richard had not divorced Elizabeth and married into a high-status Connecticut family, his descendants would not have traveled so far.

The achievements of these descendants laid the groundwork for our story's sequel, the invention of Elizabeth Tuttle as Jonathan Edwards's crazy grandmother. During the nineteenth century, Edwards acquired an iconic status in the religious history of America. As new historical memories of the nation's puritan past were constructed, theologians, evangelicals, and colonial revivalists appropriated Edwards to meet diverse cultural needs. Inhabiting the imagined landscape of old New England, his heroic figure embodied the keen intellect, moral rigor, and orderly habits that came to define the Yankee character. A new appropriation emerged when this veneration of Edwards blended with the national obsession for tracing heredity. Constructing the puritan icon's pedigree as the premier example of a superior bloodline, eugenicists deployed Edwards to promote a national policy of controlled breeding. His appearance in this new location awakened fresh memories of Elizabeth Tuttle. The story of her unhappy marriage complicated the purity of the Edwards family tree and encouraged supporters and opponents of eugenics to fashion contrasting images of the great theologian's grandmother that furthered their ideological aims. The most enduring image, which emphasized hereditary insanity and promiscuity, was imported into twentieth-century scholarship on Jonathan Edwards. This image was easily integrated into modern idealizations of Edwards because it supplied a convenient explanation for the divorce that preserved the purity of his male ancestral line. Linking his greatness to her sin, it ensured the perpetuation of the crazy-grandmother story.

Discovering that the crazy-grandmother story itself has a history permits the fashioning of a new identity for Elizabeth Tuttle. Uncovering the genealogy of this story reveals that both gender stereotypes and an inordinate love for Jonathan Edwards have shaped past understandings of the divorce. A fresh reading of the colonial records produces a less culpable and more sympathetic image of our protagonist. She was a member of a flourishing puritan family afflicted by a train of baffling providences. Her marriage was a casualty of a curious conjunction of wrong choices and inconsolable griefs. This long view should not, however, obscure the role of human agency. The Edwardses' marriage broke down because over time Elizabeth and Richard made each other's lives a misery. Richard's campaign to extricate himself from this unhappy union was a small sign of the decline of the puritan dream of a godly community that subordinated individual interests to the good of the whole. By searching for personal happiness and struggling to build a better life for himself and his children, he fulfilled a different, very American dream. We can dream that Elizabeth also found a measure of solace in her single life but, like many women, she was ill prepared to compete in the emerging market of individual self-interest. Even more than three centuries later, a world that supports the flourishing of women in her difficult situation is still struggling to be born.

NOTES

INTRODUCTION

1. Joyce Appleby, Lynn Hunt, and Margaret Jacob, *Telling the Truth about History* (New York: Norton, 1994), 259.
2. Perry Miller, *Jonathan Edwards* (1949; reprint, Amherst: Univ. of Massachusetts Press, 1981), xxxii; Joseph A. Conforti, *Jonathan Edwards, Religious Tradition, and American Culture* (Chapel Hill: Univ. of North Carolina Press, 1995), 2.
3. See, for example, John Piper, *God's Passion for His Glory: Living the Vision of Jonathan Edwards* (Wheaton, Ill.: Crossway, 2006); and John Piper and Justin Taylor, eds., *A God Entranced Vision of All Things: The Legacy of Jonathan Edwards* (Wheaton, Ill.: Crossway, 2004).
4. Ola Elizabeth Winslow, *Jonathan Edwards, 1703-1758* (1940; reprint, New York: Collier Books, 1961), 24-28; Miller, *Jonathan Edwards*, 35; George M. Marsden, *Jonathan Edwards: A Life* (New Haven: Yale Univ. Press, 2003), 22-24.
5. Laurel Thatcher Ulrich, *A Midwife's Tale: The Life of Martha Ballard, Based on Her Diary, 1785-1812* (New York: Knopf, 1990), 4-5.
6. Lisa Wilson, *Ye Heart of a Man: The Domestic Life of Men in Colonial New England* (New Haven: Yale Univ. Press, 1999), 3.
7. Edmund S. Morgan, *The Puritan Family: Religion and Domestic Relations in Seventeenth-Century New England*, rev. ed. (New York: Harper & Row, 1966); John P. Demos, *A Little Commonwealth: Family Life in Plymouth Colony* (Oxford: Oxford Univ. Press, 1970).
8. Carol F. Karlsen, *The Devil in the Shape of a Woman: Witchcraft in Colonial New England* (New York: Vintage Books, 1989), 161, 173.
9. Christopher D. Morris, *The Hanging Figure: On Suspense and the Films of Alfred Hitchcock* (Westport, Conn.: Praeger, 2002), 40-46; Donald Spoto, *The Dark Side of Genius: The Life of Alfred Hitchcock* (1983; reprint [New York]: Da Capo Press, 1999), 145.
10. Laurel Thatcher Ulrich, "The Importance of Studying Ordinary Lives: An Interview with Laurel Thatcher Ulrich," interview by Randall J. Stephens, *Historically Speaking* 10 (15 April 2009): 10.
11. Richard D. Brown, "Microhistory and the Post-Modern Challenge," *Journal of the Early Republic* 23 (Spring 2003): 5.
12. Jill Lepore, "Historians Who Love Too Much: Reflections on Microhistory and Biography," *Journal of American History* 88 (June 2001): 129, 133, 141.

13. William Gouge, *Of Domesticall Duties* (1622; reprint, Amsterdam: Theatrum Orbis Ter-
rarum, 1976), 18.

14. Thomas A. Foster, "Spellbinding Masculinity: Microhistories of Violence, Gender, and
Sexuality in the Early American Family," *William and Mary Quarterly* 61 (April 2004):
362.

15. Lepore, "Historians Who Love Too Much," 141, 138.

16. Miller, *Jonathan Edwards*, xxx.

17. Ibid., 147–48.

18. Conforti, *Jonathan Edwards*, 10.

PROLOGUE

1. William DeLoss Love, *The Colonial History of Hartford* (1935; reprint, Hartford: Centinel
Hill Press, 1974), 218–19.

2. Deposition of Timothy and Abigail Edwards; Judgment of John Woodbridge, Connecticut Archives, Crimes and Misdemeanors, 1st Ser., 1663–1789, vol. 3, Divorces, 1664–1732,
Connecticut State Library, Hartford, 236, 239 (5 March 1688, 29 December 1689); see also
237 (n.d.).

3. Richard Edwards, "A True Abreviate of the Case of Richard Edwards Respecting Elizabeth
his Late wife," Connecticut Archives, Crimes and Misdemeanors, 1st Ser., 3:235e (2 July
1689).

4. Helen Schatvet Ullmann, trans., *Connecticut Colony, Minutes of the Court of Assistants*
(Boston: New England Historic Genealogical Society, 2009), 126.

CHAPTER 1

1. John Camden Hotten, ed., *The Original Lists of Persons of Quality . . . Who Went from
Great Britain to the American Plantations, 1600–1700* (New York: Bouton, 1874), 43–56.

2. John Selwyn Herbert, *The Port of London* (London: Collins, 1947), 35, 15; William A.
Baker, *Colonial Vessels: Some Seventeenth-Century Sailing Craft* (Barre, Mass.: Barre
Publishing Co., 1962), x–xi.

3. J. H. Bird, *The Geography of the Port of London* (London: Hutchinson Univ. Library, 1957),
31–38; Joseph Guinness Broodbank, *History of the Port of London* (London: D. O'Connor,
1921), 1:54–55; Joan Parkes, *Travel in England in the Seventeenth Century* (Westport,
Conn.: Greenwood Press, 1970), 96, 103–5.

4. John Bruce, ed., *Calendar of State Papers, Domestic Series, of the Reign of Charles I*
(London: Longman, Roberts & Green, 1853–54), 6:493, 7:448; Johan Wissner, "Nicholas
Trerise, Mariner of Wapping and Charlestown," *New England Historical and Genea-
logical Register* 143 (January 1989): 27; Baker, *Colonial Vessels*, 29; G. G. Harris, *The
Trinity House of Deptford, 1514–1660* (London: Athlone, 1969), 235. According to Allison
Games, New England–bound vessels ranged anywhere from 25 to 300 tons (*Migration
and the Origins of the English Atlantic World* [Cambridge, Mass.: Harvard Univ. Press,
1999], 61).

5. Games, *Migration*, 38.

6. Hotten, *Original Lists*, 43–56; Games, *Migration*, 56, 61, 57.

7. Virginia DeJohn Anderson asserts that "[n]early nine out of ten emigrants traveled in
family groups of one sort or another" (*New England's Generation: The Great Migration
and the Formation of Society and Culture in the Seventeenth Century* [Cambridge: Cambridge Univ. Press, 199], 121). Games estimates that "at least 60 percent of travelers to New
England enjoyed the company of family members" (*Migration*, 53); Richard Archer cal-
culates that "one-third of the adult males who migrated to New England before 1650 were
single, young, and without family connections" ("New England Mosaic: A Demographic

Analysis for the Seventeenth Century," *William and Mary Quarterly* 47 [October 1990]: 481).

8. Roger Thompson, *Mobility and Migration: East Anglian Founders of New England, 1629–1640* (Amherst: Univ. of Massachusetts Press, 1994), 189. Thompson was able to connect "[o]ver one-third of the East Anglian emigrants" to "larger extended families or 'companies' of kinfolk" (ibid., 201).

9. That the three migrants were brothers is clearly indicated in their father's will. In this document, Simon Tuttle identifies Richard as "my eldest sonne"; William as "my youngest sonne," and John as "my second sonne" (Will of Simon Tuttle of Ringstead [1630], Northamptonshire Wills, 2nd Ser., Bk. O, f. 81, Northamptonshire Record Office, Northampton, England; see also Will of John Wells of Ringstead [1618], Northampton-shire Wills, 2nd Ser., Bk. M, f. 211). For a summary of genealogical information about the three brothers, see Robert Charles Anderson, *The Great Migration: Immigrants to New England, 1634–1635* (Boston: New England Historic Genealogical Society, 2011), 7:125–45.

10. Hotten, *Original Lists*, 45, 48–49; Games, *Migration*, 53–54; Keith Wrightson, *Earthly Necessities: Economic Lives in Early Modern Britain* (New Haven: Yale Univ. Press, 2000), 33.

11. Thompson, *Mobility and Migration*, 235; David Grayson Allen, "Matrix of Motivation," *New England Quarterly* 59 (September 1986): 409. As T. H. Breen and Stephen Foster note, "The traditional either/or dichotomy—*either* religion *or* economics—makes no sense" ("Moving to the New World: The Character of Early Massachusetts Immigration," *William and Mary Quarterly* 30 [April 1973]: 201). For a summary of the history of the debate, see David Cressy, *Coming Over: Migration and Communication Between England and New England in the Seventeenth Century* (Cambridge: Cambridge Univ. Press, 1987), 74–83.

12. David Grayson Allen, for example, takes an intensely local approach in *In English Ways: The Movement of Societies and the Transferal of English Local Law and Custom to Massachusetts Bay in the Seventeenth Century* (Chapel Hill: Univ. of North Carolina Press, 1981), 163–204.

13. Cressy, *Coming Over*, 86.

14. Allen, "Matrix of Motivation," 414.

15. Thompson, *Mobility and Migration*, 113.

16. Will of Simon Tuttle, Northamptonshire Wills, O, 81.

17. Wrightson, *Earthly Necessities*, 34, 72; Keith Wrightson, *English Society, 1580–1680* (New Brunswick, N.J.: Rutgers Univ. Press, 1982), 31, 33; Mildred Campbell, *The English Yeoman Under Elizabeth and the Early Stuarts* (New York: A. M. Kelley, 1968), 61, 23.

18. "The Names of All the Freehoulders Within the Seueral Hundredes of the East Devision" (2 Jac. I), in Joan Wake, ed., *A Copy of Papers Relating to Musters, Beacons, Subsidies, etc., in the County of Northampton, A. D. 1586–1623* (Kettering, England: T. B. Hart, 1926), 116.

19. Wrightson, *Earthly Necessities*, 34.

20. Joan Thirsk, ed., *The Agrarian History of England and Wales, 1500–1640*, vol. 4 of *The Agrarian History of England and Wales*, ed. H. P. R. Finberg (London: Cambridge Univ. Press, 1967), 89, 92.

21. Will of Simon Tuttle, Northamptonshire Wills, O, 81; Thirsk, *Agrarian History*, 4:92, 548–49.

22. Wrightson, *English Society*, 134–36; Wrightson, *Earthly Necessities*, 186–87; Campbell, *English Yeoman*, 104, 185–86, 69. In his will, Simon Tuttle describes several properties as "lately purchased" (Northamptonshire Wills, O, 81). Campbell notes that this phrase frequently appears in yeomen's wills, indicating that although they did farm ancient family

holdings, they "also occupied lands which they had themselves acquired through their own initiative and industry" (*English Yeoman*, 70).

23. Wrightson, *Earthly Necessities*, 77, 102, 136, 162. The Tuttles' village of Ringstead, however, was not enclosed until 1839, during a later period of parliamentary enclosure (L. F. Salzman, ed., *The History of the County of Northampton*, Victoria History of the Counties of England [1937; reprint, London: Dawsons, 1970], 4:40).

24. The commissions reported that 27,335 acres had been enclosed between 1578 and 1607, almost double the 1517 figure of 14,081 acres (Thirsk, *Agrarian History*, 4:241–42). Nevertheless, the majority of the land in Northamptonshire remained open at the end of the seventeenth century and was not enclosed until the period of parliamentary enclosure in the eighteenth and nineteenth centuries. E. M. Leonard argues that enclosure caused great distress in the Midlands because it "displaced a larger population in this part of the country than elsewhere" ("The Inclosure of Common Fields in the Seventeenth Century," *Transactions of the Royal Historical Society*, n. s., 19 [1905]: 103).

25. Thirsk, *Agrarian History*, 4:95–96; Edwin F. Gay, "The Midland Revolt and the Inquisitions of Depopulation of 1607," *Transactions of the Royal Historical Society*, n.s., 18 (1904): 232–33. See also Philip A. J. Pettit, *The Royal Forests of Northamptonshire: A Study in Their Economy, 1558–1714* (Gateshead: Northumberland Press, 1968), 141–63.

26. Roger B. Manning, *Village Revolts: Social Protest and Popular Disturbances in England, 1509–1640* (Oxford: Clarendon Press, 1988), 82, 85, 229–46.

27. W. E. Tate, "Inclosure Movements in Northampton," *Northamptonshire Past and Present* 1, no. 2 (1949): 23.

28. Games, *Migration*, 16.

29. Wrightson, *English Society*, 27; Wrightson, *Earthly Necessities*, 187, 193.

30. Thirsk, *Agrarian History*, 4:559; J. T. Smith and M. A. North, eds., *St Albans, 1650–1700: A Thoroughfare Town and Its People* (Hatfield: Hertfordshire Publications, 2003), 147.

31. Games, *Migration*, 54; Smith and North, *St. Albans*, 45. John Tuttle is identified as a mercer on the *Planter*'s passenger list, and as a draper in a second document—two commonly interchangeable occupational terms (Hotten, *Original Lists*, 45; Richard Tuttle, et al. to John Bellamy, Deed of "bargain and sale, feoffment," 20 November 1634, Stopford Sackville Archive, SS 3501, Northamptonshire Record Office, Northampton, England; Smith and North, *St. Albans*, 169).

32. I. G. Dolittle, *The Mercers' Company, 1579–1959* (London: Mercers' Company, 1994), 18–20; Wrightson, *Earthly Necessities*, 166, 199; Barry Supple, *Commercial Crisis and Change in England, 1600–1642: A Study in the Instability of a Mercantile Economy* (Cambridge: Cambridge Univ. Press, 1970), 136–37.

33. Games, *Migration*, 53. John Tuttle's first child was baptized in St. Albans in November 1628 but had been born at least a year earlier, for she is named in her grandfather's will that was written in December 1627. This suggests that John had left Ringstead and married by 1625–26 (Will of Simon Tuttle, Northamptonshire Wills, O, 81).

34. In his will Simon Tuttle refers to the "land formerly conveyed to my eldest sonne Richard," suggesting that he had received his portion before his father's death (Northamptonshire Wills, O, 81).

35. Will of Simon Tuttle, Northamptonshire Wills, O, 81. On English inheritance practices, see Keith Wrightson and David Levine, *Poverty and Piety in an English Village: Terling, 1525–1700* (1995; reprint, Oxford: Clarendon Press, 2001), 94–99.

36. Cressy, *Coming Over*, 117. But see his careful discussion of costs, pp. 107–19.

37. Deed of "bargain and sale, feoffment," SS3501.

38. Both Richard and William Tuttle are described as husbandmen on the *Planter*'s passenger list, but no conclusion about their financial status can be drawn from this term, for it was

used on the lists to designate occupation, not status, and was commonly applied to all persons, regardless of wealth, who engaged in "husbandry"—that is, the "care and cultivation of the land" (Hotten, *Original Lists,* 48, 49; Campbell, *English Yeoman,* 28–29).

39. Cressy, *Coming Over,* 88.

40. W. J. Sheils, *The Puritans in the Diocese of Peterborough, 1558–1610* (Northampton: Northamptonshire Record Society, 1979), 16. Because scribes used formulaic language, standard elements in wills, like the preamble, may not reflect the actual beliefs of the testator. But, notes Claire Cross, "amid what was increasingly becoming a stereotyped form some authentic confessions of faith can still be found" ("Wills as Evidence of Popular Piety in the Reformation Period: Leeds and Hull, 1540–1640," in *The End of Strife,* ed. David Loades [Edinburgh: T. & T. Clark, 1984], 51). See also J. D. Alsop, "Religious Preambles in Early Modern English Wills as Formulae," *Journal of Ecclesiastical History* 40 (January 1989): 19–27.

41. According to M. L. Zell, "there is far greater likelihood that an individual testator— whether or not he drafted his own will—will betray his personal religious beliefs in the specific personal requests which follow the religious preamble" ("The Use of Religious Preambles as a Measure of Religious Belief in the Sixteenth Century," *Bulletin of the Institute of Historical Research* 50 [November 1977]: 249).

42. Margaret Spufford, *Contrasting Communities: English Villagers in the Sixteenth and Seventeenth Centuries* (London: Cambridge Univ. Press, 1974), 331, 335, 325.

43. G. J. Mayhew, "The Progress of the Reformation in East Sussex, 1530–1559: The Evidence from Wills," *Southern History* 5 (1983): 53, 55.

44. Will of Simon Tuttle, Northamptonshire Wills, O, 81.

45. Deed of "bargain and sale, feoffment," SS3501. At his death in 1653, Bellamy bequeathed "my Farme house and Cottage with all my Lands, Leases, and Meadowes in Ringstead and Rounds together with all my household stuffe in Ringstead" as a life estate to his sister (Will of John Bellamye of Cotterstock, Northamptonshire, 7 February 1654, Records of the Prerogative Court of Canterbury, PROB 11/234, National Archives of the United Kingdom, London).

46. On the career of John Bellamy, see Leona Rostenberg, "The New World: John Bellamy, 'Pilgrim' Publisher of London," in *Literary, Political, Scientific, Religious, and Legal Publishing, Printing, and Bookselling in England, 1551–1700: Twelve Studies* (New York: Burt Franklin, 1965), 1:97–129; and Tai Liu, *Puritan London: A Study of Religion and Society in the City Parishes* (Newark: Univ. of Delaware Press, 1986), 62–64. Bellamy printed Edward Winslow's *Good News from New England* in 1624 and William Wood's *New England's Prospect* in 1634.

47. John Fielding, "Conformists, Puritans and the Church Courts: The Diocese of Peterborough, 1603–1642" (Ph.D. diss., University of Birmingham, 1989), 1–2.

48. Sheils, *Puritans in Peterborough,* 23, 37, 41. According to Sheils, "over half of the livings [in the diocese] were in the hands of the local gentry" (ibid., 37).

49. Salzman, *V. C. H. Northampton,* 4:44. Lewis, the third Baron Mordaunt, purchased the advowson—that is, the right of presenting a candidate to a vacant ecclesiastical benefice—in 1588, and it remained in his family until 1681 (William Page, ed., *The History of the County of Northampton,* Victoria History of the Counties of England [1930; reprint, London: Dawsons, 1970], 3:196).

50. Henry Isham Longden, *Northamptonshire and Rutland Clergy from 1500* (Northampton: Archer & Goodman, 1941), 11:141; Fielding, "Conformists, Puritans and the Church Courts," 29, 130, 156, 161n; Tom Webster, *Godly Clergy in Early Stuart England: The Caroline Puritan Movement, c. 1620–1643* (Cambridge: Cambridge Univ. Press, 1997), 229.

51. Sheils estimates that "one-third of the parishes in the diocese had direct experience of puritan evangelism" (*Puritans in Peterborough,* 145). See his map of the distribution of puritan clergy (ibid., 53) and Fielding's map of diocesan preaching centers ("Conformists, Puritans and the Church Courts," following p. 147).

52. Thirsk, *Agrarian History,* 4:489, 492; Sheils, *Puritans in Peterborough,* 119.

53. Sheils, *Puritans in Peterborough,* 24; see also Patrick Collinson, *The Elizabethan Puritan Movement* (Berkeley: Univ. of California Press, 1967), 172, 176.

54. Sheils, *Puritans in Peterborough,* 126; Fielding, "Conformists, Puritans and the Church Courts," 147–50.

55. Patrick Collinson, "Lectures by Combination: Structures and Characteristics of Church Life in 17th Century England," in *Godly People: Essays on English Protestantism and Puritanism* (London: Hamblin Press, 1983), 483–84; Fielding, "Conformists, Puritans and the Church Courts," 146.

56. Fielding, "Conformists, Puritans and the Church Courts," 154; Sheils, *Puritans in Peterborough,* 136–40.

57. Fielding, "Conformists, Puritans and the Church Courts," 122, 150.

58. Ibid., 67. By the outset of the seventeenth century, John Fielding argues, the diocese "contained two mutually antagonistic groups which subscribed to quite different opinions regarding the nature of true church" ("Arminianism in the Localities: Peterborough Diocese, 1603–1642," in *The Early Stuart Church, 1603–1642,* ed. Kenneth Fincham [Stanford, Calif.: Stanford Univ. Press, 1993], 94).

59. Fielding, "Conformists, Puritans and the Church Courts," 63; Sheils, *Puritans in Peterborough,* 79–87. According to Kenneth Fincham, ministers deprived under James I were radical puritans who refused not only to conform but also to subscribe to Archbishop Whitgift's Three Articles "which required every minister to accept the royal supremacy and the legality of the Prayer Book, the Ordinal and the Thirty-nine Articles of Religion" ("Episcopal Government, 1603–1640," in *The Early Stuart Church,* ed. Fincham, 75).

60. Fielding, "Conformists, Puritans and the Church Courts," 67–71.

61. On how the Calvinist unity of the Church of England was challenged in the 1620s by an aggressive Arminianism, see Nicholas Tyacke, "Puritanism, Arminianism, and Counter-Revolution" (*The Origins of the English Civil War,* ed. Conrad Russell [New York: Harper & Row, 1973], 119–43), and his subsequent book *Anti-Calvinists: The Rise of English Arminianism, c. 1590–1640* (Oxford: Clarendon Press, 1987).

62. Fielding, "Conformists, Puritans and the Church Courts," 92–100.

63. Kenneth Fincham, introduction to *The Early Stuart Church,* 11.

64. Richard Tuttle served as the Ringstead churchwarden in 1626 and 1629 (Donald Lines Jacobus and Edgar Francis Waterman, *Hale, House, and Related Families, Mainly of the Connecticut River Valley* [Hartford: Connecticut Historical Society, 1952], 772).

65. Fielding, "Conformists, Puritans and the Church Courts," 94, 113.

66. Webster, *Godly Clergy,* 217.

67. Paul S. Seaver, *The Puritan Lectureships: The Politics of Religious Dissent, 1560–1662* (Stanford, Calif.: Stanford Univ. Press, 1970), 90; William Urwick, *Nonconformity in Hert[fordshire], Being Lectures upon the Nonconforming Worthies of St. Albans* (London: Hazell, Watson, & Viney, 1884), 103–18, 127, 160–61.

68. Thompson, *Mobility and Migration,* 235.

69. Anderson, *New England's Generation,* 35; and "Migrants and Motives: Religion and the Settlement of New England, 1630–1640," *New England Quarterly* 58 (September 1985): 379.

70. Thompson, *Mobility and Migration,* 110.

71. See Games for a discussion of how family and friends joined to plan voyages (*Migration,* 57).

72. William Lawson Grant and James Munro, eds., *Acts of the Privy Council of England: Colonial Series, 1613–1680* (Hereford: Anthony Brothers, 1908), 1:199–201. In February 1635 Trerise successfully petitioned for the return of his bond (ibid., 1:206).

73. Cressy, *Coming Over*, 135.

74. Hotten, *Original Lists*, 43–56.

75. Cressy, *Coming Over*, 156; Games, *Migration*, 38.

76. Parkes, *Travel in England*, 15.

77. As William Whiteway recorded in his diary for January 1635, "This yeere we had an extreme hard winter with much frost, severe haile, cold raines, so that the Thames was frozen and men went and rode over it" (Quoted in Carl Bridenbaugh, *Vexed and Troubled Englishmen, 1590–1642* [New York: Oxford Univ. Press, 1968], 63n).

78. Games, *Migration*, 66.

79. According to Cressy, "of 198 recorded voyages bringing settlers to New England in the 1630s only that of the *Angel Gabriel* ended in disaster, and even then most of the passengers survived" (*Coming Over*, 148).

80. Winsser, "Nicholas Trerise," 26–27.

81. Games, *Migration*, 70.

82. Anderson, *New England's Generation*, 77.

83. By 1635 John Winthrop had discontinued his systematic record of the arrival of every ship. On 7 June 1635 he recorded, "the Lordes day there came in 7: other shippes & one to Salem & 4: more to the mouthe of the Baye with Store of Passingers & Cattle they came all within 6: weekes" (*Journal of John Winthrop, 1630–1649*, ed. Richard S. Dunn, James Savage, and Laetitia Yeandle [Cambridge, Mass.: Harvard Univ. Press, 1996], 147). Given its departure date, the *Planter* likely was among this group of ships, but no evidence exists to confirm this speculation.

84. Darrett Bruce Rutman, *Winthrop's Boston: Portrait of a Puritan Town, 1630–1649* (New York: Norton, 1972), 57, 203.

85. Richard Donald Pierce, ed., *The Records of the First Church in Boston, 1630–1868*, Colonial Society of Massachusetts, *Collections*, vol. 39 (Boston, 1961), 20.

86. Edmund S. Morgan, *Visible Saints: The History of a Puritan Idea* (Ithaca, N.Y.: Cornell Univ. Press, 1965), 99.

87. Games, *Migration*, 140–41.

88. Rutman notes that for a brief period in 1635–36, Boston linked land ownership to church membership (*Winthrop's Boston*, 78, 156–57).

89. *Boston Town Records 1634–1660, and the Book of Possessions*, Second Report of the Record Commissioners, 2nd ed. (Boston: Rockwell & Churchill, 1881), 29, 36, 43; Rutman, *Winthrop's Boston*, 73. The additional lots cost him £93.07.02. After Richard Tuttle's death, his wife was recorded as the owner of two home lots in Boston and a "Farme at Rumney Marsh" (*Boston Book of Possessions*, 7–8).

90. Richard Tuttle took the freeman's oath on 3 March 1636 (Nathaniel Bradstreet Shurtleff, ed. *Records of the Governor and Company of the Massachusetts Bay in New England* [Boston: W. White, 1853–54], 1:371); *Boston Town Recs.*, 9.

91. *Boston Town Recs.*, 35, 160n; Rutman, *Winthrop's Boston*, 225, 72–75. Richard Tuttle died in May 1640 at the age of forty-seven. For a summary of his colonial career, see Anderson, *Great Migration*, 7:136–38.

92. Allen, *In English Ways*, 132, 185, 269–79.

93. Abraham Hammatt, *The Hammatt Papers: Early Inhabitants of Ipswich, Massachusetts, 1633–1700* (1880–99; reprint, Baltimore: Genealogical Pub. Co., 1980), 375; Edward S. Perzel, "Landholding in Ipswich," *Essex Institute Historical Collections* 104, no. 4 (1968): 303, 309, 310, 323.

94. Shurtleff, *Massachusetts Bay Recs.*, 1:375. Ipswich church records for the seventeenth century are no longer extant (Harold Field Worthley, *An Inventory of the Records of the Particular (Congregational) Churches of Massachusetts Gathered 1620–1805* [Cambridge, Mass.: Harvard Univ. Press, 1970], 305).

95. Oliver Ayer Roberts, *History of the Military Company of Massachusetts, Now Called the Ancient and Honorable Artillery Company of Massachusetts, 1637–1888* (Boston: Alfred Mudge, 1895), 1:145; Shurtleff, *Massachusetts Bay Recs.*, 1:253, 308; 2:4, 35–36, 55; Thomas Franklin Waters, *Ipswich in the Massachusetts Bay* (Ipswich, Mass.: Ipswich Historical Society, 1905), 1:80.

96. On 19 December 1648, the town assessed four men, including John Tuttle, at a tax rate of 8 shillings; only one inhabitant qualified for a higher rate of 10 shillings ("Ipswich Proceedings," *New England Historical and Genealogical Register* 2 [January 1848]: 50–52). Fifteen years after settling in Ipswich, John Tuttle became entangled in an unfortunate business deal that led to his removal from New England and his ultimate relocation to Carrickfergus, Ireland, a nonconformist stronghold north of Belfast, where he apparently worked for the Irish Treasury (St. John D. Seymour, *The Puritans in Ireland, 1647–1661* [Oxford: Clarendon Press, 1969], 57). See William Aspinwall, *Notarial Records from 1644 to 1651* (Boston: Municipal Printing Office, 1903), 344–46, 423–24; W. B. Trask, ed., *Suffolk Deeds* (Boston: Rockwell & Churchill, 1880), 1:265–72; George Francis Dow, ed., *Records and Files of the Quarterly Courts of Essex County, Massachusetts* (Salem: Essex Institute, 1913), 2:141–43, 171–74, 178, 363–65); George Francis Dow, ed., *Probate Records of Essex County, Massachusetts* (Salem: Essex Institute, 1916), 1:277–78. For a summary of John Tuttle's colonial career, see Anderson, *Great Migration*, 7:125–35.

97. Richard Frothingham, *The History of Charlestown, Massachusetts* (Charlestown: C. P. Emmons, 1845), 84; Rutman, *Winthrop's Boston*, 29, 38.

98. This profile of the Charlestown "Gentry image" is developed by Ralph J. Crandall and Ralph J. Coffman in "From Emigrants to Rulers: The Charlestown Oligarchy in the Great Migration," *New England Historical and Genealogical Register* 131 (January 1977), 9–11.

99. Pierce, *Boston Church Recs.*, 21. Their children's baptismal records confirm William Tuttle's exclusion from church membership. For example, on 2 July 1637 the Boston church book records that "Jonothan the Sonne of our Sistar Elizabeth the wife of Willyam Tuttell" was baptized (ibid., 282).

100. Crandall and Coffman "From Emigrants to Rulers," 13. They estimate that between 1635 and 1640, 57 percent of Charlestown's eligible males were not church members (ibid., 12).

101. "Greene's Transcript" of the Charlestown Town Records, Charlestown Archives, 1629–1847, Town Records, vol. 2, 1629–1661 (14 July 1635, 3 October 1635, 9 February 1635/6, 17 February 1636/7, November 1637), LDS Family History Library, Microfilm No. 478190.

102. Charlestown Land Records, which lists the land holdings of town residents in 1638, does not include an entry for William Tuttle. The only indication in these records that he owned land in the Charlestown area is in the entry for John Hall, which states that Hall had four acres of farmland bordering "north upon [W]ill Tutle and the common" (*Charlestown Land Records, 1638–1802*, Third Report of the Record Commissioners [Boston: Rockwell & Churchill, 1878], 32).

103. *Boston Town Recs.*, 33. The Charlestown Town Records make no mention of William Tuttle after September 1637.

104. Games estimates that approximately two-thirds of the migrants who traveled to New England in 1635 moved at least once (*Migration*, 168–69); using a different sample, Anderson places the figure higher, at 80 percent (*New England's Generation*, 114).

105. Anderson, *New England's Generation*, 92.

106. Anderson, *New England's Generation*, 23.

107. Donald Lines Jacobus, comp., *Families of Ancient New Haven* (1922–1932; reprint, 9 vols. in 3, Baltimore: Genealogical Publishing Co., 1974), 3:1882–83.
108. Large families, like the Tuttles, that traveled to New England in 1635 were "disproportionately likely" to move from already-settled Massachusetts towns. Of those families that had initially settled in Charlestown, moreover, 51.3 percent relocated to other towns (Games, *Migration*, 172, 175–76). Of the ten Charlestown families that moved to New Haven between 1638 and 1640, all were landless like William Tuttle (see the statistical tabulation of Charlestown residents compiled by Crandall and Coffman, "From Emigrants to Rulers," 22, 25, 121, 126, 128, 130, 132, 211).
109. Isabel M. Calder, *The New Haven Colony* (New Haven: Yale Univ. Press, 1934), 44–46, 146, 50.
110. David Tuttle was baptized on 7 April 1639 (*Boston Church Recs.*, 283).
111. Charles J. Hoadly, ed., *Records of the Colony and Plantation of New-Haven, from 1638 to 1649* (Hartford: Case, Tiffany and Co., 1857), 17–18. Another forty-eight men signed the agreement at a later date (ibid., 18).
112. Edward E. Atwater, *History of the Colony of New Haven to Its Absorption into Connecticut.* (New Haven, 1881), 75–81. No record exists of the original distribution of home lots, but according to Rollin G. Osterweiss, "By the winter of 1638–39 most of the original company who had arrived in April were living on their house lots" (*Three Centuries of New Haven, 1638–1938* [New Haven: Yale Univ. Press, 1964], 12). For the layout of the original house lots in 1641, see Atwater, *History of New Haven*, 103–54.
113. Atwater, *History of New Haven*, 77. William Tuttle likely acquired the lot originally granted to Edward Hopkins, the husband of Theophilus Eaton's stepdaughter Anne Yale, following his remove to Hartford (ibid., 118–20).
114. Hoadly, *New Haven Colony and Plantation Recs.*, 43, 91, 197. According to Atwater, New Haven's first tax roll was prepared prior to the April 1641 assessment, but it must have been drawn up earlier, for it lists the Tuttle family as comprising seven people. On 22 November 1640, when the Tuttles' sixth child was baptized, the family increased to eight (*History of New Haven*, 108; Jacobus, *Families of Ancient New Haven*, 3:1883).
115. Atwater, *History of New Haven*, 80–81.
116. Franklin Bowditch Dexter, ed., *New Haven Town Records, 1649–1662*, Ancient Town Records (New Haven: Colony Historical Society, 1917), 1:54.
117. David Pulsifer, ed., *Acts of the Commissioners of the United Colonies of New England, 1643–1651*, vol. 9 of *Records of the Colony of New Plymouth* (1859; reprint, New York: AMS Press, 1968), 210, 211, 212.
118. For a description of the Delaware settlement, see Atwater, *History of New Haven*, 193–204; and Charles H. Levermore, *The Republic of New Haven: A History of Municipal Evolution* (1886; reprint, Port Washington, N.Y.: Kennikat Press, 1966), 90–99. Additional evidence of William Tuttle's dabbling in trade was his investment in a "ketch, called the *Zebulon*," which sailed out of Ipswich, his brother John's home (Petition to the Massachusetts General Court, Massachusetts Archives, SC1/series 45X, Massachusetts Archives Collection, vol. 60, Maritime, 1641–1671, 168a [Internal evidence indicates that this undated petition was written in 1650–51, the same year as the Delaware settlement]).
119. Pierce, *Boston Church Recs.*, 25; Atwater, *History of New Haven*, 101. Mrs. Elizabeth Tuttle received membership in the New Haven church in 1640 (Franklin Bowditch Dexter, *Historical Catalogue of the Members of the First Church of Christ in New Haven* [New Haven: n.p., 1914], 5).
120. Hoadly, *New Haven Colony and Plantation Recs.*, 13.
121. Cotton Mather, *Magnalia Christi Americana*, ed. Thomas Robbins (1852; reprint, New York: Russell & Russell, 1967), 1:328, 327.

122. Elizabeth Tucker Van Beek, "Piety and Profit: English Puritans and the Shaping of a Godly Marketplace in the New Haven Colony" (Ph.D. diss., University of Virginia, 1993), 471. According to Van Beek, of the 267 total church members, 65 percent were admitted in the first decade, 14 percent in the second, and 21 percent in the third (ibid., 367).

123. Hoadly, *New Haven Colony and Plantation Recs.*, 15, 137, 139, 41, 319; Dexter, *New Haven Town Recs.*, 1:80, 433, 445, 489. After the union with Connecticut, when New Haven was forced to abandon church membership as a prerequisite for freemanship, William Tuttle was elected constable and town auditor (Franklin Bowditch Dexter, ed., *New Haven Town Records, 1662–1684*, Ancient Town Records (New Haven: Colony Historical Society, 1919), 2:198, 187). For a summary of William Tuttle's colonial career, see Anderson, *Great Migration*, 7:138–45.

124. Hoadly, *New Haven Colony and Plantation Recs.*, 302, 303, 92; see also Atwater, *History of New Haven*, 543, 544, 109.

125. Elizabeth Tuttle was baptized on 9 November 1645 (Jacobus, *Families of Ancient New Haven*, 3:1884).

CHAPTER 2

1. Roger Finlay and Beatrice Shearer estimate that the population of the greater London metropolitan area was 110,00 in 1560, 355,000 in 1640, and 435,00 in 1680, while the population of east London grew from 10,000 in 1560 to 90,000 in 1640 and to 140,000 in 1680 ("Population Growth and Suburban Expansion," *London, 1500–1700: The Making of a Metropolis*, ed. A. L. Beier and Roger Finlay [London: Longman, 1986], 45). Michael J. Power, "The Urban Development of East London, 1550–1700," (Ph.D. diss., University of London, 1971), 172–97; Joseph P. Ward, "Imagining the Metropolis in Elizabethan and Stuart London," in *The Country and the City Revisited: England and the Politics of Culture, 1550–1850*, ed. Gerald Maclean, Donna Landry, and Joseph P. Ward (Cambridge: Cambridge Univ. Press, 1999), 30–31.

2. John Stowe, *A Survey of London*, ed. Charles Lethbridge Kingsford (1603; reprint, Oxford: Clarendon Press, 1908), 2:72; Michael J. Power, "East London Housing in the Seventeenth Century," in *Crisis and Order in English Towns, 1500–1700*, ed. Peter Clark and Paul Slack (London: Routledge & Kegan Paul, 1972), 246.

3. Power, "Urban Development," 50–51; Wrightson, *Earthly Necessities*, 125.

4. Paul Slack estimates that major epidemics occurred in London every fourteen years between 1540 and 1666 (*The Impact of Plague in Tudor and Stuart England* [Oxford: Clarendon Press, 1985], 151; Power, "Urban Development," 68, 70).

5. William Foster, *A Short History of the Worshipful Company of Coopers of London* (Cambridge: Cambridge Univ. Press, 1944), 14; Bob Gilding, *The Journeymen Coopers of East London: Workers' Control in an Old London Trade*, History Workshop Pamphlets (1971), 5, 14; Joseph P. Ward, *Metropolitan Communities: Trade Guilds, Identity and Change in Early Modern London* (Stanford, Calif.: Stanford Univ. Press, 1997), 33; George Unwin, *The Guilds and Companies of London* (1908; reprint, New York: Barnes and Noble, 1966), 266.

6. In his will Henry Munter identifies himself as a "citizen and cooper of London" living in East Smithfield. He also bequeathed to his grandchildren two "silver and guilt" spoons (Will of Henrie Munter, Cooper of East Smithfield, Middlesex, 8 September 1638, PROB 11/178, 96v, The National Archives of the United Kingdom, London).

7. Samuel Hopkins, *The Life and Character of the Late Reverend, Learned, and Pious, Mr. Jonathan Edwards* (1765; reprint, Northampton: S. & E. Butler, 1804), 2n.

8. The clearest indication that Richard Edwards attended university is his designation as "Richard Edwards, B.A." in the record of his employment by the Ratcliffe Free School. That he was a clergyman is confirmed by William's 1618 baptismal record, which identifies

the infant as the "son of Richard Edwards, minister, and Anne his wife" (Elizur Yale Smith, "English Ancestry of Jonathan Edwards," *New York Genealogical and Biographical Record* 70 [April 1939]: 105–6, 107). In "English Ancestry," Smith cites important parish registry data but, as Howard S. F. Randolph points out, draws some erroneous conclusions from it ("A Reply to 'The English Ancestry of Jonathan Edwards,'" *New York Genealogical and Biographical Record* 70 [July 1639]: 269–70). See also Charles Edward Banks, "The Edwards Family of Connecticut," *New York Genealogical and Biographical Record* 62 (April 1931): 116–20; and Jacobus and Waterman, *Hale, House*, 524–27.

9. Smith, "English Ancestry," 107.
10. Ibid., 105–6.
11. William Foster, *The Ratcliffe Charity, 1536–1936* (London: Allenson, [1936]), 4, 5–6, 12. See also J. S. Cockburn, H. P. F. King, and K. G. T. McDonnell, eds., *A History of the County of Middlesex*, Victoria History of the Counties of England (Oxford: Oxford Univ. Press, 1969), 1:291–93, and T. F. T. Baker, *A History of the County of Middlesex*, Victoria History of the Counties of England (Oxford: Oxford Univ. Press, 1998), 11:83–86.
12. David Cressy, "Educational Opportunity in Tudor and Stuart England," *History of Education Quarterly* 16 (Autumn 1976): 303, 307.
13. Foster, *Ratcliffe Charity*, 7.
14. Cressy, "Educational Opportunity," 307–8. According to Foster, in 1595 the schoolmaster's salary totaled 23*l*. 6*s*. 8*d*. and did not increase for many years thereafter (*Ratcliffe Charity*, 10, 14).
15. William Edwards was baptized in November 1618 at St. Botolph Aldgate, a parish in the eastern liberties outside the London wall (Smith, "English Ancestry," 107).
16. Power, "Urban Development," 68, 74.
17. Parish records indicate that "Richard Edwards, Scholemaister of Ratcliffe ffreeschoole" died of plague on 31 August 1625 (Smith, "English Ancestry," 106); Power, "Urban Development," 66.
18. Slack, *Impact of the Plague*, 177.
19. Anne gave birth to a son named John in 1621 and a daughter named Sarah in 1623 (Smith, "English Ancestry," 107).
20. No death records have been located for any of these children, but their deaths can be inferred from other documents. A 1634 letter that lists Anne Edwards Cole's children includes only William from her first marriage (James Cole to Anne Edwards Cole, 30 June 1634, Sloan MS 922, 95r–v, British Library, London). Likewise, her stepfather's will grants a bequest to no child from her first marriage but William (Will of Henrie Munter, PROB 11/178, 96v).
21. Vivien Brodsky suggests that the rate of remarriage was highest among widows of middling status, like Anne Edwards, for wealthy widows did not need to remarry and poor widows could not find a mate ("Widows in Late Elizabethan London: Remarriage, Economic Opportunity and Family Orientations," in *The World We Have Gained: Histories of Population and Social Structure*, ed. Lloyd Bonfield, Richard M. Smith, and Keith Wrightson [Oxford: Basil Blackwell, 1986], 123, 128).
22. Although life expectancy in early modern England was around thirty-eight years, in some poor London parishes it was as low as twenty-one years (Wrightson, *Earthly Necessities*, 222; Roger Finlay, *Population and Metropolis: The Demography of London, 1580–1650* [Cambridge: Cambridge Univ. Press, 1981], 108). A quarter of all children in England died before age ten, while "less than half London-born children survived to a marriageable age" (Wrightson, *English Society*, 105; Finlay and Shearer, "Population Growth," 50).
23. Brodsky, "Widows," 129.
24. Smith, "English Ancestry," 106.

25. On Wallington, see Paul S. Seaver, *Wallington's World: A Puritan Artisan in Seventeen-Century London* (Stanford, Calif.: Stanford Univ. Press, 1985).

26. Will of Julian Munter, Widow of East Smithfield, Middlesex, 8 January 1646/7, PROB 11/199, 127v, The National Archives of the United Kingdom, London.

27. Power, "Urban Development," 264–65.

28. Seaver, *Puritan Lectureships*, 199, 210, 224, 185–86, 233.

29. Seaver, *Wallington's World*, 149; Seaver, *Puritan Lectureships*, 199, 256. Julian Munter left Samuel Slater, the preacher at St. Katherine's, 20 shillings in her will (Will of Julian Munter, PROB 11/199, 127v).

30. Michael J. Power, "The Social Topography of Restoration London," in *London, 1500–1700*, ed. Beier and Finlay, 212–22.

31. Anne and James Cole had a son named after his father in 1626, a year after their marriage, and at least two more children, a daughter named Abigail and a son named Timothy, before 1634 (Smith, "English Ancestry," 109; Will of Henrie Munter, PROB 11/178, 96v).

32. James Cole to Anne Edwards Cole, 30 June 1634, Sloan MS 922, 94r–v. The autograph letters are no longer extant, but copies of the correspondence that documents James Cole's absence from London were recorded by Nehemiah Wallington in his diary and are preserved in Sloan MS 922, folios 94r–107v, 173r–176v, The British Library, London. See also Seaver, *Wallington's World*, 95–100.

33. Michael Reed, "Economic Structure and Change in Seventeenth Century Ipswich," in *Country Towns in Pre-Industrial England*, ed. Peter Clark (New York: St. Martin's Press, 1981), 103–4.

34. Craig Muldrew, *The Economy of Obligation: The Culture of Credit and Social Relations in Early Modern England* (New York: St. Martin's Press, 1998), 2, 95.

35. For a discussion of the primitive state of early modern accounting, see Muldrew, *Economy of Obligation*, 60–69. Wallington apparently kept no account book (Seaver, *Wallington's World*, 118–19).

36. *The Notebooks of Nehemiah Wallington, 1618–1654: A Selection*, ed. David Booy (Burlington: Ashgate, 2007), 148.

37. James Cole to Henry and Julian Munter, 1634, Sloan MS 922, 99r; James Cole to Anne Edwards Cole, 30 June 1634, Sloan MS, 922, 95r.

38. Muldrew, *Economy of Obligation*, 174–75, 200–1, 109–10, 205–6.

39. James Cole to Henry and Julian Munter, 1634, Sloan MS 922, 99v.

40. Donald Veall, *The Popular Movement for Law Reform, 1640–1660* (Oxford: Clarendon Press, 1970), 13–16; Roger Lee Brown, *History of the Fleet Prison, London: The Anatomy of the Fleet* (Lewiston, N.Y.: Edwin Mellen Press, 1996), x.

41. Muldrew, *Economy of Obligation*, 288–90; Veall, *Law Reform*, 145–49.

42. *Imprisonment of Men's Bodyes for Debt, as the Practice of England Now Stands* (London 1641), 21–22.

43. James Cole to Henry and Julian Munter, 1634, Sloan MS 922, 99v; James Cole to Anne Edwards Cole, n.d., Sloan MS 922, 96r.

44. Muldrew, *Economy of Obligation*, 3, 152, 274, 282.

45. Nehemiah Wallington to James Cole, 19 June 1634, Sloan MS 922, 97r, v; James Cole to Anne Edwards Cole, 29 November 1634, Sloan MS 922, 101r; James Cole to Anne Edwards Cole, n.d., Sloan MS 922, 96v.

46. Nehemiah Wallington to James Cole, 19 June 1634, Sloan MS, 922, 98r, 97r.

47. Ibid., 97v.

48. John Wallington to James Cole, 6 June 1635, Sloan MS 922, 102r, 102v.

49. James Cole to Henry and Julian Munter, 1634, Sloan MS 922, 99r, 99r–v; James Cole to Anne Edwards Cole, 29 November 1634, Sloan MS 922, 101r.

50. Alexandra Shepard, "Manhood, Credit and Patriarchy in Early Modern England, c. 1580–1640," *Past and Present* 167 (May 2000): 78, 84.

51. John Wallington to James Cole, 6 June 1635, Sloan MS 922, 102r.

52. Seaver, *Puritan Lectureships*, 111–12, 96; Norman C. P. Tyack, "The Humbler Puritans of East Anglia and the New England Movement: Evidence from the Court Records of the 1630s," *New England Historical and Genealogical Register* 138 (April 1984): 96–97.

53. Nehemiah Wallington to James Cole, 19 June 1634, Sloan MS 922, 97r, 98v; John Wallington to James Cole, 6 June 1635, Sloan MS 922, 103r.

54. Ann Hughes, *Politics, Society and Civil War in Warwickshire, 1620–1660* (Cambridge: Cambridge Univ. Press, 1987), 17.

55. Power, "Urban Development," 196.

56. Joanne Bailey, *Unquiet Lives: Marriage and Marriage Breakdown in England, 1660–1800* (Cambridge: Cambridge Univ. Press, 2003), 174. See also J. Boulton, "'It is Extreme Necessity that Makes Me Do This': Some 'Survival Strategies' of Pauper Households in London's West End During the Early Eighteenth Century," in *Household Strategies for Survival, 1600–2000: Fission, Faction, and Cooperation*, ed. Laurence Fontaine and Jürgen Schlumbohm (Cambridge: Cambridge Univ. Press, 2000), 66.

57. James Cole to Anne Edwards Cole, 30 June 1634, Sloan MS 922, 94r–v.

58. Wrightson, *English Society*, 93; Wrightson, *Earthly Necessities*, 46–47.

59. James Cole to Anne Edwards Cole, 30 June 1634, Sloan MS 922, 94v; James Cole to Henry and Julian Munter, 1634, Sloan MS 922, 99v–100r.

60. James Cole to Anne Edwards Cole, n.d., Sloan MS 922, 96v; James Cole to Henry and Julian Munter, 1634, Sloan MS 922, 100r.

61. That Anne was still in London in 1635 is suggested by John Wallington's letter to James Cole dated 6 June 1635, in which he writes, "you should be at White Chapell with your wife (Sloan MS 922, 102v).

62. David Hackett Fischer, *Albion's Seed: Four British Folkways in America* (New York: Oxford Univ. Press, 1989), 31.

63. Thompson, *Mobility and Migration*, 22; Fischer, *Albion's Seed*, 34n; Reed, "Seventeenth-Century Ipswich," 97.

64. James Cole to Anne Edwards Cole, 29 November 1634, Sloan MS 922, 101v.

65. Hughes, *Politics, Society, and Civil War*, 64–65, 72–73.

66. James Cole to Henry and Julian Munter, 1634, Sloan MS 922, 100r. According to Seaver, one of the "great men" was Lord Brooke; the other was probably either the earl of Warwick or William Fiennes, Viscount Saye and Sele, another prominent puritan aristocrat (*Wallington's World*, 191).

67. David Cressy, *Coming Over*, 40, 63, 67.

68. William Wood, *New England's Prospect*, ed. Alden T. Vaughn (1634; reprint, Amherst: Univ. of Massachusetts Press, 1977), 72–73; Cressy, *Coming Over*, 44.

69. In addition to Anne's son William, James and Anne's daughter Abigail also immigrated with her family to New England. If their youngest son, Timothy, also made the voyage, he was not living in 1652 when his father died, for the bulk of his estate was left to his daughter (Charles W. Manwaring, *A Digest of Early Connecticut Probate Records, Hartford District, 1635–1700* (Hartford: R. S. Peck, 1904), 1:108–9.). Their oldest son, James, had evidently died before they left England (James Cole to Anne Edwards Cole, 30 June 1634, Sloan MS 922, 95r–v).

70. John Winthrop, *The History of New England, from 1630 to 1649*, ed. James Savage (1825; reprint, 2 vols. in 1, New York: Arno Press, 1972), 1:136.

71. Richard S. Dunn, *Puritans and Strangers: The Winthrop Dynasty of New England, 1630–1717* (1962; reprint, New York: Norton, 1972), 66–67.

72. Love, *History of Hartford*, 2, 102–3.
73. Winthrop, *History of New England*, 1:140.
74. Bruce C. Daniels, *The Connecticut Town: Growth and Development, 1635–1790* (Middletown, Conn.: Wesleyan Univ. Press, 1979), 10. The Great and Little rivers are today called the Connecticut and Park rivers, respectively.
75. Love, *History of Hartford*, 7, 10–11, 31, 37; Winthrop, *History of New England*, 1:187.
76. Karen Ordall Kupperman, *Providence Island, 1630–1641: The Other Puritan Colony* (Cambridge: Cambridge Univ. Press, 1993), 327; George Wyllys, the future governor of the colony, was a wealthy Warwickshire landowner with ties to Brooke and Saye (ibid., 330–31).
77. Jackson Turner Maine, *Society and Economy in Colonial Connecticut* (Princeton, N.J.: Princeton Univ. Press, 1985), 6.
78. Cressy, *Coming Over,* 93.
79. Will of Henrie Munter, PROB 11/178, 96v.
80. Cressy, *Coming Over,* 123–24. According to Foster, ships always sailed with one or two coopers on board to repair barrels en route (*History of the Coopers' Company*, 14).
81. Charles J. Hoadly, ed., *Hartford Town Votes, Volume 1, 1635–1716*, Connecticut Historical Society, *Collections,* vol. 6 (Hartford, 1897), 18; Love, *History of Hartford*, 125, 126.
82. *Original Distribution of the Lands in Hartford Among the Settlers, 1639–1688*, Connecticut Historical Society, *Collections,* vol. 14 (Hartford, 1912), 195; Charles M. Andrews, *The River Towns of Connecticut: A Study of Wethersfield, Hartford, and Windsor* (Baltimore: Johns Hopkins Univ. Press, 1889), 43.
83. Hoadly, *Hartford Town Votes*, 1:16, 23, 50.
84. *Hartford Land Recs.*, 196.
85. Love, *History of Hartford*, 295, 296; Maine, *Society and Economy*, 241. The earliest inn in Hartford was located on the lot adjoining Cole's shop (Love, *History of Hartford*, 216).
86. *Hartford Land Recs.*, 195–96; Manwaring, *Probate Recs.*, 1:108–9. According to Maine, colonial craftsmen also engaged in some farming (*Society and Economy*, 29, 241, 246), and in his will Cole left to his wife "all my Cattle and Crop of Corne now on the ground" (Manwaring, *Probate Recs.*, 1:109).
87. Daniels, *Connecticut Town*, 119.
88. On 16 September 1639 William Edwards bound himself to work as a servant for a year for Hartford resident John Stone, but he probably never fulfilled the indenture for in the same year Stone sold his Hartford lands and moved to Guilford (*Note-Book Kept by Thomas Lechford . . . From June 27, 1638, to July 29, 1641*, ed. Edward E. Hale and J. Hammond Trumbull [Cambridge, Mass.: Wilson and Sons, 1885], 184; *Hartford Land Recs.*, 347; Bernard C. Steiner, *A History of the Plantation of Menunkatuck and the Original Town of Guilford, Connecticut* [Baltimore, 1897], 25; Love, *History of Hartford*, 11, 13).
89. Maine, *Society and Economy*, 7, 21.
90. Elizur Yale Smith, "The Descendants of William Edwards, Colonist to Connecticut Colony, 1639," *New York Genealogical and Biographical Record* 71 (July 1940): 219.
91. In 1631, William Spencer was listed as one of eight inhabitants of Newtown (*Records of the Town of Cambridge (Formerly Newtowne) Massachusetts, 1630–1703* [Cambridge, 1901], vi, 2).
92. Shurtleff, *Massachusetts Bay Recs.*, 1:190, 250–51; Roberts, *History of the Military Company,* 1:9, 40.
93. Love, *History of Hartford*, 54; J. Hammond Trumbull, ed., *Public Records of the Colony of Connecticut* (Hartford: Brown & Parson, 1850–68), 1:36. For a summary of William Spencer's colonial activities, see Robert Charles Anderson, *The Great Migration Begins: Immigrants to New England, 1620–1633* (Boston: New England Historical and Genealogical Society, 1995), 3:1721–25.

94. Manwaring, *Probate Recs.*, 1:36–37.
95. Mary Beth Norton, *Founding Mothers and Fathers: Gendered Power and the Forming of American Society* (New York: Vintage, 1997), 139, 140.
96. Trumbull, *Conn. Public Recs.*, 1:450; Manwaring, *Probate Recs.*, 1:36; Marylynn Salmon, *Women and the Law of Property in Early America* (Chapel Hill: Univ. of North Carolina Press, 1986), 141–43.
97. Gloria L. Maine, *Peoples of a Spacious Land: Families and Cultures in Colonial New England* (Cambridge, Mass.: Harvard Univ. Press, 2001), 84–85. According to John Faragher, in seventeenth-century Wethersfield 44.4 percent of widows under fifty years of age remarried ("Old Women and Old Men in Seventeenth-Century Wethersfield, Connecticut," *Women's Studies* 4 [December 1976]: 19).
98. Anne S. Lombard, *Making Manhood: Growing Up Male in Colonial New England* (Cambridge, Mass.: Harvard Univ. Press, 2003), 18–19.
99. When he died in 1652, James Cole left all his real property to his daughter, Abigail, his only living child, and her husband, a New Haven mariner named Daniel Sullivane. William Edwards received half his stepfather's cooper's tools (Manwaring, *Probate Recs.*, 1:109).
100. Edwards bought part of this lot from an adjoining landowner. Together with a parcel of land he acquired in exchange for land owned by William Spencer, it apparently was one of only two properties recorded to William Edwards during his lifetime (*Hartford Land Recs.*, 353–54).
101. Salmon, *Women and Property*, 22, 6. When William Edwards married Agnes Spencer, the family realty consisted of a two-acre home lot, 63 acres of pasture, 10 acres of pinefield, 13 acres of meadow, and 8.5 acres of swamp (*Hartford Land Recs.*, 352–53).
102. Hoadly, *Hartford Town Votes*, 1:77. In January 1641 the town had voted to "make a fence Leading To the mill through Mrs. Spencer's ground & give hir satisfacone for that ground" (ibid., 1:40).
103. When their mother remarried, Elizabeth Spencer was twelve years old, her sister, Sarah, was ten, and young Samuel was six (Anderson, *Great Migration Begins*, 3:1724).
104. Agnes Spencer Edwards was baptized on 6 April 1604 in Devonshire, England (Anderson, *Great Migration Begins*, 3:1724); Richard Edwards was born on 1 May 1647 (Smith, "Descendants of William Edwards," 219).
105. Lombard, *Making Manhood*, 8, 19, 98–99.
106. Faragher, "Old Women and Old Men," 19.
107. Bruce H. Mann, *Neighbors and Strangers: Law and Community in Early Connecticut* (Chapel Hill: Univ. of North Carolina Press), 6; Cornelia Hughes Dayton, *Women Before the Bar: Gender, Law, and Society in Connecticut, 1639-1789* (Chapel Hill: Univ. of North Carolina Press, 1995), 40.
108. Dayton, *Women Before the Bar*, 81, n21.
109. While he was awarded only slightly more than £21, his losses totaled almost £113.
110. Mann, *Neighbors and Strangers*, 15, 16.
111. Dayton, *Women Before the Bar*, 82.
112. Mann, *Neighbors and Strangers*, 107.
113. In two cases, Edwards as plaintiff withdrew the action; another case was settled when Edwards, as defendant, failed to appear. But the outcome of the majority of cases that were withdrawn before trial is not explicitly recorded.
114. *Records of the Particular Court of Connecticut, 1639-1663*, Connecticut Historical Society, *Collections*, vol. 22 (Hartford, 1928), 29, 192–93. In the second case, Edwards paid a substantial damage award of £5. By contrast, for the first conviction he paid only 20 shillings.

115. Helen Schatvet Ullmann, trans., *Hartford County Court Minutes, Vols. 3 and 4, 1663–1687, 1697* (Boston: New England Historic Genealogical Society, 2005), 6.
116. *Particular Ct. Recs.*, 196–97. Edwards had evidently been drawn into the controversy that eventually resulted in the division of the Wethersfield church. See Trumbull, *Conn. Public Recs.*, 1:319–20, and Paul R. Lucas, *Valley of Discord: Church and Society Along the Connecticut River, 1636–1725* (Hanover, N.H.: Univ. Press of New England, 1976), 50–51, 75–77.
117. Finding some substance to the charge, the magistrates removed Clark as secretary until the next election (Trumbull, *Conn. Public Recs.*, 1:401, 405).
118. Mann, *Neighbors and Strangers*, 17–20.
119. *Particular Ct. Recs.*, 185, 199, 206–7, 164, 186–87; Trumbull, *Conn. Public Recs.*, 1:309; *Hartford Land Recs.*, 411–13; Love, *History of Hartford*, 43; Richard P. Gildrie, *The Profane, the Civil, and the Godly: The Reformation of Manners in Orthodox New England, 1679–1749* (University Park: Pennsylvania State Univ. Press, 1994), 75. Neither the uncivil carriage nor the defamation charge came to trial, but Edwards was convicted of unjust molestation.
120. Robert St. George, "'Heated' Speech and Literacy in Seventeenth-Century New England," in *Seventeenth-Century New England*, ed. David D. Hall and David Grayson Allen, Colonial Society of Massachusetts, *Publications*, vol. 63 (Boston, 1984), 295. Edwards twice made slander charges against men suing him for payment, but he lost both suits (*Particular Ct. Recs.*, 39–40, 60, 67).
121. David D. Hall, ed. *Witch-Hunting in Seventeenth-Century New England: A Documentary History, 1638–1695* (Boston: Northeastern Univ. Press, 1991), 161–62; Karlsen, *Devil in the Shape of a Woman*, 140. On the Hartford hunt, see Hall, *Witch-Hunting*, 147–63, and John Putnam Demos, *Entertaining Satan: Witchcraft and the Culture of Early New England* (New York: Oxford Univ. Press, 1982), 340–67.
122. Demos, *Entertaining Satan*, 76–79, 86–89, 38–39, 53–54, 353.
123. No family connection can be shown between James Cole, William Edwards's stepfather, and Ann Cole, the possessed girl who sparked the Hartford witch-hunt. Several years before the hunt began, however, John Cole, the girl's father, had purchased the home lot and farmlands that James Cole's daughter, Abigail, had inherited after her father's death (Manwaring, *Probate Recs.*, 1:50, *Hartford Land Recs.*, 486). Another small hint connecting William Edwards to the witch-hunt is the complaint he made against Jacob Mygatt, whose mother had provided important testimony in Elizabeth Seager's witchcraft trial (Hall, *Witch-Hunting*, 160). Edwards accused Mygatt of swearing "by the life of God, or By God that he would plauge Edwardses wife." The meaning of this odd threat is unclear, but because Mygatt allegedly made it during the hunt it suggests that he may have suspected Agnes Edwards of witchcraft. In response, Mygatt charged Edwards with a series of speech and behavior offenses (Ullmann, *Hartford County Ct. Minutes*, 13, 6).
124. *Hartford Land Recs.*, 294–95, 415; Lucius R. Paige, *History of Cambridge, Massachusetts, 1630–1877* (Boston: H. O. Houghton, 1877), 481. Neither copy of the mortgage indicates that it was paid. However, land records subsequent to the date of the mortgage list William Edwards's home lot on the green as an abutter (*Hartford Land Recs.*, 408, 523), and it appears that this was the home lot transferred to his wife in 1663 (*Hartford Land Recs.*, 354).
125. *Hartford Land Recs.*, 353, 144, 39, 168, 459, 494. When he died William Spencer owned land in Concord, Massachusetts, worth £120, which was also sold sometime prior to 1654 (Trumbull, *Conn. Public Recs.*, 1:451; Brian Donahue, *The Great Meadow: Farmers and the Land in Colonial Concord* [New Haven: Yale Univ. Press, 2004], 80, 108, 271 n.21). The only land Edwards acquired through purchase during his marriage was a small, perhaps quarter-acre, augmentation of his house lot on the town green (*Hartford Land Recs.*, 353).

NOTES

126. Lombard, *Making Manhood*, 10.
127. *Hartford Land Recs.*, 354; Manwaring, *Probate Recs.*, 1:109.
128. Laurel Thatcher Ulrich, *Good Wives: Image and Reality in the Lives of Women in Northern New England, 1650–1750* (New York: Vintage Books, 1991), 49–50.
129. Aspinwall, *Notarial Recs.*, 113–14.
130. William Blackstone, *Commentaries on the Laws of England* (1765; reprint, Chicago: Univ. of Chicago Press, 1979), 1:430.
131. Salmon, *Women and Property*, xv, 82, 123–32. After his wife assumed ownership of the family property, Edwards's court appearances rapidly declined, and after 1670, his involvement in litigation ceased (Ullmann, *Hartford County Ct. Minutes*, 122–24). Later in life he also achieved a few traditional markers of manhood. At forty he became a member of the Connecticut horse troop and was admitted freeman (Trumbull, *Conn. Public Recs.*, 1:309, 315). He also served in a few small positions of public responsibility in Hartford (Hoadly, *Hartford Town Votes*, 1:152, 154; Ullmann, *Hartford County Ct. Minutes*, 398). He died sometime after March 1686, when he witnessed a mortgage (*Hartford Land Recs.*, 563).
132. *Hartford Land Recs.*, 197. James Cole had stipulated in his will that his daughter and son-in-law care for his widow by providing her an "upper roome" in the dwelling house they had inherited. Abigail Cole, however, did not long outlive her father, and her husband soon remarried. After his death in the summer of 1655, his second wife sold the Cole property (Manwaring, *Probate Recs.*, 1:50, 109; *Hartford Land Recs.*, 486).
133. Manwaring, *Probate Recs.*, 1:292; Ullmann, *Hartford County Ct. Minutes*, 269–70.
134. *Particular Ct. Recs.*, 85–86. According to the terms of William Spencer's will, his son was to receive half this sum, while his two daughters were to split the other half (Manwaring, *Probate Recs.*, 1:36–37).
135. Will of Richard Spencer of London, 17 March 1645, in "Genealogical Gleanings in England," by Henry F. Waters, *New England Historical and Genealogical Register* 45 (July 1891): 232. See also Aspinwall, *Notarial Recs.*, 141.
136. By 1650 Elizabeth had married and moved from Hartford with her husband, William Wellman; six years later her younger sister, Sarah, was living in the neighboring colony of New Netherlands with her husband, John Case (Anderson, *Great Migration Begins*, 3:1724; Manwaring, *Probate Recs.*, 1:104).
137. Samuel Spencer and his wife, Sarah, raised eight children (Lucius Barnes Barbour, *Families of Early Hartford, Connecticut* [Baltimore: Genealogical Publishing Co., 1977], 557). Becoming a freeman soon after marriage, he held a variety of town offices, including constable and selectman. In 1695, he opened an inn, having been granted permission to sell drink by retail (Trumbull, *Conn. Public Recs.*, 2:518; Hoadly, *Hartford Town Votes*, 1:215, 227, 232, 261, 240).
138. Dayton, *Women Before the Bar*, 176, 163. "New England magistrates in this early period," Dayton observes, "often approached lascivious carriage cases as if they were attempted rape cases; they severely punished the man and sometimes declined to bring charges against the woman" (ibid., 177n).
139. Ullmann, *Hartford County Ct. Minutes*, 77.
140. New England weddings usually took place in the bride's home (Bruce Daniels, *Puritans at Play: Leisure and Recreation in Colonial New England* [New York: St. Martin's Press, 1995], 118). That Elizabeth Tuttle married Richard Edwards in New Haven is confirmed by the fact that their marriage was recorded in the vital records for that town (Jacobus, *Families of Ancient New Haven*, 3:1884).
141. In Wethersfield, the average age at first marriage for men was 28 years; in Andover it was 26.7 years for second-generation males, and in Plymouth 26.1 years. Only five second-generation males in Andover, Massachusetts, married before reaching the age of majority

(Faragher, "Old Women and Old Men," 17; Philip J. Greven, *Four Generations: Population, Land, and Family in Colonial Andover, Massachusetts* [Ithaca, N.Y.: Cornell Univ. Press, 1970], 33–34; Demos, *A Little Commonwealth*, 151, 193).

142. Anderson, *Great Migration*, 7:137, 291; Manwaring, *Probate Recs.*, 1:141–42.

143. Ullmann, *Hartford County Ct. Minutes*, 95. Richard and Elizabeth Edwards were one of the last couples fined £5 for this offense; by 1669, convicted couples most commonly paid £3.

144. Robert V. Wells, "Illegitimacy and Bridal Pregnancy in Colonial America," in *Bastardy and Its Comparative History*, ed. Peter Lazlett, Karla Oosterveen, and Richard M. Smith (Cambridge, Mass.: Harvard Univ. Press, 1980), 351.

145. Dayton, *Women Before the Bar*, 173–87. According to Dayton, before 1690 men charged with fornication routinely confessed to their crime and were given a punishment equal to that of the accused woman. Because the law allowed the court to enjoin marriage on convicted couples, many who were not already married did marry subsequent to conviction. Few men, however, challenged what was generally believed to be the godly and manly response to premarital pregnancy (ibid., 173–207).

146. Lombard, *Making Manhood*, 63–64.

147. Laurel Thatcher Ulrich and Lois Stabler, "'Girling of It' in Eighteenth-Century New Hampshire," in *Families and Children*, ed. Peter Benes, Annual Proceedings of the Dublin Seminar for New England Folklife (Boston: Boston Univ. Press, 1987), 30.

148. Richard Godbeer, *Sexual Revolution in Early America* (Baltimore: Johns Hopkins Univ. Press, 2002), 3; see also 33–38.

149. Dayton, *Women Before the Bar*, 188. Only eleven married couples were convicted of fornication in New Haven County between 1670 and 1689 (ibid., 182), while in Hartford County in the same period at least twenty-four were convicted, although the two towns had comparable populations (Jay Mack Holbrook, *Connecticut 1670 Census* [Oxford, Mass.: Holbrook Research Institute, 1977], iii).

150. Dayton, *Women Before the Bar*, 222–23; Godbeer, *Sexual Revolution*, 246–49.

151. Ullmann, *Hartford County Ct. Minutes*, 95.

152. John D. Cushing, ed., *Earliest Laws of the New Haven and Connecticut Colonies, 1639–1673* (Wilmington, Del.: Michael Glazier, 1977), 80; Dayton, *Women Before the Bar*, 158.

153. Ullmann, *Hartford County Ct. Minutes*, 177–78, 61.

154. Ullmann, *Hartford County Ct. Minutes*, 95, emphasis added.

155. Jacobus, *Families of Ancient New Haven*, 2:1480; Hoadly, *New Haven Colony and Plantation Recs.*, 17, 91; Dexter, *Historical Catalogue of the New Haven Church*, 4, 7.

156. Dexter, *New Haven Town Recs.*, 2:91, 228–29. For charges of drunkenness, see ibid., 189, 198, 276.

157. Lawrence Stone, *Road to Divorce: England, 1530–1987* (Oxford: Oxford University Press, 1990), 233, 241–42, 246, 247. The criminal conversation suit that Henry Howard, the 7th Duke of Norfolk, brought in 1692 against his wife's lover was part of a protracted campaign to secure a Parliamentary divorce (ibid., 313–17, 251).

158. New Haven County Court Records, 1666–1855, vol. 1, September 1666–November 1698, Connecticut State Library, Hartford, 13, 20, 22 (10 June 1667; 11 November 1668; 9 June 1669).

159. Laura Gowing, *Common Bodies: Women, Touch, and Power in Seventeenth-Century England* (New Haven: Yale Univ. Press, 2003), 118–22, 140–41, 145–47; and Mary E. Fissell, *Vernacular Bodies: The Politics of Reproduction in Early Modern England* (Oxford: Oxford Univ. Press, 2004), 152–53.

160. Ulrich, *Good Wives*, 97.

161. St. George, "'Heated' Speech," 297, 321–22.

162. Richard Edwards states in his first divorce petition that Elizabeth Tuttle's parents took responsibility for the child, and this arrangement is confirmed by William Tuttle's will, which also provides the name of the child ("A True Abreviate," Conn. Archives, Crimes and Misdemeanors, 1st Ser., 3:235a; "Mr. Tuttle's Will and Inventory," New Haven County Ct. Recs., 1:61 [11 June 1673]).

163. Dawn Keetley discusses "paternity uncertainty" as a cause of homicidal violence in marriage in "Homicidal Envy: The Case of Richard Henry Dana, Sr.'s *Paul Felton*," *Early American Literature* 41 (June 2006): 282.

CHAPTER 3

1. *New Haven Town Recs.*, 1:38–40, 165, 104, 116–17, 481; 2:79–80, 90.

2. Morgan, *The Puritan Family*, 88–89.

3. Gildrie, *Profane, Civil, and Godly*, 2–3, 43, 64, 106. On the protracted adolescence of colonial youth, see Greven, *Four Generations*, 72–99.

4. Roger Thompson, *Sex in Middlesex: Popular Mores in a Massachusetts County, 1649–1699* (Amherst: Univ. of Massachusetts Press, 1986), 71, 89, 93; Ross W. Beales, "In Search of the Historical Child: Miniature Adulthood and Youth in Colonial New England," *American Quarterly* 27 (October 1975): 394–98.

5. *New Haven Town Recs.*, 1:55–56, 178–79, 45–52; 2:188, 198; Charles J. Hoadly, ed., *Records of the Colony or Jurisdiction of New Haven, from May 1653 to the Union* (Hartford: Case, Lockwood, 1858), 139.

6. Thompson, *Sex in Middlesex*, 83. Thompson demonstrates in his analysis of Middlesex families that "adolescent sexual offenses transcended class and church lines" and "were emphatically not the preserve of a small subculture where family government had failed" (ibid., 104).

7. Thompson, *Sex in Middlesex*, 104–5; Gildrie, *Profane, Civil, and Godly*, 107.

8. Greven, *Four Generations*, 98, 99 n, 78, 34–35.

9. Ibid., 130–31; "Mr. Tuttle's Will and Inventory," New Haven County Ct. Recs., 1:61. William Tuttle's sons, whose portions were £50 each, had received prior to his death the following amounts: John, £105.9.4 (the eldest received a double portion); Thomas, £20; Jonathan, £50; David, £26.17.06; Joseph, £19; Simon, £19; Benjamin, £3.10.0; Nathaniel, 0. His daughters, whose portions were £40 each, had received the following amounts, presumably as dowries: Anne, £37.09.08; Sarah, £40.06.05; Mercy, £32.00.04. Elizabeth had received her full portion of £25, which was less than her sisters', presumably to compensate for the cost of raising her child.

10. *New Haven Town Recs.*, 1:276, 330, 481; 2:32, 14, 437.

11. William Tuttle must have died between March and June of 1673, for three months before his estate went through probate he had appeared at the New Haven town meeting ("Mr. Tuttle's Will and Inventory," New Haven County Ct. Recs., 1:61; *New Haven Town Recs.*, 2:309).

12. According to Maine, the "median age at death in Hartford was 62½ years and in Windsor, fully 70" (*Society and Economy*, 7). While Greven estimates for Andover that "slightly more than half (51.1 per cent) reached the age of seventy" (*Four Generations*, 27), Faragher states that in Wethersfield 30 percent lived to such an old age ("Old Women and Old Men," 13).

13. "Mr. Tuttle's Will and Inventory," New Haven County Ct. Recs., 1:61; "An Inventory of the Estate of Mr. William Tuttle," New Haven Town Records., Probate Records, vol. 1, 1647–87, Connecticut State Library, 158 (n.d.).

14. New Haven County Ct. Recs., 1:77, 85, 88, 100, 126 (10 June 1674, 9 June 1675, 19 November 1675, 3 January 1676, 8 June 1681).

15. Gildrie, *Profane, Civil, and Godly*, 49.

16. Nathaniel Tuttle married in 1682, and by 1697 he was living in Wyndam, Connecticut, where his last child was born (Jacobus, *Families of Ancient New Haven*, 3:1884–85).

17. Simon Tuttle signed the original Wallingford covenant in 1669 and was granted an eight-acre house lot, as was his brother David (Charles H. S. Davis, *History of Wallingford, Connecticut* [Meriden, 1870], 76–78, 81, 911).

18. New Haven granted Simon Tuttle a shop lot in 1678 (*New Haven Town Recs.*, 2:373). His first child was born in New Haven in 1680; soon thereafter, he and his family moved to Wallingford, where the rest of his children were born (Jacobus, *Families of Ancient New Haven*, 3:1884–85).

19. "New Haven Code of 1656," in Cushing, *Earliest Laws*, 50. Connecticut law stated that "no young man that is neither married nor hath any servant, nor is a publique officer, shall keep howse of himself without the consent of the Towne" (Trumbull, *Conn. Public Recs.*, 1:538–39).

20. Donald Lines Jacobus, "Tuttle, Pantry, Judson, Hurd: An Important Correction," *The American Genealogist* 30 (January 1954): 9–10. That Benjamin Tuttle was living in Stamford with his sister Sarah by 1676 is clear from the records of his murder trial; that he had earlier resided with his sister Hannah is suggested by the fact that a portion of his estate was in Stratford at the time of his execution (Ullmann, *Ct. of Assistants Minutes*, 50–51, 53).

21. Jeanne Majdalany, *The Early Settlement of Stamford, Connecticut, 1641–1700* (Bowie, Md.: Heritage Books, 1991), 190.

22. Samuel Orcutt, *A History of the Old Town of Stratford and the City of Bridgeport, Connecticut* (New Haven: Tuttle, Morehouse, and Taylor, 1886), 1:269–73; William Howard Wilcoxson, *History of Stratford, Connecticut, 1639–1939* (Bridgeport: Brewer-Borg, 1940), 201; Estelle S. Feinstein, *Stamford, from Puritan to Patriot: The Shaping of a Connecticut Community, 1641–1774* (1976), 103–23.

23. Elizabeth Tuttle to the Conn. Ct. of Assistants, Connecticut Archives, Private Controversies, 1st Ser., 1642–1717, vol. 1, Connecticut State Library, 148 (26 May 1678).

24. Benjamin Tuttle's Deed of Gift to Elizabeth Edwards, Conn. Archives, Private Controversies, 1st Ser., 1:146 (20 April 1677).

25. Greven, *Four Generations*, 155, 158.

26. As the oldest son of an original proprietor, John Slauson would also have qualified for proprietorship (Feinstein, *Puritan to Patriot*, 107).

27. Christine Daniels, "Intimate Violence Now and Then," in *Over the Threshold: Intimate Violence in Early America*, ed. Christine Daniels and Michael V. Kennedy (New York: Routledge, 1999), 3.

28. Ulrich, *Good Wives*, 18, 13, 20–21; Maine, *Peoples of a Spacious Land*, 215.

29. Although night watch had been kept in the colonies since the earliest days of settlement, with the outbreak of King Philip's War the Connecticut General Court ordered "that in the several plantations of this Colony there be kept a sufficient watch in the night, which watch is to be continued from the shutting in of the evening till the sun rise" (Trumbull, *Conn. Public Recs.*, 2:361).

30. This summary of events is drawn from "A Veardit of a Jourey's Inquest," Connecticut Archives, Crimes and Misdemeanors, 1st Ser., vol. 1, 1663–1706, Connecticut State Library, 80 (18 November 1676).

31. Bradley Chapin, *Criminal Justice in Colonial America, 1606–1660* (Athens: Univ. of Georgia Press, 1983), 112. Four Indians were convicted of murder prior to 1660, at least two of whom were executed (Cornelia H. Dayton and Randolph Roth, comp., "Connecticut Adult Homicides, 1639–1797," Historical Violence Database, Criminal Justice Research Center, Ohio State University, http://cjrc.osu.edu).

32. Peter Abbott (8 October 1667), Henry Green (25 May 1675), Benjamin Tuttle (29 May 1677), John Stoddard (3 October 1678), Abigail Thompson (2 May 1706). In addition to these five colonists, an African named Cloyes Negro (25 May 1675) and a New Haven woman named Ruth Briggs (1667) were also executed (Ullmann, *Hartford County Ct. Minutes*, 79; Ullmann, *Ct. of Assistants Minutes*, 40, 48, 55–56, 389–96). Daniel A. Hern has reconstructed the circumstances of Ruth Briggs's infanticide case in *Legal Executions in New England: A Comprehensive Reference, 1623–1960* (London: McFarland, 1999), 41–44. According to Dayton and Roth's calculations, seven Indians were executed in Connecticut during this period ("Connecticut Homicides").

33. The maps of the early Stamford land holdings drawn by Majdalany place Bishop's and Slauson's lots on the eastern side of town near the meetinghouse lot (*Early Settlement of Stamford*, n.p.).

34. John Bishop to Increase Mather, in Massachusetts Historical Society, *Collections*, 4th Ser., vol. 8 (Boston: Wiggin & Lunt, 1868), 298–99. The date given for the letter in this volume (2 m. 26. 76; i.e., 26 April 1676) must be an error, for the murder occurred some seven months later, as did the fire in Boston that is also mentioned in the letter. Although the original MS of the letter is damaged, the date appears to be 12 m. 26. 76, i.e., 26 February 1677 (Prince Collection, Boston Public Library, Boston, Massachusetts).

35. As G. S. Rowe and Jack D. Marietta observe, because "[n]eighbors seem to have been almost constantly present in households," they were not really "outsiders." Violence between neighbors should by extension be considered a form of intimate violence ("Personal Violence in a 'Peaceable Kingdom': Pennsylvania, 1682–1801," *Over the Threshold*, ed. Daniels and Kennedy, 30).

36. Chapin, *Criminal Justice*, 141.

37. Ullmann, *Hartford County Ct. Minutes*, 79; Ullmann, *Ct. of Assistants Minutes*, 40, 113, 390; "Examination of John Stodder," Conn. Archives, Crimes and Misdemeanors, 1st Ser., 1:109a, 110 (25, 27 July 1678). How Briggs killed her infant is unknown.

38. "Examination of John Stodder," Conn. Archives, Crimes and Misdemeanors, 1st Ser., 1:109b.

39. The fact that Abbott committed the crime while his family slept indicates that it did not occur in the immediate aftermath of a quarrel but that he deliberated at least for a brief period of time. In this regard it resembles the familicides discussed by Daniel A. Cohen in "Homicidal Compulsion and the Conditions of Freedom: The Social and Psychological Origins of Familicide in America's Early Republic," *Journal of Social History* 28 (Summer 1995): 725–64.

40. Alden T. Vaughn, *New England Frontier: Puritans and Indians, 1620–1675*, 3rd ed. (Norman: Univ. of Oklahoma Press, 1994), 38; Douglas E. Leach, *Flintlock and Tomahawk: New England in King Philip's War* (1958; reprint, New York: Norton, 1966), 5.

41. "A Veardit of a Jourey's Inquest," Conn. Archives, Crimes and Misdemeanors, 1st Ser., 1:80. As Roger Lane notes, the "hue and cry" dates at least from medieval England, where "anyone unable personally to stop the killing was supposed to raise a 'hue and cry,' calling on all other members of the town or vill to form a posse and chase the killer" (*Murder in America: A History* [Columbus: Ohio State Univ. Press, 1997], 12).

42. Feinstein, *Puritan to Patriot*, 53–58; Majdalany, *Early Settlement of Stamford*, 16, 22–24; Hoadly, *New Haven Colony and Plantation Recs.*, 135, 146, 482; Hoadly, *New Haven Colony or Jurisdiction Recs.*, 458–63.

43. Edmund Andros to Esopus [Kingston], New York, 19 October 1675, *Books of General Entries of the Colony of New York, 1674–1688*, ed. Peter R. Christoph and Florence A. Christoph, vol. 3 of *New York Historical Manuscripts: English* (Baltimore: Genealogical Publishing Co., 1982), 81.

44. Leach, *Flintlock and Tomahawk*, 240, 122. Stoddard claimed to have seen two Indians running from the house after he killed his infant stepbrother. They were apprehended and presented for the murders alongside Stoddard but were not indicted (Conn. Archives, Crimes and Misdemeanors, 1st Ser., 1:109a, 112b, 113 [3 October 1678, 26 July 1678]; Ullmann, *Ct. of Assistants Minutes*, 56–57).

45. On the development of the American axe, see Gary Kulik, "American Difference Revisited: The Case of the American Axe," in *American Material Culture: The Shape of the Field*, ed. Ann Smart Martin and J. Ritchie Garrison (Knoxville: Univ. of Tennessee Press, 1997), 26–36; and Henry J. Kauffman, *American Axes: A Survey of Their Development and Their Makers* (Brattleboro, Vt.: Stephen Greene Press, 1972), 1–4.

46. Paul B. Kebabian, *American Woodworking Tools* (Boston: Little, Brown, 1978), 34; Mark Atchison, e-mail communication with author, 28 June 2011. In contrast, Squampum's weapon is described as a "broad Axx" (Ullmann, *Ct. of Assistants Minutes*, 113), and one of Stoddard's weapons is described as a "hatchet" ("Examination of John Stodder," Conn. Archives, Crimes and Misdemeanors, 1st Ser., 1:109a).

47. Ian MacLachlan, "Humanitarian Reform, Slaughter Technology, and Butcher Resistance in Nineteenth-Century Britain," in *Meat, Modernity, and the Rise of the Slaughterhouse*, ed. Paula Young Lee (Durham: Univ. of New Hampshire Press, 2008), 112–17; Virginia D. Anderson, e-mail communication with author, 31 July 2009.

48. [James Plumptre], *The Experienced Butcher* (London, 1816), 138.

49. Randle Holme, *The Academy of Armory . . . with the Instruments Used in All Trades and Sciences, Together with Their Terms of Art* (Chester, England, 1688), 3:315, 87; Martha Sulya, e-mail communication with author, 10 September 2009.

50. Lombard, *Making Manhood*, 8–11. Although historians of murder often assert that young, single men commit a disproportionate number of homicides, in seventeenth-century Connecticut this generalization does not hold. Of the six English colonists executed for murder before 1711, two were married men, two were women, and two were single men. Colonial Pennsylvania also does not fit the common profile (Jack D. Marietta and G. S. Rowe, *Troubled Experiment: Crime and Justice in Pennsylvania, 1682–1800* [Philadelphia: Univ. of Pennsylvania Press, 2006], 113). According to Lombard, youths tended to engage in demonstrative violence against authority, not in homicide (ibid., 134–40).

51. Court records for Fairfield County, Connecticut, in the seventeenth century have been lost; if Benjamin ran into trouble with the law while living in either Stratford or Stamford no record of the charges remains.

52. Michael Dalton, *The Countrey Justice, Containing the Practice of Justices of the Peace in Their Sessions* (1622; reprint, New York: Arno Press, 1972), 275.

53. "Certificate Concerning John Stother's Wicked Course," Conn. Archives, Crimes and Misdemeanors, 1st Ser., 1:114 (3 October 1678).

54. Ullmann, *Ct. of Assistants Minutes*, 391–96.

55. New England "clergymen assumed an intimate relationship among sins and a natural progression from one to another" (Daniel A. Cohen, *Pillars of Salt, Monuments of Grace: New England Crime Literature and the Origins of American Popular Culture, 1674–1860* [New York: Oxford Univ. Press, 1993], 87).

56. The Connecticut Code of 1672 stipulates that "whensoever any Person shall come to any very suddain, untimely, or un-natural Death; The next Magistrate, or the Constable of that Town, shall forthwith Summon a Jury of *Twelve* discreet men, to enquire of the Cause and Manner of his Death" (Cushing, *Earliest Laws*, 93).

57. Holly Brewer, *By Birth or Consent: Children, Law, and the Anglo-American Revolution in Authority* (Chapel Hill: Univ. of North Carolina Press, 2005), 162, 163.

58. "A Veardit of a Jourey's Inquest," Conn. Archives, Crimes and Misdemeanors, 1st Ser., 1:80.
59. Statement of William Jones, Assistant, Conn. Archives, Crimes and Misdemeanors, 1st Ser., 1:83 (29 May 1677). See also the statements of Benjamin Tuttle, Richard Law, and Samuel and Elizabeth Elmer (ibid., 1:81, 82, 84).
60. Ullmann, *Ct. of Assistants Minutes*, 48.
61. "A Veardit of a Jourey's Inquest," Conn. Archives, Crimes and Misdemeanors, 1st Ser., 1:80.
62. Conn. Archives, Crimes and Misdemeanors, 1st Ser., 1:81, 82 (29 May 1677, 23 November 1677); E. B. Huntington, *History of Stamford, Connecticut* (1868; reprint, Camden, Me.: Picton Press, 1992), 276–77.
63. "A Veardit of a Jourey's Inquest," Conn. Archives, Crimes and Misdemeanors, 1st Ser., 1:80.
64. Martin Ingram, "'Scolding Women Cucked or Washed': A Crisis in Gender Relations in Early Modern England?" in *Women, Crime and the Courts in Early Modern England,* ed. Jennifer Kermode and Garthine Walker (Chapel Hill: Univ. of North Carolina Press, 1994), 48, 57–58, 63; D. E. Underdown, "The Taming of the Scold: The Enforcement of Patriarchal Authority in Early Modern England," in *Order and Disorder in Early Modern England*, ed. Anthony Fletcher and John Stevenson (Cambridge: Cambridge Univ. Press, 1985), 119, 23, 123.
65. Dayton, *Women Before the Bar,* 299–300.
66. Jane Kamensky, *Governing the Tongue: The Politics of Speech in Early New England* (New York: Oxford Univ. Press, 1997), 22.
67. Louis P. Masur, *Rites of Execution: Capital Punishment and the Transformation of American Culture, 1776–1865* (New York: Oxford Univ. Press, 1989), 27.
68. Irene Quenzler Brown and Richard D. Brown, *The Hanging of Ephraim Wheeler: A Story of Rape, Incest, and Justice in Early America* (Cambridge, Mass.: Harvard Univ. Press, 2003), 38.
69. Increase Mather, *A Sermon Occasioned by the Execution of a Man Found Guilty of Murder,* 2nd ed. (Boston, 1687), 11.
70. Karen Halttunen, *Murder Most Foul: The Killer and the American Gothic Imagination* (Cambridge, Mass.: Harvard Univ. Press, 1998), 25.–32.
71. Puritan ministers in New England inherited the practice of visiting prisoners in jail from their English predecessors (Lawrence W. Towner, "True Confessions and Dying Warnings in Colonial New England," in *Sibley's Heir: A Volume in Memory of Clifford Kenyon Shipton* [Boston: Colonial Society of Massachusetts, 1982], 525; Cohen, *Pillars of Salt,* 44).
72. According to Cohen, "crowds at local gallows reportedly numbered well into the thousands" (*Pillars of Salt,* 3).
73. After sentencing Tuttle, the Court of Assistants noted that "the reverend Mr. Collins is desired & appointed to preach the lecture that day the execution is done" (Ullmann, *Ct. of Assistants Minutes,* 48). Although other hangings may also have been preceded by sermons, Tuttle's execution appears to be the only time the Court of Assistants named the preacher. In the poetic encomium he composed on the death of Nathaniel Collins, Cotton Mather praised him for "How deep his Sermons were" and "how fraught the Pulpit was of Grace, of Gravity, of Wisdom" when he preached ("An Elegy on the Much-to-be-Deplored Death of that Never-to-be-Forgotten Person, The Reverend Nathaniel Collins" [Boston, 1685], 11). For a sketch of the life of Nathaniel Collins, see John Langdon Sibley, *Biographical Sketches of the Graduates of Harvard College* (Cambridge, Mass.: Charles William Sever, 1881), 2:58–60.

74. Cohen, *Pillars of Salt*, 7.
75. Love, *History of Hartford*, 286.
76. For descriptions of the execution day ritual, see Wayne C. Minnick, "The New England Execution Sermon, 1639–1800," *Speech Monographs* 35 (March 1968): 79–80; and Ronald A. Bosco, "Lectures at the Pillory: The Early American Execution Sermon," *American Quarterly* 30 (Summer 1978): 159–60.
77. According to Minnick, nine ministers took Luke 23:42–43 as their text, making it the most popular text for execution sermons, while three chose Rom. 6:23 and two chose Num. 35:16 ("New England Execution Sermon," 81).
78. Cohen, *Pillars of Salt*, 84; Halttunen, *Murder Most Foul*, 13.
79. Mather, *Sermon Occasioned*, 2; Samuel Danforth, *The Cry of Sodom Enquired Into* (Cambridge, 1674), 11.
80. Increase Mather, *The Wicked Man's Portion* (Boston, 1675), 16.
81. Cohen, *Pillars of Salt*, 84. According to Cohen, "The theological understanding of crime as resulting from God's just abandonment of the sinner to his own corrupt impulses was present in one form or another in virtually all early execution discourses" (ibid., 84).
82. Mather, *Sermon Occasioned*, 21.
83. Cotton Mather, *Pillars of Salt: A History of Some Criminals Executed in this Land, for Capital Crimes* (Boston, 1699), 17, 18.
84. Joshua Moodey, *An Exhortation to a Condemned Malefactor* (Boston, 1686), 62. The discourse Cotton Mather appends to *Pillars of Salt* takes as its topic the "Dreadful Justice of God, in Punishing of Sin, with Sin" (*Pillars of Salt*, 1).
85. Halttunen, *Murder Most Foul*, 93.
86. Ibid., 14–15.
87. Mather, *Sermon Occasioned*, 15.
88. Peter Lake observes that murder "turns the world upside down" in *The Antichrist's Lewd Hat: Protestants, Papists and Players in Post-Reformation England* (New Haven: Yale Univ. Press, 2002), xxi, 54.
89. Peter J. Thuesen, *Predestination: The American Career of a Contentious Doctrine* (New York: Oxford Univ. Press, 2009), 62, 2, 86.
90. Cohen, *Pillars of Salt*, 48.
91. Jacobus, *Families of Ancient New Haven*, 3:1881–85, 1619. In his study of seventeenth-century Wethersfield, Faragher found that widowers under fifty "waited a median of less than twelve months before remarrying" ("Old Women and Old Men," 19). John Slauson's first child with his second wife was born in 1680, suggesting that he waited at least three years to remarry (Majdalany, *Early Settlement of Stamford*, 190–91).
92. New Haven County Ct. Recs., 1:107 (27 February 1677); *New Haven Town Recs.*, 2:359–60; Elizabeth Tuttle to the Conn. Ct. of Assistants, Conn. Archives, Private Controversies, 1st Ser., 1:148.
93. "An Inventory of the Estate of John Tuttle, Sen.," New Haven Town Recs., Probate Recs., 1:195 (12 November 1683); New Haven County Ct. Recs., 1:143 (6 December 1683).
94. New Haven County Ct. Recs., 1:158, 182 (11 November 1685, 12 November 1690); "An Inventory of the Estate of Joseph Tuttle, Sr.," New Haven Town Recs., Probate Recs., vol. 2, 1689–1703, 58 (30 October 1690).
95. Elizabeth Tuttle to the Conn. Ct. of Assistants, Conn. Archives, Private Controversies, 1st Ser., 1:148.
96. New Haven County Ct. Recs., 1:154–158 (10 June 1685, 28 July 1685, 28 September 1685, 11 November 1685). Thomas, Joseph, and Nathaniel Tuttle were named the administrators of the estate and were likely the active participants in the contest, with Jonathan, David,

and Simon taking subordinate roles. Although Elizabeth Tuttle's will has not survived, an inventory of her estate appears in the New Haven Town Recs., Probate Recs., 1:209 (3 February 1684).

CHAPTER 4

1. New Haven County Ct. Recs, 1:158 (11 November 1685), emphasis added.
2. Davis, *History of Wallingford*, 81. The bill of sale for his Wallingford property includes a six-acre home lot and an eight-acre parcel on the river (Wallingford Town Records, 1670–1754, Connecticut State Library, 192 [23 March 1693]).
3. As Robert V. Wells and Michael Zuckerman observe, "The proportion never marrying is one of the most difficult of the marriage patterns with which to deal." They found a high number of bachelors and spinsters among a small sample of middle-colony Quakers (12.1 percent and 15.9 percent, respectively), but they assert that the percentages were significantly lower in colonial New England ("Quaker Marriage Patterns in a Colonial Perspective," *William and Mary Quarterly* 29 [July 1972]: 426–28, 432–33).
4. Thomas A. Foster, *Sex and the Eighteenth-Century Man: Massachusetts and the History of Sexuality in America* (Boston: Beacon Press, 2006), 101. The disproportionate number of bachelors in Cornelia H. Dayton's study of Hampshire County guardianship returns suggests the "key role of wives in blunting the impact of a male household head's mental illness and thus obviating the need for an outsider to be appointed as guardian" ("Frames of Distraction: Investigating the 'Signs and Tokens' of Insanity in Early New England" [paper presented at the Bloomington Eighteenth-Century Workshop, May 2002], 5).
5. Mary Ann Jimenez, *Changing Faces of Madness: Early American Attitudes and Treatment of the Insane* (Hanover, N.H.: Univ. Press of New England, 1987), 40–41, 65; Dayton, "Frames of Distraction," 3–5, 7–9. On the rise of the asylum, see, in addition to Jimenez, Gerald N. Grob, *The Mad Among Us: A History of the Care of America's Mentally Ill* (New York: Macmillan, 1994).
6. Jimenez, *Changing Faces of Madness*, 33.
7. Matthew Hale, *The History of the Pleas of the Crown* (1736; reprint, Clark, N.J.: Lawbook Exchange, 2003), 1:29, 31. Although this work was published in the eighteenth century, Hale wrote *Pleas of the Crown* before his death in 1676. In Nigel Walker's estimation, its chapter on the "defect of idiocy, madness and lunacy" represents the "most detailed description of seventeenth-century [legal] practice" regarding the insane (*Crime and Insanity in England: Vol. 1, The Historical Perspective* [Edinburgh: Edinburgh Univ. Press, 1968], 34).
8. New Haven County Ct. Recs., 1:168 (3 August 1687); Dayton, "Frames of Distraction," 3.
9. New Haven County Ct. Recs., 1:186, 214 (10 June 1691, 19 June 1693). David Tuttle alone set his "hand and seal" to the deed of sale for his Wallingford property, indicating that the court judged him competent to make a legally binding agreement (Wallingford Town Recs., 192 [24 March 1693]).
10. New Haven County Ct. Recs., 1:203 (1 November 1692); "An Inventory of the Estate of David Tuttle of New Haven (who is non Compos Mentis)," New Haven Town Recs., Probate Recs., 2:122 (9 November 1682).
11. Larry D. Eldridge, "'Crazy Brained': Mental Illness in Colonial America," *Bulletin of the History of Medicine* 70 (Autumn 1996): 377–78.
12. L. Stephen O'Brien, *Traumatic Events and Mental Health* (Cambridge: Cambridge Univ. Press, 1981), 122–23, 2, 125, 152.
13. Michael MacDonald, *Mystical Bedlam: Madness, Anxiety, and Healing in Seventeenth-Century England* (Cambridge: Cambridge Univ. Press, 1981), 72, 77.

14. Richard Burton, *The Anatomy of Melancholy* (1621; London: Dent, 1964), 1:358.
15. O'Brien, *Traumatic Events*, 165.
16. Gordon E. Geddes, *Welcome Joy: Death in Puritan New England* (Ann Arbor, Mich.: UMI Research Press, 1981), 94.
17. Jacobus, *Families of Ancient New Haven*, 3:1884.
18. Morgan, *The Puritan Family*, 76; Gildrie, *Profane, Civil, and Godly*, 93.
19. Dexter, *New Haven Town Recs.*, 2:91–94.
20. Jacobus, *Families of Ancient New Haven*, 3:1883–84; Daniels, *Puritans at Play*, 117–18.
21. Jacobus fails to include the birth of the third child, Samuel, who must have been born in 1674 given that he was seventeen in 1691 (*Families of Ancient New Haven*, 1:346).
22. Davis, *History of Wallingford*, 78, 81, 662; "Mr. Tuttle's Will and Inventory," New Haven County Ct. Recs., 1:61.
23. Gideon Brown was born in New Haven in July 1685 and died sometime prior to 1691 (Jacobus, *Families of Ancient New Haven*, 1:346; "An Inventory of the Estate of Samuel Brown," New Haven County Ct. Recs., 1:195 [11 November 1691]).
24. Ulrich, *Good Wives*, 20.
25. Sarah Tuttle married Joseph Doolittle on 24 April 1690 (Jacobus, *Families of Ancient New Haven*, 1:346).
26. Ulrich, *Good Wives*, 18.
27. This reconstruction of the murder is drawn from the records of Mercy Brown's trial (Conn. Archives, Crimes and Misdemeanors, 1st Ser., 1:165–67, 171 [29, 30 June 1691; 2 October 1691]).
28. Gouge, *Of Domesticall Duties*, 358.
29. Ulrich, *Good Wives*, 155.
30. Cotton Mather describes the characteristics of the "virtuous mother" in *Ornaments for the Daughters of Zion* (1741; reprint, Delmar, N.Y.: Scholars' Facsimiles, 1978), 99–110.
31. 21 Jas. I, c. 27 (1624); quoted in Peter C. Hoffer and N. E. H. Hull, *Murdering Mothers: Infanticide in England and New England, 1558–1803* (New York: New York Univ. Press, 1984), 20. A similar infanticide statute was adopted in Massachusetts in 1696 and in Connecticut in 1699 (ibid., 38).
32. Hoffer and Hull, *Murdering Mothers*, 108–9, 107.
33. Phillip J. Resnick coined the term "neonaticide" in "Murder of the Newborn: A Psychiatric Review of Neonaticide" (*American Journal of Psychiatry* 126 [April 1970]: 58). See also George B. Palermo, "Murderous Parents," *International Journal of Offender Therapy and Comparative Criminology* 4 (April 2002): 124.
34. Conn. Archives, Crimes and Misdemeanors, 1st Ser., 1:166.
35. Conn. Archives, Crimes and Misdemeanors, 1st Ser., 1:82, 179 (1 October 1691). According to Edwin Powers, colonial indictments usually "brought in the Devil as a sort of codefendant" (*Crime and Punishment in Early Massachusetts, 1620–1692: A Documentary History* [Boston: Beacon Press, 1966], 560).
36. Jimenez, *Changing Faces of Madness*, 12–13.
37. Conn. Archives, Crimes and Misdemeanors, 1st Ser., 1:166, 167.
38. Conn. Archives, Crimes and Misdemeanors, 1st Ser., 1:181 (1 October 1691).
39. Conn. Archives, Crimes and Misdemeanors, 1st Ser., 1:173, 175a–b, 177, 174a, 176, 169 (1, 6, 7 October 1691; 25 September 1691).
40. Jimenez, *Changing Faces of Madness*, 14, 22.
41. MacDonald, *Mystical Bedlam*, 5, 113.
42. Norton, *Founding Mothers and Fathers*, 19–20.
43. MacDonald, *Mystical Bedlam*, 165.
44. Conn. Archives, Crimes and Misdemeanors, 1st Ser., 1:83.

45. Depositions of John and Jemimah Hall, Aaron Blanchard, and Elizabeth Wade, New London County Superior Court Files, Box 1, file 4 (7 February 1712), R. G. 3, Connecticut State Library; Dayton, "Frames of Distraction," 7–8.

46. MacDonald, *Mystical Bedlam,* 140–41.

47. Conn. Archives, Crimes and Misdemeanors, 1st Ser., 1:175a, 171.

48. MacDonald, *Mystical Bedlam,* 142–45.

49. Julius H. Rubin, *Religious Melancholy and the Protestant Experience in America* (New York: Oxford Univ. Press, 1994), 27, 47.

50. Conn. Archives, Crimes and Misdemeanors, 1st Ser., 1:169, 167, 170 (n.d.).

51. P. T. d'Orban, "Women Who Kill Their Children," *British Journal of Psychiatry* 134 (June 1979): 565; Phillip J. Resnick, "Child Murder by Parents: A Psychiatric Review of Filicide," *American Journal of Psychiatry* 126 (September 1969): 329. Altruistic filicides are often committed by suicidal mothers who kill their children to protect them from a mother-less future. However, the evidence in Brown's case, although suggestive, is insufficient to conclude that this homicide was an interrupted suicide-filicide.

52. Geddes, *Welcome Joy,* 147.

53. Conn. Archives, Crimes and Misdemeanors, 1st Ser., 1:172 (n.d.).

54. Conn. Archives, Crimes and Misdemeanors, 1st Ser., 1:166, 181, 178 (n.d.).

55. Josephine Stanton and Alexandra Simpson, "Filicide: A Review," *International Journal of Law and Psychiatry* 25 (January–February 2002): 3. Resnick introduced the term "altruism" to describe the "most important factor that distinguishes filicide from other homicides" ("Child Murder by Parents," 329).

56. Ania Wilczynski, *Child Homicide* (London: Greenwich Medical Media, 1997), 55–56; Josephine Stanton, Alexandra Simpson, and Trecia Wouldes, "A Qualitative Study of Filicide by Mentally Ill Mothers," *Child Abuse and Neglect* 24 (November 2000): 1456.

57. Liza H. Gold, "Clinical and Forensic Aspects of Postpartum Depression," *Journal of the American Academy of Psychiatry and Law* 29 (September 2001): 346; Christine Alder and Ken Polk, *Child Victims of Homicide* (Cambridge: Cambridge Univ. Press, 2001), 62.

58. Conn. Archives, Crimes and Misdemeanors, 1st Ser., 1:178; Alder and Polk, *Child Victims,* 162.

59. According to Hale, a "person of non sane memory [who] commit[s] a homicide during such his insanity" can be "tried after the recovery of his understanding" (*Pleas of the Crown,* 1:35).

60. The court papers from the Wyar trial include two bills of indictment, one returned *ignoramus* ("We do not know") and the other *billa vera* ("true bill"). Given that she proceeded to trial, the grand jury apparently voted to indict when instructed to reconsider their earlier *ignoramus* (New London Superior Ct. Files, Box 1, File 4 [25 March 1712]).

61. Ullmann, *Ct. of Assistants Minutes,* 135, 136. The words "horribly and most unnaturally" appear to be an addition to the standard language of an indictment, emphasizing the shocking nature of the crime.

62. Chapin, *Criminal Justice,* 37, 40; Richard Moran, "The Origin of Insanity as a Special Verdict: The Trial for Treason of James Hadfield (1800)," *Law and Society Review* 19, no. 3 (1985): 488.

63. Ullmann, *Ct. of Assistants Minutes,* 136.

64. Henry de Bracton, *On the Laws and Customs of England,* ed. George E. Woodbine, trans. Samuel E. Thorne (c. 1250; Cambridge, Mass.: Harvard Univ. Press, 1968), 2:384; Thomas Maeder, *Crime and Madness: The Origins and Evolution of the Insanity Defense* (New York: Harper & Row, 1985), 3. See also Walker, *Crime and Insanity,* 1:26.

65. Ullmann, *Ct. of Assistants Minutes,* 136.

66. Conn. Archives, Crimes and Misdemeanors, 1st Ser., 1:181.

67. Connecticut allowed attorneys to represent defendants in civil and misdemeanor criminal cases, but not felonies (Edgar J. McManus, *Law and Liberty in Early New England: Criminal Justice and Due Process* [Amherst: Univ. of Massachusetts Press, 1993], 93–97).

68. Dayton, *Women Before the Bar*, 1.

69. "The Body of Liberties" (1641), No. 52, in William H. Whetmore, ed., *The Colonial Laws of Massachusetts* (Boston: Rockwell & Churchill, 1889), 45; Powers, *Crime and Punishment*, 439–40.

70. Trumbull, *Conn. Public Recs.*, 1:515. Rhode Island adopted a statute explicitly addressing the criminal liability of insane persons (John D. Cushing, ed. *The Earliest Acts and Laws of the Colony of Rhode Island and Providence Plantations, 1647–1719* [Wilmington, Del.: Michael Glazier, 1977], 19).

71. McManus, *Law and Liberty*, 105.

72. Hale, *Pleas of the Crown*, 1:32–33, 29; Walker, *Crime and Insanity*, 1:35; Maeder, *Crime and Madness*, 9.

73. Hale, *Pleas of the Crown*, 1:30–33; Edward Coke, *Third Part of the Institutes of the Laws of England* (1644, 1797; reprint, Buffalo: William S. Hein, 1986), 6. According to Walker, Hale found only total insanity exculpatory (*Crime and Insanity*, 1:38–39).

74. Walker, *Crime and Insanity*, 1:35; McManus, *Law and Liberty*, 12.

75. Dalton, *The Countrey Justice*, 223–24; Hale, *Pleas of the Crown*, 1:30; Edward Coke, *First Part of the Institutes of the Laws of England, or a Commentary Upon Littleton* (1628; reprint, Union, N.J.: Lawbook Exchange, 1999), 2:247b.

76. Conn. Archives, Crimes and Misdemeanors, 1st Ser., 1:180. This document is dated 3 October 1691, two days after the Court of Assistants convened to hear Mercy Brown's case.

77. Hale, *Pleas of the Crown*, 1:31. Given that in 1691 the colonists still employed the Julian calendar, the phase of the moon and the position of the sun on the day of the murder must be calculated for the Gregorian calendar date of 3 July, not 23 June, 1691. The night before the murder the first quarter moon would have been visible in the Connecticut sky; however, Mercy Brown would not have seen it when she arose the next morning, because the summer solstice had occurred about ten days earlier. With the sun rising early, she likely was walking to her neighbor's house for fire around 5:30 a.m. (Cheri Adams, personal conversation with author, 18 March 2010.).

78. Hale, *Pleas of the Crown*, 1:31–32. In a landmark case dating from 1724, the judge instructed the jury that a "madman as is to be exempted from punishment" must be "totally deprived of his understanding, and doth not know what he is doing, no more than an infant, or a wild beast" (quoted in Walker, *Crime and Insanity*, 1:56). This "wild-beast test" denied that any degree of "partial insanity" was exculpatory.

79. Hale, *Pleas of the Crown*, 1:30; Coke, *Third Part of the Institutes*, 6.

80. Hale, *Pleas of the Crown*, 1:35. As Ania Wilczynski observes, "[I]mages of criminal women tend to be polarized to two extremes, the 'mad' and the 'bad'" ("Images of Women Who Kill Their Infants: The Mad and the Bad," *Women and Criminal Justice* 2, no. 2 [1991]: 72).

81. Thomas W. Jodziewicz, "A Stranger in the Land: Gershom Bulkeley of Connecticut," *Transactions of the American Philosophical Society* 78, no. 2 (1988): 10–17; Trumbull, *Conn. Public Recs.*, 3:218; [Annie E. Trumbull], ed., *Records of the Particular Court of the Colony of Connecticut. Administration of Sir Edmond Andros, Royal Governor, 1687–1688* (Hartford, 1935), 3.

82. Although Bulkeley had composed *Will and Doom* by 1692, it did not appear in print until 1895 (Connecticut Historical Society, *Collections*, vol. 3 [Hartford, 1895], 69–269).

83. Bulkeley, *Will and Doom*, 90, 112, 192.

84. Cushing, *Earliest Laws*, 68; Powers, *Crime and Punishment*, 252, 303–6; McManus, *Law and Liberty*, 187–91.

85. Bulkeley, *Will and Doom*, 109, 101–2.

86. Mann, *Neighbors and Strangers*, 79. Connecticut law made provision for a special verdict (Cushing, *Earliest Laws*, 111). The court papers from the Brown trial preserve a special verdict written in the proper form (Conn. Archives, Crimes and Misdemeanors, 1st Ser., 1:172v [n. d.]).

87. Bulkeley, *Will and Doom*, 230–32; Bulkeley to the Court of Assistants, Conn. Archives, Crimes and Misdemeanors, 1st Ser., 1:182a (5 October 1691).

88. Conn. Archives, Crimes and Misdemeanors, 1st Ser., 1:182b.

89. Barbara J. Shapiro, *"Beyond Reasonable Doubt" and "Probable Cause": Historical Perspectives on the Anglo-American Law of Evidence* (Berkeley: Univ. of California Press, 1991), 4; Thomas A. Green, "A Retrospective on the Criminal Trial Jury, 1200–1800," in *Twelve Good Men and True: The Criminal Trial Jury in England, 1200–1800*, ed. J. S. Cockburn and Thomas A. Green (Princeton N.J.: Princeton Univ. Press, 1988), 369.

90. As Walker notes, "Since the petty jury consisted of local men, it was perfectly reasonable to ask them to declare . . . whether the accused had really been mad when he committed the offense" (*Crime and Insanity*, 1:26); R. A. Houston, *Madness and Society in Eighteenth-Century Scotland* (Oxford: Clarendon Press, 2000), 237–38.

91. Conn. Archives, Crimes and Misdemeanors, 1st Ser., 1:182c; Bulkeley, *Will and Doom*, 230. Hale contradicted Bulkeley on this point of law, asserting that "if a man be a lunatick, and hath his *lucida intervalla*, and this be sufficiently proved, yet the law presumes the acts or offenses of such a person to be committed in those intervals, wherein he hath the use of reason, unless by circumstances or evidences it appears they were committed in the time of his distemper" (*Pleas of the Crown*, 1:33–34). Bulkeley cites *Beverly's Case of Non Compos Mentis* (*The Reports of Sir Edward Coke*, ed. John Henry Thomas and John Farquhar Fraser [1826; reprint, Union, N.J.: Lawbook Exchange, 2002], 2:571 [pt. IV, 124a–b]).

92. Edward Randolph to the Lords of Trade, 10 January 1690, *Calendar of State Papers, Colonial Series*, ed. J. W. Fortescue (1901; reprint, Vaduz: Kraus Reprint, 1964), 13:205. Massachusetts had in 1689 sentenced fourteen persons to death in order to "meet the possible threat of a challenge to its legitimacy" (David Thomas Konig, *Law and Society in Puritan Massachusetts: Essex County, 1629–1692* [Chapel Hill: Univ. of North Carolina Press, 1979], 168).

93. Bulkeley, *Will and Doom*, 230, 229.

94. Conn. Archives, Crimes and Misdemeanors, 1st Ser., 1:174a–b, 175a–b, (6, 7 October 1691); Ullmann, *Ct. of Assistants Minutes*, 136.

95. Wallingford Town Recs., 172 (1 September 1691); New Haven County Ct. Recs., 1:195 (11 November 1691).

96. Bulkeley, *Will and Doom*, 232–33.

97. Ibid., 234–35; Richard Godbeer, *Escaping Salem: The Other Witch Hunt of 1692* (New York: Oxford Univ. Press, 2005), 127–28, 122–23. In *Will and Doom* Bulkeley cites the Disborough case as further evidence of the irregularity of the Connecticut judicial system.

98. Hall, *Witch-Hunting*, 350.

99. The members of Disborough's committee were Samuel Willis, William Pitkin (members of Connecticut's moderate faction), and Nathaniel Stanley (a radical Democrat). All three had supported the restoration of charter government (Hall, *Witch-Hunting*, 351; Richard R. Johnson, *Adjustment to Empire: The New England Colonies, 1675–1715* [New Brunswick, N.J.: Rutgers Univ. Press, 1981], 110–11).

100. Ullmann, *Ct. of Assistants Minutes*, 152.

101. The court order states that "She Shall be kept in Custody as the Magistrates of New Haven, with Thomas Trowbridge, or any two of them Shall order from time to time" (Ullmann, *Ct. of Assistants Minutes*, 152). A Tuttle genealogist notes that "Mercy was living as

late as 1695, in New Haven, perhaps with Thomas Trowbridge" (George Frederick Tuttle, *The Descendants of William and Elizabeth Tuttle* [Rutland: Tuttle & Co., 1883], 540).

CHAPTER 5

1. Charles J. Hoadly, *Public Records of the Colony of Connecticut* (Hartford: Case, Lockwood, and Brainard, 1868–90), 4:59.
2. Dayton, *Women Before the Bar*, 105, 112.
3. Stone, *Road to Divorce*, 25, 191, 192, 312, 301, 307, 383; Dayton, *Women Before the Bar*, 108–9.
4. Stone, *Road to Divorce*, 347. Massachusetts magistrates for a brief period in the eighteenth century "declined to dissolve valid marriages and decreed separate bed and board for petitioners who formerly and subsequently would have been granted divorce" (Nancy F. Cott, "Divorce and the Changing Status of Women in Eighteenth-Century Massachusetts," *William and Mary Quarterly* 33 [October 1976]: 590).
5. Stone, *Road to Divorce*, 348, 142; Dayton, *Women Before the Bar*, 109–10.
6. George Elliott Howard, *A History of Matrimonial Institutions* (1904; reprint, New York: Humanities Press, 1964), 2:331; K. Kelly Weisberg, "'Under Great Temptations Heer': Women and Divorce in Puritan Massachusetts," *Feminist Studies* 2, no. 2/3 (1975): 186–87.
7. Trumbull, *Conn. Public Recs.*, 2:328.
8. According to Dayton's calculation, "Connecticut magistrates considered and granted nearly 1,000 divorce petitions" between 1670 and 1799; by comparison, the governor and Council of Massachusetts granted "fewer than 150 marital separations" in the same period (*Women Before the Bar*, 112, 108, 113, 125).
9. Middle age was apparently a common time for colonial men to want a separation from their wives, with forty-five being the average age of men petitioning for divorce in eighteenth-century Connecticut (Cornelia Hughes Dayton, "Women Before the Bar: Gender, Law, and Society in Connecticut, 1710–1790" [Ph.D. diss., Princeton University, 1986], 311–12).
10. Edwards, "A True Abreviate," Conn. Archives, Crimes and Misdemeanors, 1st Ser., 3:235b.
11. Demos explores how conflicts not resolvable by the colonial legal system lingered for years and at times gave rise to witchcraft accusations (*Entertaining Satan*, 297–98).
12. William Whately, *A Bride-Bush: Or, A Direction for Married Persons. Plainly Describing the Duties Common to Both, and Peculiar to Each of Them* (London, 1619), 1, 33.
13. Gouge, *Of Domesticall Duties*, 225. The duty to love primarily belonged to the husband, for scripture commands, "Husbands, love your wives, even as Christ also loved the church" (Eph. 5:25; cf. Col. 3:19). But wives likewise had a reciprocal duty to love their husbands (see Titus 2:4).
14. That Richard and Elizabeth Edwards were in 1673 living on the town's north side, where his parents and grandmother also lived, is indicated in town records for that year (Hoadly, *Hartford Town Votes*, 1:168).
15. Gouge, *Of Domesticall Duties*, 29–30.
16. Lombard, *Making Manhood*, 98.
17. Ullmann, *Hartford County Ct. Minutes*, 92.
18. Whately, *Bride-Bush*, 88, 89; Lombard, *Making Manhood*, 100.
19. Ulrich, *Good Wives*, 13.
20. Colonial craftsmen commonly located their shops on the family lot. The inventory of Richard Edwards's estate indicates his shop was near his house at the time of his death ("An Inventory of the Estate belonging to Mr. Richard Edwards, late of Hartford,

Deceased," Hartford Probate Packets, 1641–1880, vol. 508, No. 1824 [2 May 1718], Connecticut State Library).

21. Ulrich, *Good Wives*, 36–38.

22. Daniels, *Puritans at Play*, 142.

23. To discourage excessive consumption, the unlicensed sale of "Wyne" and "strong water" had been prohibited in Connecticut as early as 1643, and the sale of alcohol to the native population was outlawed in 1654 (Trumbull, *Conn. Public Recs.*, 1:100, 254–55; see also ibid., 2:119). That women participated in informal trading activities is explicitly recognized in the text of the 1654 statute, which prohibited "any person whatsoever, male or feamale" from selling alcohol to Indians (ibid., 1:255).

24. Ullmann, *Hartford County Ct. Minutes*, 138–39.

25. Edwards's second conviction, for which he was fined £5, was for selling "six gallons drink by retale" and "enterteining persons unseasonably" (Ullmann, *Hartford County Ct. Minutes*, 138). For his first offense he had sold a quart of liquor, and Elizabeth a pint.

26. Lombard, *Making Manhood*, 18.

27. Gouge, *Of Domesticall Duties*, 497–98.

28. Smith, "Descendants of William Edwards," 221–22. See also Hopkins, *Life and Character*, 1; and Deposition of Timothy and Abigail Edwards, Conn. Archives, Crimes and Misdemeanors, 1st Ser., 3:236.

29. Lombard, *Making Manhood*, 113.

30. The term "little commonwealth" was frequently used by domestic conduct writers in the early modern period to describe the family. See, for example, Robert Cleaver, *A Godlie Forme of Household Government: For the Ordering of Private Families, According to the Direction of God's Word* (London, 1600), 13; and Gouge, *Of Domesticall Duties*, 18.

31. Trumbull, *Conn. Public Recs.*, 2:105, 1:315; David H. Fowler, "Connecticut's Freemen: The First Forty Years," *William and Mary Quarterly*, 15 (July 1958): 314. When Richard Edwards qualified for freemanship in 1669 a man had to be twenty-one years of age, have an estate valued at £20, and be "of civill, peaceable and honest conversation" (Trumbull, *Conn. Public Recs.*, 1:389).

32. Hoadly, *Hartford Town Votes*, 1:168, 204; Ullmann, *Hartford County Ct. Minutes*, 196, 218, 306.

33. Dayton, "Women Before the Bar," 315.

34. Merril D. Smith, *Breaking the Bonds: Marital Discord in Pennsylvania, 1730–1830* (New York: New York Univ. Press, 1991), 46.

35. Edwards, "A True Abreviate," Conn. Archives, Crimes and Misdemeanors, 1st Ser., 3:235a, emphasis added.

36. Bailey, *Unquiet Lives*, 1.

37. Many documents in Richard Edwards's own hand have been preserved in the colonial records; a comparison clearly shows that he composed his own divorce petitions.

38. Trumbull, *Conn. Public Recs.*, 1:47; see Love, *History of Hartford*, 287.

39. *Hartford Land Recs.*, 353.

40. John Talcott notes this expenditure, and another payment to Edwards, in the January 1680 entries of his account book (Account Book of the Treasurer of Connecticut, John Talcott, Treasurer, 1673–1712, 57, 62 [1, 14 January 1680], Connecticut State Library). In May 1675, the Court of Assistants convicted Henry Green of murdering a neighbor's child but apparently refrained from executing him. Benjamin Tuttle must have shared the dungeon with this fellow axe-murderer, who was evidently kept in confinement from 1675 until his death in 1680 (Ullmann, *Ct. of Assistants Minutes*, 39–40).

41. *Hartford Land Recs.*, 197.
42. Powers, *Crime and Punishment*, 228.
43. Conn. Archives, Private Controversies, 1st Ser., 1:147 (4 October 1677).
44. Benjamin Tuttle's Deed of Gift to Elizabeth Edwards, Conn. Archives, Private Controversies, 1st Ser., 1:146.
45. Ibid.
46. Conn. Archives, Private Controversies, 1st Ser., 1:147, 148; Ullmann, *Ct. of Assistants Minutes*, 50–51, 53, 80–81.
47. Mabel Edwards was baptized on 13 December 1685 (*Historical Catalogue of the First Church in Hartford, 1633–1855* [Hartford, 1855], 165).
48. Norton, *Founding Mothers and Fathers*, 19–20, 52, 78–80. See also Nancy F. Cott, *Public Vows: A History of Marriage and the Nation* (Cambridge, Mass.: Harvard Univ. Press, 2000), 29–30.
49. Edwards, "A True Abreviate," Conn. Archives, Crimes and Misdemeanors, 1st Ser., 3:235b–c.
50. Godbeer, *Sexual Revolution*, 54, 55.
51. M. W. Perkins, *Christian Oeconomie: Or, A Short Survey of the Right Manner of Erecting and Ordering a Familie*, trans. Thomas Pickering (London, 1609), 111.
52. Gouge, *Of Domesticall Duties*, 221–22. The term comes from Paul's first letter to the Corinthians: "Let the husband render unto the wife due benevolence: and likewise the wife unto the husband" (7:3).
53. Perkins, *Christian Oeconomie*, 121, 122.
54. Amanda Porterfield, *Female Piety in Puritan New England: The Emergence of Religious Humanism* (New York: Oxford Univ. Press, 1992), 2, 20.
55. Dayton, *Women Before the Bar*, 108.
56. Anthony Fletcher, *Gender, Sex, and Subordination in England, 1500–1800* (New Haven: Yale Univ. Press, 1995), 19.
57. Gouge, *Of Domesticall Duties*, 77, 423.
58. See the chart complied by Dayton listing divorce cases heard by the Connecticut Court of Assistants and their grounds (*Women Before the Bar*, 330–33).
59. Edwards, "A True Abreviate," Conn. Archives, Crimes and Misdemeanors, 1st Ser., 3:235d–f. Edwards was evidently familiar with the 1635 account of the life of Galeacius Caracciolus, relating the circumstances of his divorce and remarriage (*The Italian Convert: Newes from Italy of a Second Moses, or the Life of Galeacius Caracciolus, the Noble Marquis of Vico* [London, 1635], 37–50).
60. Dissimilarity and embarrassment are two primary criteria that New Testament scholars use when judging the historicity of the sayings of Jesus recorded in the gospels. See John P. Meier, *A Marginal Jew: Rethinking the Historical Jesus, Vol. 1, The Roots of the Problem and the Person* (New York: Doubleday, 1991), 168–74.
61. Alexandra Shepard, *Meanings of Manhood in Early Modern England* (Oxford: Oxford Univ. Press, 2003), 57.
62. Elizabeth Foyster, "A Laughing Matter? Marital Discord and Gender Control in Seventeenth-Century England," *Rural History* 4 (April 1993): 8, 11.
63. Cleaver, *A Godlie Forme of Household Government*, 159.
64. Laura Gowing, *Domestic Dangers: Women, Words, and Sex in Early Modern London* (Oxford: Clarendon Press, 1996), 232–76.
65. Edwards, "A True Abreviate," Conn. Archives, Crimes and Misdemeanors, 1st Ser., 3:235a. The two magistrates were Thomas Welles (d. 1668) and John Talcott (d. 1688), the latter the father of the woman Edwards would marry as soon as the divorce was granted (Jacobus and Waterman, *Hale, House*, 783, 751). Edwards also claimed that Talcott supported

his account in a letter Talcott wrote to a "Mr. Ra[n]dolph," but no copy of this letter was preserved in the court papers ("A True Abreviate," 3:235a).

66. Dayton, *Women Before the Bar*, 185.

67. Gail Sussman Marcus, "'Due Execution of the Generall Rules of Righteousnesse': Criminal Procedure in New Haven Town and County, 1638–1658," in *Saints and Revolutionaries: Essays on Early American History,* ed. David D. Hall, John M. Murrin, and Thad W. Tate (New York: Norton, 1984), 112; and John M. Murrin, "Magistrates, Sinners, and a Precarious Liberty: Trial by Jury in Seventeenth-Century New England," in ibid., 175; Dayton, *Women Before the Bar,* 29, 181.

68. Blackstone, *Commentaries,* 1:434, 442–45.

69. Ullmann, *Hartford County Ct. Minutes,* 75. The County Court also ordered Elizabeth Williams's husband to pay a sum to her father for the maintenance of the child, suggesting that the magistrates were uncertain of its paternity.

70. According to Dayton, "Seventeenth-century magistrates, but not their eighteenth-century successors, decided to draw the line when asked by husbands to expand the concept of fraudulent contract to include a wife's premarital conception of a child by another man" (*Women Before the Bar,* 125–26).

71. Edwards, "A True Abreviate," Conn. Archives, Crimes and Misdemeanors, 1st Ser., 3:235a–b.

72. Dayton, "Women Before the Bar," 352–53; Edwards, "A True Abreviate," Conn. Archives, Crimes and Misdemeanors, 1st Ser., 3:235d.

73. Gouge, *Of Domesticall Duties,* 229.

74. Lynda E. Boose, "Scolding Brides and Bridling Scolds: Taming the Woman's Unruly Member," *Shakespeare Quarterly* 42 (Summer 1991): 195.

75. Edwards, "A True Abreviate," Conn. Archives, Crimes and Misdemeanors, 1st Ser., 3:235g, c; Gowing, *Domestic Dangers,* 198–99.

76. John Dod and Robert Cleaver, *A Plain and Familiar Exposition of the Ten Commandments* (London, 1635), 262.

77. Ulrich, *Good Wives,* 97; Karlsen, *Devil in the Shape of a Woman,* 155–57, 174–77.

78. Hoadly, *Hartford Town Votes,* 1:217, 206.

79. *Historical Catalogue,* 165; Shepard, *Meanings of Manhood,* 59–60; Fletcher, *Gender, Sex and Subordination,* 58–62.

80. Clifford K. Shipton, *Sibley's Harvard Graduates* (Cambridge, Mass.: Harvard Univ. Press, 1933), 4:93.

81. Gouge recommends that a "man ought to doe what he can to containe" himself while his wife is nursing an infant (*Of Domesticall Duties,* 224). Postpartum abstinence was likely a method of spacing births, but it also expressed the popular belief that sex could dry up a lactating woman's milk (Angus McLauren, *Reproductive Rituals: The Perception of Fertility in England from the Sixteenth Century to the Nineteenth Century* [London: Methuen, 1984], 66–70).

82. Edwards, "A True Abreviate"; Deposition of Timothy and Abigail Edwards, Conn. Archives, Crimes and Misdemeanors, 1st Ser., 3:235c, 236.

83. Shipton observes that during the "first quarter of 1688 an ominous mark appears against [Timothy Edwards's] name in the 'punishments' column, and shortly thereafter he disappears from the record" (*Sibley's Harvard Graduates,* 4:94).

84. Dayton, *Women Before the Bar,* 105.

85. Ullmann, *Ct. of Assistants Minutes,* 126, 129; Hoadly, *Conn. Public Recs.,* 4:37.

86. Dayton, *Women Before the Bar,* 115; Dayton, "Women Before the Bar," 290, 370–71.

87. Jacobus and Waterman, *Hale, House,* 748–49, 751–52; S. V. Talcott, comp., *Talcott Pedigree in England and America* (Albany: Weed, Parsons, 1876), 22–24, 32–37.

88. The record of Mary Talcott's fornication conviction is published in [Trumbull], *Particular Ct. Recs., Andros Admin.*, 10.

89. Dayton, *Women Before the Bar*, 173, 206, 224.

90. Ullmann, *Hartford County Ct. Minutes,* 393, 405. Because judicial records for the Dominion period in Connecticut are incomplete, the record of Edwards's subsequent appearance may also have been lost.

91. Edwards began gathering evidence in support of his petition a month before Mary Talcott's fornication presentment, for in May 1688 Timothy and Abigail Edwards gave their deposition swearing that "our Mother for many Years hath demeaned and behaved her selfe with very Great obstinacy and averseness against our Father Richard Edwards" (Conn. Archives, Crimes and Misdemeanors, 1st Ser., 3:236).

92. Cleaver, *A Godlie Forme of Household Government*, 158. This purpose is clearly articulated in the biblical injunction that commands, "to avoid fornication, let every man have his own wife, and let every woman have her own husband" (I Cor. 7:2).

93. Richard Edwards's Petition to the General Assembly, Conn. Archives, Crimes and Misdemeanors, 1st Ser., 3:238a (n.d.); Edwards, "A True Abreviate," ibid., 3:235i, h.

94. Linda K. Kerber, *Women of the Republic: Intellect and Ideology in Revolutionary America* (1980; reprint, New York: Norton, 1986), 173; Smith, *Breaking the Bonds*, 22–23.

95. According to Dayton, spouses contested a divorce action to protest "being assigned the role of guilty party and thus implicitly suggesting that the tables should be turned and he or she should be receiving the divorce decree" ("Women Before the Bar," 318).

96. Court of Assistants Records, 45, 64–65; Dayton, *Women Before the Bar,* 127.

97. Ullmann, *Ct. of Assistants Minutes,* 45, 64–65, 287, 317; Conn. Archives, Crimes and Misdemeanors, 1st Ser., 3:262; Dayton, *Women Before the Bar,* 127, 119.

98. Edwards, "A True Abreviate," Conn. Archives, Crimes and Misdemeanors, 1st Ser., 3:235b, f, c.

99. Ullmann, *Ct. of Assistants Minutes,* 150; Thomas A. Foster, "Deficient Husbands: Manhood, Sexual Incapacity, and Male Marital Sexuality in Seventeenth-Century New England," *William and Mary Quarterly*, 56 (October 1999), 735–40; Smith, *Breaking the Bonds*, 80. For a nineteenth-century case in which a husband forced his wife to have sex despite her painful pelvic disorder, see Robert L. Griswold, "Sexual Cruelty and the Case for Divorce in Victorian America," *Signs* 11 (Spring 1986): 529–41.

100. Gouge, *Of Domesticall Duties*, 223; Perkins, *Christian Oeconomie*, 100.

101. Dayton, "Women Before the Bar," 314; Henry S. Cohn, "Connecticut's Divorce Mechanism: 1636–1969, *American Journal of Legal History* 14 (January 1970), 40; Ullmann, *Ct. of Assistants Minutes*, 126.

102. Pitkin's Complaint, Conn. Archives, Crimes and Misdemeanors, 1st Ser., 1:162–63 (15, 18 May 1691).

103. Hoadly, *Conn. Public Recs.*, 4:53.

104. Dayton, *Women Before the Bar*, 114, 143.

105. Hoadly, *Conn. Public Recs.*, 4:53.

106. According to Dayton, of fifty-seven divorce petitions filed in New Haven and Connecticut colonies from 1639 to 1710, thirty-three were based solely on grounds of desertion, and another nine cited desertion aggravated by adultery; only four petitioners were unsuccessful (*Women Before the Bar*, 117).

107. Dayton, *Women Before the Bar*, 148.

108. Edwards's Petition, Conn. Archives, Crimes and Misdemeanors, 1st Ser., 3:238a.

109. Dayton, "Women Before the Bar," 321.

110. Dayton identifies one analogous argument, made subsequent to Edwards's case in 1705, by a wife named Mary Sage, in which two male supporters testified that "about the time

he willfully deserted and Left her," her husband "was compos mentis" (Conn. Archives, Crimes and Misdemeanors, 1st Ser., 3:275). According to Dayton, by the mid–eighteenth century Connecticut magistrates no longer considered mental illness a bar to divorce (*Women Before the Bar*, 125 n., 151).

111. Edwards's Petition, Conn. Archives, Crimes and Misdemeanors, 1st Ser., 3:238a.

112. MacDonald, *Mystical Bedlam*, 126.

113. Dayton, "Women Before the Bar," 316.

114. Conn. Archives, Crimes and Misdemeanors, 1st Ser. 3:239 (13 October 1691).

115. "Judgment of Mr. John Woodbridge," Conn. Archives, Crimes and Misdemeanors, 1st Ser., 3:239 (29 December 1689).

116. In its May 1691 ruling the Assembly appointed six ministers to serve on this council, one of whom was "Mr. Woodbridge," most likely Timothy Woodbridge, the Hartford pastor (Hoadly, *Conn. Public Recs.*, 4:52). But both Timothy and his brother John, the Wethersfield pastor, had supported Edwards's suit from the outset (Conn. Archives, Crimes and Misdemeanors, 1st Ser., 3:237, 239).

117. Edwards's Petition, Conn. Archives, Crimes and Misdemeanors, 1st Ser., 3:238b.

118. Frances E. Dolan, *Dangerous Familiars: Representations of Domestic Crime in England, 1550–1700* (Ithaca, N.Y.: Cornell Univ. Press, 1994), 39; Gowing, *Domestic Dangers*, 202.

119. Whether Edwards wrote his second petition before or after the second murder is unclear because the document is undated. If after, then he exploited the tragedy for his own gain, if before, he benefited from conjunction of fortuitous circumstances.

120. Hoadly, *Conn. Public Recs.*, 4:59.

121. Kerber, *Women of the Republic*, 172.

122. Edwards, "A True Abreviate," Conn. Archives, Crimes and Misdemeanors, 1st Ser., 3:235h.

CHAPTER 6

1. Marsden, *Jonathan Edwards*, 35; Sereno Edwards Dwight, *The Life of President Edwards* (New York: Carvill, 1830), 653.

2. Timothy Edwards, "Some Things Written for My Own Use and Comfort, Concerning the Life and Death of My Very Dear and Ever Honoured Father, Mr. Richard Edwards, Late of Hartford, Who Departed this Life, April 20, 1718," Jonathan Edwards Papers, f. 16–A.1, Franklin Trask Library, Andover-Newton Theological School, Newton Centre, Mass., [32], [30]. Because only the first eleven pages of this eighty-six-page MS are paginated, subsequent page numbers appear in the notes in brackets.

3. Charles E. Hambrick-Stowe, *The Practice of Piety: Puritan Devotional Disciplines in Seventeenth-Century New England* (Chapel Hill: Univ. of North Carolina Press, 1982), 229.

4. Lewis Bayly, *The Practice of Piety: Directing a Christian How to Walk, That He May Please God* (London, 1654), 391.

5. Edwards, "Some Things Written," [30], [32–33], [42].

6. Ibid., [82], [84], [85].

7. Bayly, *Practice of Piety*, 378.

8. Estate of Richard Edwards, 1718, Hartford Probate Packets, 1641–1880, #1824, Connecticut State Library, Hartford, Connecticut.

9. William Perkins, *Directions on How to Live Well, and to Die Well*, in Richard Rogers et al., *A Garden of Spiritual Flowers* (London, 1631), n.p.

10. Bayly, *Practice of Piety*, 415, 417.

11. Edwards, "Some Things Written," [29].

12. Blackstone, *Commentaries*, 2:502–3; Bruce Mann and Bridgette Williams-Searle, e-mail communications with author, 7 June 2006.

13. Wilson, *Ye Heart of a Man*, 158.

14. Faragher found that 84.2 percent of men in colonial Wethersfield who lost their spouses before age fifty remarried; if older men are included in the sample, the figure drops to 66.6 percent ("Old Women and Old Men," 18–19; correction for misprint in text supplied by Faragher [e-mail communication with author, 3 May 2006]).

15. *Early Hartford Vital Records*, Connecticut Historical Society, *Collections*, vol. 14 (Hartford, 1912), 589. Only three sons lived to adulthood.

16. Fletcher, *Gender, Sex, and Subordination*, 58–59.

17. *Historical Catalogue of the Hartford Church*, 39–40.

18. Estate of Lieut. Col. John Talcott, 1688, Hartford Probate Records, 1641–1880, #5373; Hartford County Court and Probate Records, 1677-1706, vol. 5, 1689–1697, Connecticut State Library, 8 (20 November 1689), 45-46 (inventory); Manwaring, *Probate Recs.*, 1:509–10.

19. Mary's brother Joseph Talcott attempted to claim his right under English intestacy law to the whole of their father's realty. With the overthrow of the Dominion, the suit failed and the estate was eventually distributed according to longstanding colonial practice, which gave a double portion to the eldest son. Mary likely received approximately £29 in personal and £150 in real property (Ullmann, *Ct. of Assistants Minutes*, 124–25, 128; Hoadly, *Conn. Public Recs.*, 4:48; Conn. Archives, Private Controversies, 1st Ser., 4:47–48 [15 May 1691]).

20. Estate of Richard Edwards, Hartford Probate Packets, #1824.

21. Ullmann, *Hartford County Ct. Minutes*, 165, 361, 387, 401–2, 430; Ullmann, *Ct. of Assistants Minutes*, 100, 105, 127.

22. Hartford County Ct. Recs., 5:48-49 (7 December 1692); Bulkeley, *Will and Doom*, 263–65.

23. In a letter to the Connecticut General Assembly dated 30 March 1687, John Talcott and his brother Samuel recommended that the government submit to the king's demand (*New England Historical and Genealogical Register* 23 [April 1869]: 174).

24. Hartford County Ct. Recs., 5:73, 119 (6 September 1694, 8 November 1696); and vol. 6, 1697–1706, 13, 23, 37, 49 (3 March 1698, 13 April 1698, 1 September 1698); Ullmann, *Hartford County Ct. Minutes*, 450; Ullmann, *Ct. of Assistants Minutes*, 202, 214–16, 220, 237, 240; Hoadly, *Conn. Public Recs.*, 4:127, 210–11.

25. Edward Coke, *Second Part of the Institutes of the Laws of England* (1642; reprint, New York: Garland, 1979), 683; Howard, *A History of Matrimonial Institutions*, 1:351–54. Massachusetts expressly prohibited marriage to a "dead wife's sister" in 1679; this type of marriage was not legalized in Connecticut until 1793 (ibid., 2:213, 397). For the scripture rule, see Lev. 18:16; 20:21.

26. Conn. Archives, Crimes and Misdemeanors, 1st Ser., 3:245, 246, 522, 253a, b; Ullmann, *Ct. of Assistants Minutes*, 164. The brief for this case is in Edwards's hand and rivals in length and complexity his own divorce petitions.

27. Hoadly, *Conn. Public Records*, 4:305, 468; Dayton, *Women Before the Bar*, 34, and n.29; Hartford County Ct. Recs., 6:263 (6 April 1705); Dwight Loomis and J. Gilbert Calhoun, *Judicial and Civil History of Connecticut* (Boston: Boston History Co., 1895), 157–58.

28. Manwaring, *Probate Recs.*, 2:58–59; Ullmann, *Ct. of Assistants Minutes*, 465; Hoadly, *Conn. Public Recs.*, 5:48.

29. Estate of Richard Edwards, Hartford Probate Packets, #1824; Hoadly, *Conn. Public Records*, 4:499. Elected governor in 1724, Talcott remained in office until 1735 (ibid., 6:484).

30. Ullmann, *Ct. of Assistants Minutes*, 390–96.

31. Gershom Bulkeley to Fitz-John Winthrop, 2 September 1707; Fitz-John Winthrop to the Connecticut General Assembly, 23 September 1707 (*Winthrop Papers*, Massachusetts Historical Society, *Collections*, 6th Ser., vol. 3 [Boston, 1889], 399, 403). Although the records

are vague, Thompson apparently was executed in May 1708 (Hoadly, *Conn. Public Recs.,* 5:12, 28, 62, 65).

32. Dayton, *Women Before the Bar,* 47–48; Mann, *Neighbors and Strangers,* 85, 93–94.
33. Edwards owned *The Reports of Sir Henry Hobart Lord Chief Justice of the Common Pleas* . . . (London, 1741); Richard Hutton, *The Young Clarks Guide . . . Very Useful and Necessary for All, but Chiefly for those that Intend to Follow the Atturney's Practice* (London, 1670); Gerard Malynes, *Consuetudo, Vel, Lex Mercatoria, or, The Ancient Law-Merchant* . . . (London, 1622); and Thomas Smith, *The Commonwealth of England and the Manner of Government Thereof* . . . (London, 1640). A book listed as the "The Compleat Attorney" may be William Booth, *The Compleat Solicitor, Entering-Clerk, and Attorney: Fully Instructed in the Practice, Methods, and Clerkship of all His Majesties Courts* . . . (London, 1683). A sixth work, listed as "The Old Boston Law Book," cannot be identified.
34. Edwards, "Some Things Written," 2, [71].
35. Although in unusual circumstances the guilty party was allowed to remarry, in practice he or she was denied this privilege (Dayton, *Women Before the Bar,* 113, 120, n.26).
36. Deposition of Timothy and Abigail Edwards, Conn. Archives, Crimes and Misdemeanors, 1st Ser., 3:236.
37. Edwards, "Some Things Written," 10, [18].
38. Cotton Mather, *Parentator: Memoirs of Remarkables in the Life and the Death of the Ever-Memorable Dr. Increase Mather. Who Expired, August 23, 1723* (Boston, 1724), in *Two Mather Biographies: "Life and Death" and "Parentator,"* ed. William J. Scheick (Bethlehem, Pa.: Lehigh Univ. Press, 1989), 75.
39. Timothy Edwards made this indirect reference to the divorce in an eight-page variant of the first fourteen pages of "Some Things Written" (Connecticut Historical Society, Hartford, Connecticut); he omitted it from the full biography.
40. Edwards, "Some Things Written," 1, 3, 6, 7, 4.
41. Edwards, "Some Things Written," [39]; Edwards, "A True Abreviate," Conn. Archives, Crimes and Misdemeanors, 1st Ser., 3:235b.
42. Wilson, *Ye Heart of a Man,* 15.
43. Scheick, introduction to *Two Mather Biographies,* 11, 15–16.
44. Edwards, "Some Things Written," [8], [17], [20], [21], [13], [19], [12], [23].
45. Edwards, "Some Things Written," [12], [14], [23].
46. Scheick points out that Cotton Mather made a similar move in *Parentator,* although for very different reasons (introduction to *Two Mather Biographies,* 24–26).
47. Edwards, "Some Things Written," 1, [31], [38], [42].
48. Morgan, *Visible Saints,* 70, 91. See also Michael McGiffert, *God's Plot: Puritan Spirituality in Thomas Shepard's Cambridge,* rev. ed. (Amherst: Univ. of Massachusetts Press, 1994), 19–21.
49. Edwards, "Some Thing Written," 1.
50. Ibid., [74], [63], 1, [86].
51. Although listed with the Harvard class of 1691, Timothy Edwards received both his B.A. and his M.A. at the 1694 commencement (Shipton, *Sibley's Harvard Graduates,* 4:94).
52. Kenneth P. Minkema, "Hannah and Her Sisters: Sisterhood, Courtship, and Marriage in the Edwards Family in the Early Eighteenth Century," *New England Historical and Genealogical Register* 146 (January 1992): 35. Interestingly, after naming the first girl Esther, her maternal grandmother's name, they named their second child Elizabeth, presumably after her paternal grandmother.
53. Minkema, "Hannah and Her Sisters," 41, 36, 46, 45, 55; Hannah Edwards Wetmore, Diary, 1736–1739, Jonathan Edwards Papers, MSS 151, Box 24, f. 1377, Beinecke Rare Book and Manuscript Library, Yale University, New Haven, Conn.

54. David D. Hall, *The Faithful Shepherd: A History of the New England Ministry in the Seventeenth Century* (New York: Norton, 1974), 270, 273–74.

55. "A Register of the Rules and Resolves of the North Association of the County of Hartford," 1 June 1725, United Church of Christ, Connecticut Conference, Archives, Hartford, 17; "The Complaint of John Moore, Jun., of Windsor," 15 March 1725, Hartford Superior Court, Divorce Files, 1740–1794, RG3, Connecticut State Library; John A. Stoughton, *Windsor Farmes: A Glimpse of an Old Parish* (Hartford: Clark & Smith, 1883), 71–73; Alison Duncan Hirsch, "The Thrall Divorce Case: A Family Crisis in Eighteenth-Century Connecticut," *Women and History* 4 (Winter 1982): 51–52.

56. Roger Wolcott, "A Narrative of the Troubles in the Second Church in Windsor, from the Year 1735 to the Year 1741," Roger Wolcott Papers, box 3, f. 6, Connecticut Historical Society, 10, 11; Kenneth P. Minkema, "The Edwardses: A Ministerial Family in Eighteenth-Century New England" (Ph.D. diss., University of Connecticut, 1988), 128, 131.

57. Ruling of the Ministerial Council Called by the Windsor First Society, 13 February 1734, Hartford Superior Ct., Divorce Files, 1740–1795; Hirsch, "The Thrall Divorce Case," 67, 53, 56. See William Ames, *Conscience with the Power and Cases Thereof* (London, 1643), 209.

58. "Som Few Considerations Concerning Wedlock," 13 November 1713; "Resolve of the Hartford Clergy," n.d., New Haven Superior Court, Divorce Files, 1712–1718, Connecticut State Library; Dayton, *Women Before the Bar*, 142–43.

59. Timothy Edwards, "Ecclesiastical Minutes and Notes From Various Authors, 1738–1758," Jonathan Edwards Papers, f. 1730–1739, 1 (5, 7 September 1738), Trask Library; Connecticut Archives, Crimes and Misdemeanors, 1st Series, vol. 4, 1737–1755, Connecticut State Library, 16 (9 February 1737), 14 (29 April 1735); Minkema, "The Edwardses," 115.

60. Edwards, "A True Abreviate," Conn. Archives, Crimes and Misdemeanors, 1st Ser., 235b–c, e.

61. John Read, "Plea for Merriman," n.d., New Haven Superior Ct., Divorce Files, 1712–1718; Dayton, *Women Before the Bar*, 144.

62. "The Humble Petition of Hannah the Late wife and Companion of Captain John Merriman," n.d.; "Resolve of the New Haven Clergy," 17 July 1717, New Haven Superior Ct., Divorce Files, 1712–1718. The Hartford County pastors, including Timothy Edwards, took a similar position ("Resolve of the Hartford Clergy," ibid.); Dayton, *Women Before the Bar*, 144. Connecticut did not recognize spousal cruelty as a statutory ground for divorce until 1843 (ibid.).

63. Ruling of the Ministerial Council, 13 February 1734; Deposition of Timothy Edwards, 9 September 1735, Hartford Superior Ct., Divorce Files, 1740–1795.

64. Dayton, *Women Before the Bar*, 159–61, 206–8.

65. Ava Chamberlain, "Jonathan Edwards and the Politics of Sex in Eighteenth-Century Northampton," in *Jonathan Edwards at 300: Essays on the Tercentenary of His Birth*, ed. Harry S. Stout, Kenneth P. Minkema, and Caleb J. D. Maskell (Landham, Md.: Univ. Press of America, 2005), 112–18. For the scripture rule, see Ex. 22:16–17 and Deut. 22:28–29.

66. Massachusetts Archives, SC1/series 45X, Massachusetts Archives Collection, vol. 9, Domestic Relations, 1613–1774, 296 (28 May 1746), 299 (n.d.), 301 (n.d.). On this case, see Roy Carpenter, "Sexual Politics in Eighteenth-Century Pelham, Massachusetts: The Jonathan Edwards Clan, Divorce Law, and the Eleanor Gray Case," *Jonathan Edwards Studies* 1, no. 1 (2011): 22–44, 58–89, http://jestudies.yale.edu/index.php/journal.

67. The *"Blank Bible,"* ed. Stephen J. Stein, vol. 24, pt. 2 of *The Works of Jonathan Edwards*, gen. ed. Harry S. Stout (New Haven: Yale Univ. Press, 2006), 835.

68. Massachusetts Archives Collection, 9: 300 (n.d.), 317 (4 February 1747).

69. *A Faithful Narrative of the Surprising Work of God*, in C. C. Goen, ed., *The Great Awakening*, vol. 4 of *The Works of Jonathan Edwards*, gen. ed. John E. Smith (New Haven: Yale Univ. Press, 1972), 195.

70. Barbara Welter, "The Cult of True Womanhood: 1820–1860," *American Quarterly* 18 (Summer 1966): 152.
71. Nancy F. Cott, "Passionlessness: An Interpretation of Victorian Sexual Ideology, 1790–1850," in *A Heritage of Her Own: Toward a New Social History of American Women* (New York: Simon & Schuster, 1979), 173.

CHAPTER 7

1. Hopkins, *Life and Character*, v, iii, 2. It is unlikely that Anne Edwards Cole actually assisted in making a ruff for Queen Elizabeth, for she was a young girl in 1603 when the monarch died. The assertion that Richard and Elizabeth Edwards had seven children is also difficult to explain. Some genealogists speculate the couple had a child who died young, born perhaps during the four-year gap between Abigail and Elizabeth, but no record supports this conjecture.
2. Dwight, *Life of President Edwards*, 10, 654, emphasis added. This biography was published in 1829 as the first volume of Dwight's ten-volume *Works of President Edwards* (New York: S. Convese, 1829–30). Dwight was a fifth-generation descendant of William Edwards; Richard was his great-great-grandfather.
3. Henry Bamford Parkes, *Jonathan Edwards: The Fiery Puritan* (New York: Minton, Balch, 1930), 27, 28. Parkes was apparently the first biographer to include information about the divorce in an account of Jonathan Edwards's ancestry. A. V. G. Allen, the author of the only substantive biography published between Dwight's and Parkes's, fails to mention Richard Edwards's two wives and emphasizes Jonathan Edwards's maternal inheritance as the principal source of his religious genius (*Jonathan Edwards* [Boston: Houghton Mifflin, 1889], 1–3).
4. Parkes, *The Fiery Puritan*, 28.
5. The nineteenth-century reputations of Jonathan Edwards's youngest son, Pierpont, and his grandson Aaron Burr were well expressed by the phrenologist Orson S. Fowler: "For ages to come will these two names . . . be coupled with seductions the most artful and successful, with sexual indulgence the most gross and unparalleled on record, as well as with the ruin of females the most lovely and unblemished" (*Hereditary Descent: Its Laws and Facts Applied to Human Improvement* [New York: Fowler & Wells, 1847], 148–49). John A. Stoughton first described the "peculiar disposition" of Jonathan Edwards's sister Martha, who married a Tuttle, and two of her daughters, who inherited the "peculiarities of the Tuttle blood." Their alleged opium addiction cannot be substantiated (*Windsor Farmes*, 67–68).
6. Louis Leonard Tucker, *Clio's Consort: Jeremy Belknap and the Founding of the Massachusetts Historical Society* (Boston: Massachusetts Historical Society, 1990), 63–65.
7. Hoadly, *Conn. Public Recs.*, 9:15; 13:367, 424.
8. Christopher P. Bickford, "Public Records and the Private Historical Society: A Connecticut Example," *Government Publications Review* 8A, no. 4 (1981): 315; Sylvie J. Turner, "The Connecticut Archives," *Connecticut Historical Society Bulletin* 33 (July 1968): 81–82; George S. Godard, "Public Libraries and Records," *History of Connecticut in Monographic Form*, ed. Norris Galpin Osborn (New York: States History Co., 1925), 5:541–41.
9. Connecticut General Assembly, *Resolutions and Private Acts, 1851* (Hartford: Boswell & Faxon, 1851), 187; Catherine Hickey Handy, "The Connecticut State Library, 1851–1936" (M.A. thesis, Southern Connecticut State University, 1965), 20–21, 97; Godard, 524–25.
10. Joseph A. Conforti, *Imagining New England: Explorations of Regional Identity from the Pilgrims to the Mid-Twentieth Century* (Chapel Hill: Univ. of North Carolina Press, 2001), 113, 94.
11. Conforti, *Jonathan Edwards*, 4, 9, 10.

12. Conforti, *Imagining New England*, 204–5.
13. Allen, *Jonathan Edwards*, 7; Conforti, *Jonathan Edwards*, 160, 145.
14. On the establishment of an American school of genealogy, see François Weil, "John Farmer and the Making of American Genealogy," *New England Quarterly* 80 (September 2007): 408–34.
15. Dwight, *Life of President Edwards*, 653; Nathaniel Goodwin, *Genealogical Notes, or Contributions to the Family History of Some of the First Settlers of Connecticut and Massachusetts* (1856; reprint, Baltimore: Genealogical Publishing Co., 1969), 49. Goodwin does not explicitly state that Elizabeth Tuttle died prior to Richard Edwards's second marriage but implies it in the same way as had Hopkins.
16. Tuttle, *Descendants of William and Elizabeth Tuttle*, 347, vii; William H. Edwards, *Timothy and Rhoda Ogden Edwards of Stockbridge, Mass., and Their Descendants* (Cincinnati: Robert Clark, 1903), 1.
17. Michael Kammen, *Mystic Chords of Memory: The Transformation of Tradition in American Culture* (New York: Vintage Books, 1993), 38.
18. Conforti, *Jonathan Edwards*, 169.
19. *The Memorial Volume of the Edwards Family Meeting at Stockbridge, Mass., September 6–7, 1870* (Boston: Congregational Pub. Society, 1871), 12, 21–22, 184.
20. Conforti, *Jonathan Edwards*, 175–83, 184.
21. Alice Morse Earle, *The Sabbath in Puritan New England*, 11th ed. (New York: Scribner's, 1913), 327.
22. David D. Hall and Alan Taylor, "Reassessing the Local History of New England," in *New England: A Bibliography of Its History*, ed. Roger Parks (Hanover, N.H.: Univ. Press of New England, 1989), xxviii.
23. Stoughton, *Windsor Farmes*, v, vi.
24. Ibid., 69, n.1; 68; 39, n.4; 39; v. In the 1859 edition of *The History of Ancient Windsor* the author, Henry R. Stiles, makes no mention of the divorce in his account of the Edwards genealogy (588); the revised, two-volume edition, appearing in 1891–92, includes the divorce and a reference to Stoughton's account of the incident in *Windsor Farmes* (2:194, and note).
25. Hall and Taylor, "Reassessing the Local History of New England," xxv.
26. John C. Waller, "'The Illusion of an Explanation': The Concept of Hereditary Disease, 1770–1870," *Journal of the History of Medicine and Allied Sciences*, 57 (October 2002), 410–11; and "Ideas of Heredity, Reproduction and Eugenics in Britain, 1800–1875," *Studies in History and Philosophy of Biological and Biomedical Sciences*, 32 (September 2001), 466, 479–80.
27. Jacobus, *Families of Ancient New Haven*, 3:1884. See also Jacobus and Waterman, *Hale, House*, 524–35, 770–75. *Families of Ancient New Haven* was first published serially in the *New Haven Genealogical Register* from 1922 to 1932.
28. Donald Lines Jacobus, *Genealogy as Pastime and Profession*, 2nd ed., rev. (Baltimore: Genealogical Pub. Co., 1968), 17, 18, 105; the assessment of Jacobus's standing as a genealogist comes from Milton Rubincam's introduction to *Genealogy as Pastime and Profession*, p. 2.
29. Galton formed "eugenics" from the Greek word meaning "good in stock, hereditarily endowed with noble qualities" (*Inquiries into Human Faculty and Its Development* [1883; reprint, New York: AMS Press, 1973], 17, n.1); Mark H. Haller, *Eugenics: Hereditarian Attitudes in American Thought* (New Brunswick, N.J.: Rutgers Univ. Press, 1984), 8, 17.
30. Francis Galton, *Hereditary Genius: An Inquiry into Its Laws and Consequences* (1869; reprint, New York: Horizon Press, 1952), 1, 296, 60; Preface to the 1892 ed., in ibid., xxvii.

31. Daniel J. Kevles, *In the Name of Eugenics: Genetics and the Uses of Human Heredity* (1985; reprint, Cambridge, Mass.: Harvard Univ. Press, 1995), 64.

32. Christine Rosen, *Preaching Eugenics: Religious Leaders and the American Eugenics Movement* (New York: Oxford Univ. Press, 2004), 113; Haller, *Eugenics*, 80.

33. Kenneth M. Ludmerer, *Genetics and American Society: A Historical Analysis* (Baltimore: Johns Hopkins Univ. Press, 1972), 42.

34. Kevles, *In the Name of Eugenics*, 85; Haller, *Eugenics*, 77.

35. Robert L. Dugdale, *The Jukes: A Study in Crime, Pauperism, Disease, and Heredity*, 4th ed. (1877, 1910; reprint, New York: Arno Press, 1970), 14–15, 25–26. "Juke" was a pseudonym apparently taken from a word meaning "to roost" that "refers to the habit of fowls to have no home, no nest, no coop" (Albert E. Winship, *Jukes-Edwards: A Study in Education and Heredity* [Harrisburg, Pa.: R. L. Myers, 1900], 8–9).

36. Steven A. Gelb, "Myths, Morons, Psychologists: The Kallikak Family Revisited," *The Review of Education* 11 (Fall 1985): 255. In his analysis of the Juke family, Dugdale principally employed the environmental approach of Benedict Morel, who maintained that unhealthy environments caused "degeneracy." Nevertheless, as hereditarian arguments became more common in the late nineteenth century, his and other family studies were employed to support a rigid hereditarian view (Charles E. Rosenberg, *No Other Gods: On Science and American Social Thought*, rev. ed. [Baltimore: Johns Hopkins Univ. Press, 1997], 43–46; Elof Axel Carlson, "R. L. Dugdale and the Jukes Family: A Historical Injustice Corrected," *BioScience* 30 [August 1980]: 535–39).

37. Arthur H. Estabrook, *The Jukes at 1915* (Washington: Carnegie Institute, 1916), 52–67, 85.

38. For a selection of the most important family studies, see Nichole Hahn Rafter, ed., *White Trash: The Eugenic Family Studies, 1877–1919* (Boston: Northeastern Univ. Press, 1988).

39. Henry H. Goddard, *The Kallikak Family* (1912; reprint, New York: Arno Press, 1973), 77.

40. Haller, *Eugenics*, 21.

41. Winship, *Jukes-Edwards*, 15, 16, 19; *National Cyclopedia of American Biography* (New York: J. T. White, 1891, 1921), 2:119–20. Prior to Winship's publication, the Edwards family had been identified as an example of superior heredity. See, for example, Fowler, *Hereditary Descent*, 189–91.

42. George A. Gordon, "The Significance of Edwards To-Day," *Jonathan Edwards: A Retrospect; Being the Addresses Delivered in Connection with the Unveiling of a Memorial . . . ,*" ed. H. Norman Gardiner (Boston: Houghton Mifflin, 1901), 54; George C. Eggleston, *The American Immortals: The Record of Men . . . whose Names are Inscribed in the Hall of Fame* (New York: Putnam's, 1901), x.

43. Winship, *Jukes-Edwards*, 60, 10–11, 32–33, 36. Like Dugdale, Winship employed a mixed environmental-hereditarian analysis. He admitted that the Jukes would have been "immensely improved by education and environment" and that the Edwards family could not have "maintained its record without education, training, and environment" (ibid., 54).

44. Henry M. Boies, *The Science of Penology: The Defense of Society Against Crime* (New York: Putnam's Sons, 1901), 327–28.

45. Patricia Cline Cohen, *A Calculating People: The Spread of Numeracy in Early America* (Chicago: Univ. of Chicago Press, 1982), 205, 207–11.

46. Herbert Eugene Walter, *Genetics: An Introduction to the Study of Heredity* (New York: Macmillan, 1917), 230; James E. Peabody and Arthur E. Hunt, *Biology and Human Welfare* (New York: Macmillan, 1927), 547.

47. "The Jukes-Edwards Contrast," *Journal of Education* 50 (24 August 1899): 128. The series began in the 14 September 1899 issue, under the title "Education and Ignorance: The Jukes versus Jonathan Edwards," and ran until 15 February 1900.

48. Steven Selden, *Inheriting Shame: The Story of Eugenics and Racism in America* (New York: Teachers College Press, 1999), 65; George William Hunter, *A Civic Biology: Presented in Problems* (New York: American Book Co., 1914), 263–64. According to Selden, various editions of Hunter's text were among the most popular high school biology texts used in pre-war classrooms (ibid., 70).

49. Paul Popenoe and Roswell H. Johnson, *Applied Eugenics* (New York: Macmillan, 1918), 161; Selden, *Inheriting Shame*, 48–57.

50. Ignatius W. Cox, "The Folly of Human Sterilization," *Scientific American* 151 (October 1934): 189; Frederick Adams Woods, "Heredity and the Hall of Fame," *Popular Science Monthly* 82 (May 1913): 446; Edith A. Winship, "The Human Legacy of Jonathan Edwards," *The World's Work* 6 (May–October 1903): 3981–84; H. N[orman] G[ardiner] and R[ichard] We[bster], "Jonathan Edwards," *Encyclopaedia Britannica*, 11th ed. (Cambridge: Cambridge Univ. Press, 1910–11), 9:5, n.1.

51. Albert E. Wiggam, *Fruit of the Family Tree* (Indianapolis: Bobbs-Merrill, 1924), 15, 16–18.

52. Harvey W. Wiley, "The Rights of the Unborn," *Good Housekeeping* (October 1922): 171–72.

53. Lothrop Stoddard, *The Revolt Against Civilization: The Menace of the Under Man* (New York: Scribner's, 1922), 260–61, 262.

54. Phillips E. Osgood, "Eugenics: The Refiner's Fire" (9 May 1926), American Eugenics Society Records, American Philosophical Association, Philadelphia, Penn., 5; Rosen, *Preaching Eugenics*, 124–25, 113–14.

55. Winship, *Jukes-Edwards*, 22.

56. E. Carleton MacDowell, "Charles Benedict Davenport, 1866–1944: A Study of Conflicting Influences," *Bios* 27 (March 1946): 4–5; Amzi Benedict Davenport, *A History and Genealogy of the Davenport Family* (New York: S. W. Benedict, 1851) and *A Supplement to The History and Genealogy of the Davenport Family* (Stamford, Conn.: W. W. Gillespie, 1876).

57. Charles Benedict Davenport, *Heredity in Relation to Eugenics* (New York: Henry Holt, 1911), 239.

58. Charles B. Davenport and Harry H. Laughlin, "How to Make a Eugenical Family Study," *Eugenics Record Office Bulletin, No. 13* (Cold Spring Harbor, N.Y., 1915), 9. For a complete list of traits, see Charles B. Davenport, "The Trait Book," *Eugenics Record Office Bulletin, No. 6* (Cold Spring Harbor, N.Y., 1912). The elaborate card file system maintained at the Eugenics Record Office is today part of the genetics collection of the American Philosophical Society Library.

59. Ludmerer, *Genetics and American Society*, 50–51.

60. Davenport, *Heredity in Relation to Eugenics*, 51, 55, 181–203.

61. Davenport, *Heredity in Relation to Eugenics*, 225–26. Davenport cites as his source for this information a "manuscript furnished by a reputable genealogist" that is "deposited at the Eugenics Record Office" (ibid., 227, n.1, 228, n.1). This manuscript is no longer a part of the Eugenics Record Office files held by the American Philosophical Society and cannot now be identified.

62. Jonathan Edwards's ten sisters evidently approximated his height, for Timothy Edwards famously quipped that he had "sixty feet of daughters" (Minkema, "Hannah and Her Sisters," 35). According to Timothy Edwards, his father was of "middle stature" (abridgement of "Some Things Written," 1).

63. Davenport, *Heredity in Relation to Eugenics*, 227, 226, 183, 228.

64. Ibid., 226, 183, 227.

65. Jacobus, *Genealogy as Pastime and Profession*, 104.

66. Davenport, *Heredity in Relation to Eugenics*, 227.

67. Davenport, "How to Make a Eugenical Family Study," 29; Arthur Holmes, "The First Law of Character Making," in *Eugenics: Twelve University Lectures* (New York: Dodd, Mead, 1914), 209.

68. Kevles, *In the Name of Eugenics*, 78. Other duplex family studies include Gertrude C. Davenport, "Hereditary Crime" (1907) and Elizabeth S. Kite, "Two Brothers" (1912), in Rafter, *White Trash*, 66–80.

69. Goddard, *The Kallikak Family*, 50, 29, 68–69.

70. Goddard, *The Kallikak Family*, 52, 68.

71. Davenport, *Heredity in Relation to Eugenics*, 226.

72. Wiggam, *Fruit of the Family Tree*, 16, 17, 20.

73. Wendy Kline, *Building a Better Race: Gender, Sexuality, and Eugenics from the Turn of the Century to the Baby Boom* (Berkeley: Univ. of California Press, 2001), 11; Popenoe and Johnson, *Applied Eugenics*, 246–54. See also the chapter "The Lost Children of the Colleges" in Ellsworth Huntington and Leon F. Whitney, *The Builders of America* (New York: William Morrow, 1927), 42–53.

74. Wiggam, *Fruit of the Family Tree*, 303, 302.

75. Kevles, *In the Name of Eugenics*, 77–79; Kline, *Building a Better Race*, 19, 21–22; Florence H. Danielson and Charles B. Davenport, *The Hill Folk: Report on a Rural Community of Hereditary Defectives*, in Rafter, *White Trash*, 89; see also Goddard's discussion of feeble-mindedness and hereditary "harlotry" in *The Kallikaks*, 54–62.

76. Kline, *Building a Better Race*, 34, 39, 42.

77. The movement's other major legislative accomplishment was the passage of the federal Immigration Restriction acts of 1921 and 1924. Harry H. Laughlin, Charles Davenport's colleague at the Eugenics Record Office, worked closely with the House Committee on Immigration and Naturalization to promote these bills (Phillip R. Reilly, *The Surgical Solution: A History of Involuntary Sterilization in the United States* [Baltimore: Johns Hopkins Univ. Press, 1991], 63–65).

78. Reilly, *Surgical Solution*, 25, 26, 33, 87, 97; Charles B. Davenport, "State Laws Limiting Marriage Selection Examined in the Light of Eugenics," *Eugenics Record Office Bulletin, No. 9* (Cold Spring Harbor, N.Y., 1913), 45; Harry H. Laughlin, *Eugenical Sterilization in the United States* (Chicago: Chicago Psychopathic Laboratory, 1922), 15.

79. Ludmerer, *Genetics and American Society*, 75–78.

80. Kevles, *In the Name of Eugenics*, 145.

81. Eugene Smith, "'Hereditary' Criminals," *New York Times*, 2 November 1909; Smith was responding to an editorial criticizing the pending legislation that had run in the paper on 29 October 1909. Daniel Davenport, "'Hereditary' Crime"; editorial, "Race Homicide"; obituary, "Daniel Davenport, Noted Lawyer, Dead," *New York Times*, 5 November 1909; 14 November 1909; 10 March 1931.

82. Daniel Davenport to W. O. Burr, 6 December 1909, carbon copy of original letter, Baldwin Family Papers, General Correspondence, Group 55, 1st Ser., Box 57, Folder 730, Yale University MS Collection, New Haven, Conn.

83. Walter, *Genetics*, 260.

84. John Langdon-Davies, *The New Age of Faith* (Garden City, N.Y.: Garden City Publishing, 1925), 150–51.

85. Ibid., 148; Walter, *Genetics*, 261.

86. Harvey Wickham, *The Misbehaviorists: Pseudo-Science and the Modern Temper* (New York: Dial Press, 1930), 216, 217.

87. J. B. S. Haldane, *Heredity and Politics* (New York: Norton, 1938), 88; Langdon-Davies, *The New Age of Faith*, 156; Raymond Pearl, *The Present Status of Eugenics* (Hanover, N.H.: The Sociological Press, 1928), 20.

88. Clarence Darrow, "The Edwardses and the Jukeses," *The American Mercury* 6 (October 1925): 148, 149, 153, 151, 152, 153. The "battle royal" between Clarence Darrow and William Jennings Bryan occurred in July 1925. In his opposition to eugenics, however, Darrow aligned himself with Bryan, who had in his closing argument in the Scopes trial denounced eugenics as a pernicious product of evolutionary theory. Darrow's opposition to eugenics was so well established by 1925 that Charles Davenport and other prominent eugenicists, who had, as evolutionary biologists, advised the American Civil Liberties Union in its preparation of Scopes's defense, refused to appear as expert witnesses in the trial (Edward J. Larson, *Summer for the Gods: The Scopes Trial and America's Continuing Debate Over Science and Religion* [Cambridge, Mass.: Harvard Univ. Press, 1997], 99, 271, n.64, 113, 135).

89. Haller, *Eugenics*, 82–85; Kevles, *In the Name of Eugenics*, 173; Ludmerer, *Genetics and American Society*, 79–85.

90. Winslow, *Jonathan Edwards*, 26, 27, 28.

91. Winslow, *Jonathan Edwards*, 27.

92. [Trumbull], *Particular Ct. Recs., Andros Admin.*, 10.

93. Winslow, *Jonathan Edwards*, 27.

94. Miller, *Jonathan Edwards*, xxx, 35; Iain H. Murray, *Jonathan Edwards: A New Biography* (Edinburgh: Banner of Truth Trust, 1987), 4; Marsden, *Jonathan Edwards*, xvii, 22–23. Although Marsden quotes from Richard Edwards's divorce petitions to support his assertions, he extracts these quotations from Winslow's biography and Kenneth P. Minkema's unpublished intergenerational study of the Edwards family. Minkema is the only modern biographer after Winslow to directly consult the court records documenting Richard Edwards's divorce; nevertheless, his analysis does not substantially differ from Winslow's (Minkema, "The Edwardses," 24–26).

CONCLUSION

1. New Haven County Ct. Recs., 1:217 (1 December 1693); Jacobus, *Families of Ancient New Haven*, 3:1883.

2. Norton, *Founding Mothers and Fathers*, 243, 252.

3. New Haven County Ct. Recs., 1:217.

4. Michael MacDonald and Terence R. Murphy, *Sleepless Souls: Suicide in Early Modern England* (Oxford: Clarendon Press, 1990), 31, 46.

5. Geddes, *Welcome Joy*, 99–100; Howard I. Kushner, *Self-Destruction in the Promised Land: A Psychocultural Biology of American Suicide* (New Brunswick, N.J.: Rutgers Univ. Press, 1989), 21–22. In England, the personal estate of the family of a convicted *felo de se* was forfeited to the Crown, and the corpse was thrown into a pit at a crossroads and a stake was driven through its body. It is unclear how common profane burial of suicides was in colonial New England. In both New and old England, such penalties did not apply if the suicide was ruled *non compos mentis* at the time of the act (MacDonald and Murphy, *Sleepless Souls*, 15).

6. MacDonald and Murphy, *Sleepless Souls*, 42.

7. Ibid., *Sleepless Souls*, 259–60.

8. New Haven County Ct. Recs., 1:217.

9. Rosenberg, *No Other Gods*, 29–30; Waller, "Illusion of an Explanation," 436–38.

10. Fletcher, *Gender, Sex, and Subordination*, 44–45; Roy Porter, *Mind-Forge'd Manacles: A History of Madness in England from the Restoration to the Regency* (Cambridge, Mass.: Harvard Univ. Press, 1987), 39–40, 45–46.

11. Edwards, *A Faithful Narrative*, in Goen, *The Great Awakening*, 4:206; MacDonald and Murphy, *Sleepless Souls*, 53.

12. MacDonald and Murphy, *Sleepless Souls,* 133; Jimenez, *Changing Faces of Madness,* 12, 65.

13. Waller, "'Illusion of an Explanation,'" 410; Waller, "Ideas of Heredity," 463–68.

14. Waller, "'Illusion of an Explanation,'" 416.

15. Lindsey Kent and Simon Baron-Cohen, "Genes in Mind?" in *Davenport's Dream: 21st Century Reflections on Heredity and Eugenics,* ed. Jan A. Witkowski and John R. Inglis (Cold Spring Harbor, N.Y.: CSH Laboratory Press, 2008), 151; Allan V. Horwitz, *Creating Mental Illness* (Chicago: Univ. of Chicago Press, 2002), 142–46.

16. Kevles, *In the Name of Eugenics,* 49; Maynard V. Olson, "Davenport's Dream," in Witkowski and Inglis, *Davenport's Dream,* 80.

17. Elof A. Carlson, "The Eugenic World of Charles Benedict Davenport," in Witkowski and Inglis, *Davenport's Dream,* 72.

18. Daniel R. Weinberger and David Goldman, "Psychiatric Genetics in an Era of Relative Enlightenment," in Witkowski and Inglis, *Davenport's Dream,* 129, 127.

19. Holly Peay and Jehannine Austin, *How to Talk with Families About Genetics and Mental Illness* (New York: Norton, 2011), 21.

20. John P. Demos, "Demography and Psychology in the Historical Study of Family-Life: A Personal Report," in *Household and Family in Past Time: Comparative Studies in the Size and Structure of the Domestic Group Over the Last Three Centuries in England, France, Serbia, Japan and Colonial North America, with Further Materials from Western Europe,* ed. Peter Laslett and Richard Wall (Cambridge: Cambridge Univ. Press, 1972), 563.

21. Frances E. Dolan, *Marriage and Violence: The Early Modern Legacy* (Philadelphia: Univ. of Pennsylvania Press, 2008), 3, 45, 5.

22. Shipton, *Sibley's Harvard Graduates,* 4:94.

INDEX

Page numbers in italics refer to figures. Those followed by n refer to notes, with note number.

ABOUT THE AUTHOR

Ava Chamberlain is Associate Professor of Religion at Wright State University in Dayton, Ohio. She is the editor of *The "Miscellanies," Nos. 501–832*, vol. 18 of *The Works of Jonathan Edwards*, gen. ed. Harry S. Stout (New Haven: Yale University Press, 2000).